Black Sox in the Courtroom

Black Sox in the Courtroom

The Grand Jury, Criminal Trial and Civil Litigation

WILLIAM F. LAMB

McFarland & Company, Inc., Publishers
Jefferson, North Carolina, and London

Library of Congress Cataloguing-in-Publication Data

Lamb, William F., 1947–
Black Sox in the courtroom : the grand jury, criminal trial and civil litigation / William F. Lamb.
p. cm.
Includes bibliographical references and index.

ISBN 978-0-7864-7268-0
softcover : acid free paper ♾

1. Cicotte, Edward (Edward V.) — Trials, litigation, etc. 2. Illinois — Trials, litigation, etc. 3. Chicago White Sox (Baseball team) — Trials, litigation, etc. 4. Trials (Conspiracy) — Illinois — Chicago. 5. Baseball — Corrupt practices — United States. 6. Baseball — Betting — United States. 7. World Series (Baseball) (1919) I. Title.

KF224.C49L36 2013
345.773'02097711 — dc23 2013005783

British Library cataloguing data are available

On the cover: A 1919 Chicago White Sox team photograph; (foreground) gavel image © 2013 iStockphoto/Thinkstock

Manufactured in the United States of America

McFarland & Company, Inc., Publishers
Box 611, Jefferson, North Carolina 28640
www.mcfarlandpub.com

Acknowledgments

In no small measure, this work benefited from the generous assistance of others. In rough alphabetical order, the author would like to thank Professor Albert Alschuler and Law Librarian Marcia Lehr of the Northwestern University School of Law for their tutelage on circa 1920 Illinois criminal law; Teri Blasko of the Saratoga (NY) Public Library for providing access and guidance on review of the library's gambling archives; baseball authors Susan Dellinger and Rick Huhn for careful review and informative feedback on the original manuscript; Black Sox expert Bob Hoie for exacting scrutiny of the text and for background information on various individuals mentioned therein; Dave Holmgren and Walt Wilson for obtaining follow-up information in Des Moines and Chicago; Conrad Kowal, executive director of the Chicago Baseball Museum, for providing access to the transcript of the Jackson civil trial; Elizabeth and Tom Lamb for helping their computer-challenged father get the manuscript in proper form; Arlene Marcley, executive director of the Shoeless Joe Jackson Museum and Library for providing access to designated excerpts of the Gene Carney papers; Tim Newman for bringing the trained eye of a Black Sox-knowledgable civil attorney to the manuscript draft and for sharing his notes on the Cannon documents; Mike Nola, official historian of the Shoeless Joe Jackson Virtual Hall of Fame, for providing access to his treasure trove of regional Black Sox reportage and for filling in obscure details of the scandal saga; Deb Ross of the Laconia (NH) Public Library for procuring trial-related reportage from Chicago and Milwaukee; Jim Weaver of New Hampshire Correctional Industries for enhancing the photographic images displayed in this work; and the staffs at the Giamatti Research Center in Cooperstown, the Chicago History Museum, the Chicago Public Library/Harold Washington branch, and the National Archives in Chicago for their patient help. The author is indebted to them all.

Table of Contents

Preface

On the afternoon of October 9, 1919, the enduring infamy of eight members of the Chicago White Sox was secured by a seemingly unremarkable event: a grounder to second. But more than the execution of a routine play was at stake. For the instant that the toss to first was safely handled, the Cincinnati Reds were World Series champions. And a dark, surreptitious objective had been achieved as well — the prearranged outcome of baseball's ultimate competition.

Only ten days before, a Cincinnati triumph would have been deemed a significant upset. Although a solid club, the new champs had been decided underdogs — until betting odds inexplicably shifted in the Reds' favor on the eve of Game One. The erratic, uninspired play of the highly touted White Sox was also a puzzlement. For much of the Series, the Chicago side bore little resemblance to the powerhouse that had captured the American League flag. Almost immediately after the final out was recorded, muffled rumblings about the integrity of the team's play found public voice, with syndicated sports columnist Hugh Fullerton being the most vocal skeptic. Still, it would take almost another year and an altogether different Chicago baseball contretemps — the rumored fix of a meaningless late 1920 regular-season game between the Cubs and the Philadelphia Phillies — to bring exacting scrutiny to bear on the suspiciously-played Fall Classic of 1919.

This work endeavors to provide an accounting of the judicial proceedings — grand jury, criminal trial, and civil litigation — spawned by the outcome of the 1919 Series. It does not, however, purport to be the definitive exposition of the Black Sox scandal. Nor will judgment be rendered on the accused players. Rather, the goal of this work is a modest one: to provide a thorough, non-partisan, and reliable account of how the Black Sox controversy played out in court. To that end, chapters on the judicial components of the affair — each markedly different in process and objective — will contain educational paragraphs. Therein, presumably unfamiliar legal concepts like the mandate of grand jury secrecy, extradition requirements, 1919 Illinois conspiracy law, the principle of condonation, and others will be explained in lay terms. An understanding of these somewhat arcane matters is crucial to comprehension of what took place in the courtroom. The narrative of judicial events will also be accompanied by description of simultaneous happenings outside of court. Use of this format is intended to afford the reader a broader picture of the factual/legal landscape as the proceedings unfolded. In addition, commentary, particularly on the legal impact of certain events, will be incorporated into the historical narrative. The text is densely sourced and annotated, with notes, many of them substantive, placed at the end of each chapter for convenient perusal. Finally, appended to the text is a glossary to help identify and keep straight the sizable cast of characters involved in the Black Sox case.

In a practical sense, this work is a reclamation project, for only fragments of the original judicial record survive. To the extent possible, these official excerpts serve as the narrative's primary source. In this regard, immeasurable assistance in piecing together events was afforded by review of the extant but difficult-to-access transcript of the 1924 trial of Joe Jackson's breach of contract suit against the White Sox, made available to the author via the kind offices of Conrad Kowal, executive director of the Chicago Baseball Museum. Equally valuable was examination of once-lost Black Sox criminal case documents obtained in December 2007 by the Chicago History Museum and now available for public inspection. Particularly revelatory were museum-held notes that memorialize statements made in and about the Cook County Courthouse by Eddie Cicotte and the now-recovered transcript of grand jury testimony by Lefty Williams. Unavoidably, a complete telling of the story also required use of contemporary newspaper reportage and ensuing Black Sox literature.

Ultimately, the aim of this book is not to change minds about whether Cicotte pitched to win Game 4 or about the fairness of Buck Weaver's banishment from baseball. Rather, it seeks to provide a comprehensive, non-argumentative account of relevant judicial proceedings so that continuing discussions of Black Sox controversies might be better informed.

1

Prelude to Infamy

At the core of the Black Sox scandal rests the longstanding, often toxic, relationship between baseball and professional gamblers. Given ample treatment of the subject elsewhere,[1] no useful purpose is served by exhaustive commentary here. Suffice it to say that once baseball evolved from sporting exercise for young gentlemen into a competition where the outcome was seriously contested, the game became a fit object for high-stakes gambling and, hence, temptation. According to respected early baseball historian Bill Ryczek, ballplayers and gamblers were likely in cahoots as early as 1862.[2] Three years later, three members of the New York Mutuals were expelled, at least temporarily, from organized club play for game-fixing.[3] The National Association, the first professional baseball league, was plagued by gambling-related problems throughout its five season (1871–1875) existence,[4] and the second campaign of its successor, the National League, was marred by late-season game dumping by the pennant-contending Louisville Grays.[5] The permanent banishment of four accused Louisville players by NL President William Hulbert had some deterrent effect, but with ballplayers and gamblers regularly rubbing elbows in hotel lobbies, railway cars, saloons, and the like, gambling and baseball could not be separated in perpetuity.

Post-season championship play enjoyed no immunity from gamblers. In fact, the very first modern World Series of 1903 was jeopardized by attempts to induce Boston catcher Lou Criger to throw Series games. In an affidavit signed twenty years after the fact, Criger revealed that he had rejected a $12,000 bribe offered by a gambler named Anderson.[6] Two seasons after the Criger incident, there was murmured controversy over the legitimacy of the shoulder injury that kept Philadelphia A's pitching ace Rube Waddell out of action in the 1905 World Series. More openly reported was an unsuccessful attempt to bribe umpires Bill Klem and Jimmy Johnstone prior to the famous 1908 pennant-deciding playoff game between the Chicago Cubs and the New

York Giants. But NL investigation of the incident was less than vigorous, resulting only in the banishment of Dr. Joseph Creamer, the Giants team physician, from all major and minor league clubhouses.[7] Thereafter, degrees of suspicion would attend the Boston Braves sweep of the prohibitively favored A's in the 1914 World Series and the Red Sox Series' victory over the Cubs four autumns later.[8] By then, however, rumor of gambler influence over Series-bound players had become commonplace, a matter given little credence by the sporting press. The game's monitors had become complacent, largely dismissive of the notion that gambling posed a threat to baseball's integrity. Indeed, mention of the betting odds was a stock feature of newspaper reportage on important contests like the World Series. Illustrative is the caption for Chicago sports editor Harvey Woodruff's column on the eve of the 1919 Series: "If Your Money Goes on the Sox, the Odds are 13–20."[9]

Indifference to gambling-related corruption pervaded the press box as the contestants made ready for the World Series of 1919. The eagerly awaited match would feature clubs representing two of baseball's most storied venues. Cincinnati was, of course, the home of the game's first openly professional team, the original Red Stockings of Harry and George Wright, Ross Barnes, Cal McVey, and other pioneer-era luminaries. That team's undefeated nationwide campaign of 1869 had brought glory to Cincinnati and done much to popularize the game of baseball. Subsequent incarnations of the Reds joined the National League as a charter member in 1876 and captured the inaugural American Association pennant in 1882. After that, Cincinnati nines fell on hard times, going without a baseball championship for the next 36 years.

Since 1902, the NL Reds had been owned by a local consortium headed by yeast manufacturing millionaire and one-time Cincinnati mayor Julius Fleischmann. The club president was August "Garry" Herrmann, a personable city politico and small-stake franchise shareholder. Herrmann also served as chairman of the National Commission, major league baseball's three-man governing body. After decades of mediocrity, the Reds had begun to make progress under manager Christy Mathewson, the longtime Giants hurling star who took the Cincinnati helm midway through the 1916 season. First-division finishes in 1917 and 1918 followed, but Mathewson would not see the Reds through to a pennant. Late in the 1918 season, he had resigned his post to accept overseas World War I duty as a U.S. Army officer. During the 1919 World Series, Mathewson would be stationed in the press box as special Series correspondent for the *New York Times.*

The club that Mathewson had assembled was inherited by Pat Moran, a tough, hard-drinking 43-year-old former catcher who had guided the Philadelphia Phillies to the 1915 NL pennant. Reds center fielder Edd Roush, the reigning NL batting champion (.341) and a future Hall of Famer, was the team's only real star. But infield cornermen Heinie Groh (.310) and Jake Daubert (.276 and a two-time NL batting champ) were first-rate and the remainder of the lineup was sound, particularly on defense. Key to the Reds' success, however, was a deep and talented pitching staff. Available for Series duty were Slim Sallee (21–7, 2.06 ERA), Hod Eller (20–9, 2.39), Dutch Ruether (19–6, 1.82), Ray Fisher (14–5, 2.17), Jimmy Ring (10–9, 2.26), and Dolf Luque (9–3, 2.63). With the starters rarely turning in a sub-par performance, the Moran squad had posted a sparkling 96–44 record, cruising to the 1919 NL pennant a full nine games ahead of the runner-up Giants.

Although the Reds were a fine team, few observers placed them in the same class as their Series opposition. Like Cincinnati, Chicago traced its baseball lineage back to pre–National Association days. The Windy City had also hosted a charter member of the National League, the team eventually known as the Cubs. The White Sox were the local upstart, having come to town in 1900 as a member of Ban Johnson's then minor American (née Western) League. Since the club's inception, the Sox had been owned and operated by Charles A. Comiskey, the son of a Chicago alderman and a former player who had risen to sporting prominence in the mid–1880s as first baseman/captain of the American Association champion St. Louis Browns. In 1906, the World Series upset of an NL-dominant, 116-game-winning Cubs team by a White Sox squad of Hitless Wonders (a .230 regular-season team batting average) had pretty much put Comiskey's Pale Hose on equal footing with its intra-city rival.

In 1917, the White Sox returned to glory, capturing another World Series crown in six games over the Giants. Unlike the earlier Sox champs, this Chicago lineup had plenty of offensive firepower. Left fielder Joe Jackson and second baseman Eddie Collins were batting stars of the first magnitude. The Sox were also potent at third (Buck Weaver), first (Chick Gandil), and center (Happy Felsch), while scrappy backstop Ray Schalk handled a standout pitching corps headed by Eddie Cicotte, Red Faber, and rookie Claude "Lefty" Williams.[10] But while the team performed seamlessly on the field, the Chisox clubhouse was rife with discord, with much of the roster divided into two cliques. One faction was headed by Ivy Leaguer (Columbia) Eddie Collins, polished and self-assured to the point of arrogance. Aligned with "Cocky" Collins were outfielders Shano Collins (no relation) and Nemo Leibold, Faber, and Schalk. In the other camp were poorly educated, hardscrabble types, united by envy, if not outright hatred, of the better-paid and socially superior Collins.[11] The unquestioned leader of this faction was tough guy Gandil, an off-season boilermaker and one-time pugilist. Gandil's running mates included Cicotte, the boisterous but amiable duo of Weaver and Felsch, weak-hitting but hard-asnails shortstop Swede Risberg, and utilityman Fred McMullin, a West Coast buddy of Risberg and the only one of this crew to have finished high school.[12] Road roommates Jackson and Williams, both introverted and malleable, sometimes socialized with the Gandil group but more often kept to themselves.

Far removed from his own playing days, team owner Comiskey had grown distant from his players, with the exception of team captain Eddie Collins. His preference was to administer club affairs from above while lavishing attention — via personal access, sumptuous post-game buffets, and a well-stocked liquor cabinet — upon Chicago sports scribes, most of whom revered Comiskey. The White Sox front office was insular as well, populated by club treasurer J. Louis Comiskey, the nearly 400 lb. son of the owner, as well as trusted Comiskey loyalists like former Western League president Norris O'Neill and club secretary Harry Grabiner. By 1919, the longstanding distance between club brass and players meant that few, if any, of the current White Sox felt any emotional attachment to their employer. For most, playing baseball for the Chicago White Sox was a matter of livelihood, not loyalty.

The salary, star status, and social superiority of White Sox captain Eddie Collins (left) created resentment in manager Kid Gleason's clubhouse.

The separation between team officials and Sox players had only been aggravated by the entry of the United States into World War I in April 1917. Among those heeding the call to arms was veteran Sox righthander Jim Scott, whose early enlistment in Army officer training was applauded by the vocally patriotic Comiskey. It was reported that Comiskey paid Scott for the remainder of the 1917 regular season and accorded the hurler a full Series player's share, as well.[13] In 1918, U.S. Provost Marshal Enoch Crowder's "work or fight" directive put many of the able-bodied young men playing professional baseball on the spot. Early in the season's campaign, staff mainstay Red Faber enlisted in the Navy. Then in June, Joe Jackson, Lefty Williams, Happy Felsch, and back-up catcher Byrd Lynn left the club for defense plant jobs. But unlike entry into the military, ballplayers seeking defense industry employment were not admired. As did many Americans, Charles Comiskey regarded those avoiding military service as slackers. Remarking upon the quartet's departure for defense plants, the Chisox boss sneered, "I don't even consider them fit to play on my ball club."[14] Much more likely to garner Comiskey's approval was the conduct of Eddie Collins, who left the club in mid–August to join the Marines. Several weeks later, the roster-depleted Sox staggered home a sixth place (57–67) finisher in the war-shortened 1918 campaign. Soon thereafter, Comiskey dismissed manager Clarence "Pants" Rowland, the unknown who had guided the Sox to a world championship only a season earlier. His replacement at the helm was 52-year-old William "Kid" Gleason, a 22-year playing veteran who had been a coach on the 1917 Sox club.

Although the defense plant jumpers were welcomed back by Gleason in 1919, the defections had further divided Comiskey from his charges. Another sore spot was player salaries. The accepted wisdom that Comiskey was a notably tight-fisted team owner is erroneous, thoroughly refuted by actual player salary data now readily available. Generally speaking, Comiskey paid White Sox players the prevailing wage, and then some.[15] Indeed, depending on the criteria applied, the 1919 Chicago White Sox had either the second- or third-highest player payroll in major league baseball. Only the New York Yankees, and perhaps the Boston Red Sox, paid their players more, and the payrolls of those three teams were no more than a few thousand dollars apart. White Sox salaries, however, were noticeably imbalanced, with Eddie Collins receiving a $15,000 annual stipend, a legacy of Federal League-generated salary inflation, that was more than twice the wage of any teammate. Still, a number of other Chisox veterans — Buck Weaver, Ray Schalk, Eddie Cicotte[16] — were among the highest-paid players at their respective positions. But other Sox, particularly Lefty Williams, and, to a lesser extent, Joe Jackson and Chick Gandil, were paid less than their talents would have commanded had normal salary conditions prevailed in early 1919. The problem was that the situation had not been normal. Base salaries had been depressed by war jitters and, earlier, by the demise of the rival Federal League. The 1919 season, moreover, had been approached with caution by the major league magnates, who were concerned about the game's capacity to recover its pre-war popularity. Misgivings on that score had prompted reduction of the 1919 regular-season schedule to 140 games, with player salaries trimmed accordingly.

Whatever the resentments harbored privately by certain players, the

Contemporaries considered the 1919 Chicago White Sox one of baseball's greatest teams.

reunited White Sox were every bit as much a juggernaut as the 1917 world champions. The offense, paced by stars Jackson (.351) and Collins (.319), received ample support from Leibold (.302), Weaver (.296), and Felsch (.275). The 1919 Sox posted an American League-leading .287 team batting average while pacing the circuit in runs scored (668). The Sox also swiped a league-best 150 bases. The pitching staff was equally good. Cicotte (29–7, 1.82 ERA), Williams (23–11, 2.64), and mid-season call-up Dickie Kerr (13–7, 2.89) had been sterling. With intermittent help from Faber (11–9, 3.83) and second-liners Bill James, Grover Lowdermilk, and Roy Wilkinson, Sox hurlers had notched the most complete games (87) and issued the fewest walks (342) in the AL. To make the package complete, the 1919 Chicago White Sox were also an excellent defensive team, placing second in league standings in fielding percentage (.969), double plays (116), and fewest errors committed (176). Guided with a steady hand by manager Gleason, the Sox finished a pennant-winning season at 88–52, good for a 3½ game final margin over the Cleveland Indians.[17]

Despite its deep pitching staff and a better regular-season record, the National League champion Cincinnati Reds were lightly regarded by Series prognosticators. Although Edd Roush and Heinie Groh were commonly adjudged first-rate players, few placed them in the same class as Shoeless Joe Jackson and Eddie Collins. Other head-to-head comparisons largely favored the White Sox, although Reds first baseman Jake Daubert probably rated a slight edge over Gandil and the two shortstops (Larry Kopf and Risberg) were both considered non-entities. The main worry of Chicago supporters was the pitching staff, where more than 300 regular season innings were feared to have drained life from Eddie Cicotte's 35-year-old right arm. In addition, Red Faber, a three-game winner during the 1917 Series but plagued by season-long illness and arm miseries, had been declared unavailable. As during much of the 1919 regular season, Faber's spot in the Series rotation would be taken by the undersized (5'7", 155 lb.) Kerr. Notwithstanding these concerns, Sox backers took comfort in the recent history of post-season play. Since 1910, the American League pennant winner had captured all but one World Series crown, the stunning upset of the A's by the 1914 Miracle Boston Braves being the anomaly. Otherwise, the NL side had not put up much of a fight, with only the 1912 New York Giants able to extend Series play to the limit before succumbing.

With the above considerations weighing on the minds of odds-makers, the White Sox were installed as solid Series favorites, with Chicago favored by anywhere from an outlandish 5 to 1, to a more rational 7 to 5.[18] But little wagering activity was in evidence, as Reds backers were scarce. As noted by one observer, "A few bets have been made [on Cincinnati] at 8 to 5 but the money wagered is small compared to that of other years. ... It is doubtful if there has ever been a series in which so few bets have been made. Everyone seems to want to take the White Sox."[19] Then with the teams in Cincinnati preparing for Game One, betting on the Reds surged, converting the NL champs from decided underdogs into a slight Series favorite. This sudden and unanticipated shift in wagering preference was noted with concern by the country's bookmakers and betting commissioners.[20] It also had a disquieting effect on certain baseball insiders. Something, it seemed, was afoot.

Notes

1. For a comprehensive treatment of the connection between baseball and the gambling fraternity, see Daniel E. Ginsburg, *The Fix Is In: A History of Baseball Gambling and Game Fixing Scandals* (Jefferson, NC: McFarland, 1995).

2. See William J. Ryczek, *Baseball's First Inning: A History of the National Pastime Through the Civil War* (Jefferson, NC: McFarland, 2009), 197–198.

3. As discussed in John Thorn, *Baseball in the Garden of Eden: The Secret History of the Early Game* (New York: Simon & Schuster, 2011), 127–129.

4. For an authoritative treatment of the National Association, see William J. Ryczek, *Blackguards and Red Stockings: A History of the National Association, 1871–1875* (Wallingford, CT: Colebrook Press, 1992).

5. For a complete account of the Louisville scandal, see William A. Cook, *The Louisville Grays Scandal of 1877: The Taint of Gambling at the Dawn of the National League* (Jefferson, NC: McFarland, 2005).

6. Criger disclosed the bribe attempt in a 1923 affidavit. For more detail, see the Criger obituary, circulated by the Associated Press, May 15, 1934.

7. The league's investigation of the incident, directed by Giants owner John T. Brush, was more than content to scapegoat the expendable team physician and leave more important club actors unscathed. For a fuller account of the matter, see David W. Anderson, *More than Merkle: A History of the Best and Most Exciting Baseball Season in Human History* (Lincoln: University of Nebraska Press, 2000), 210–222.

8. A wafer-thin argument that the 1918 World Series may have been fixed is proffered in Sean Deveney, *The Original Curse: Did the Cubs Throw the 1918 World Series to Babe Ruth's Red Sox and Incite the Black Sox Scandal?* (New York: McGraw-Hill, 2010).

9. *Chicago Tribune,* September 29, 1919.

10. For an overview of the 1917 White Sox season, see Warren N. Wilbert and William C. Hageman, *The 1917 White Sox: Their World Championship Season* (Jefferson, NC: McFarland, 2004).

11. For more on the rival Sox factions, see Rick Huhn, *Eddie Collins: A Baseball Biography* (Jefferson, NC: McFarland, 2008), 141–142.

12. McMullin was a graduate of Los Angeles High School while Gandil spent a year or two at Oakland High. The rest did not go beyond the eighth grade, if they got that far.

13. See *Chicago Tribune,* June 12, 1918.

14. As quoted in the *Chicago Tribune,* June 12, 1918. Elsewhere, Comiskey was reported as vowing to use "every ounce of my strength and the last cent I have" to keep defense plant jumpers Jackson, Williams, and Felsch "out of organized baseball forever." See *Salt Lake Telegram,* September 17, 1918.

15. See Bob Hoie, "1919 Baseball Salaries and the Mythically Underpaid Chicago White Sox," *Base Ball: A Journal of the Early Game,* Vol. 6, No. 1, Spring 2012, 17–34.

16. In popular lore, Cicotte is portrayed as the victim of a miserly Comiskey. But via the Haupert Player Salary Database and other now available salary information, Bob Hoie calculates that, between salary and bonus payments, Cicotte was paid better in 1918–1919 than any other major league pitcher, save Walter Johnson.

17. Statistics utilized in this work are taken from http://www.Baseball-Reference.com; *Total Baseball,* 7th ed., John Thorn, et al., editors (Kingston, NY: Total Sports, 2001), and *The Baseball Encyclopedia,* 4th ed., Joseph Reichler, editor (New York: Macmillan, 1979).

18. As noted by Black Sox expert Gene Carney, there is no consensus among baseball historians regarding the precise odds on the 1919 World Series. But researchers agree that the early betting line clearly favored the White Sox. See Gene Carney, *Burying the Black Sox: How Baseball's Cover-Up of the 1919 World Series Fix Almost Succeeded* (Washington, DC: Potomac Books, 2006), 308, n. 6.

19. *Washington Post,* September 28, 1919.

20. The now-forgotten appellation *betting commissioner* was a fluid term, its meaning dependent on circumstances. In certain contexts, betting commissioner was a synonym for a race track bookmaker, then a lawful profession in most places. In other contexts, a betting commissioner served as a middleman between parties who wished to bet against each other, but sought to do so discreetly. Or a betting commissioner might be the agent of a particular well-heeled client who did not care to do his betting personally.

2

The 1919 World Series

Notwithstanding pre-season misgivings about the game's vitality, major league magnates had voted to expand the 1919 World Series into a best-of-nine-game match, a format not used since the inaugural modern Series of 1903. The Series would begin in Cincinnati on October 1 and be played on consecutive days thereafter to a finish. Capacity crowds were anticipated, as the majors had enjoyed an explosion in attendance. The pennant-winning Reds had attracted 532,501 regular-season fans for their home games, more than 2½ times the draw of 1918. The White Sox had done even better, drawing 627,186, a more than threefold increase over the previous season. Thus, a financial bonanza was in the offing for the 1919 Series participants.

Interest in the Series was heightened by the prediction of experts. Among those making their views known were rival managers Kid Gleason and Pat Moran, engaged by a *Washington Post* syndicate to provide daily Series copy.[1] To no one's surprise, Sox leader Gleason brimmed with confidence, convinced that he had "the best baseball team in the world."[2] In Gleason's opinion, his club had no weaknesses. "In Eddie Cicotte and Claude Williams, I have the two greatest pitchers in the game today," Kid boasted.[3] The Chicago infield defense of Buck Weaver, Swede Risberg, Eddie Collins, and Chick Gandil was also nonpareil, superior even to the celebrated Philadelphia A's $100,000 infield of a decade earlier.[4] Left fielder Joe Jackson, "one of the greatest hitters today and one of the best that ever played," was easily the Series' premier batsman, while center fielder Happy Felsch, "another fence buster," was (with apologies to Cleveland's Tris Speaker) "the best defensive outfielder in the American League."[5] Touting his Sox as "the gamest bunch I ever saw on a ballfield" and certain that his "gang was ready to do its best,"[6] Kid Gleason was the picture of pre–Series confidence.

Although expressing a quiet confidence in his own team, Reds manager Moran was considerably more subdued in his assessments. Moran was also deferential to the opposition, concurring with those who had pronounced the White Sox "great in every department."[7] "But the Reds are great, too — don't forget," the Cincinnati skipper hastened to add.[8] In Moran's view, the depth of the Reds pitching staff gave his club the edge in a nine-game match. He also thought that his players matched up well position-by-position against their more highly regarded counterparts. Moran concluded his pre–Series columns with some uncharacteristic swagger. The Reds would not be playing just to win the Series, but "to win by the biggest score possible. It will be our aim in every game to demonstrate real superiority over the White Sox. And I am confident that we will do it."[9]

Moran's faith in his team was shared by few in the game's inner precincts. And those looking on from the outside were not impressed by the Reds' chances either, given what the experts were saying. Included within the ranks of baseball cognoscenti publicly predicting a relatively easy White Sox triumph was syndicated sportswriter Hugh Fullerton of the *Chicago Herald Examiner.* For years, newspapers around the country had carried Fullerton's closely analyzed "dope" on World Series combatants. And it was not just home team bias or a long friendship with club owner Charles Comiskey that led Fullerton to gravitate toward the White Sox. Like many veteran observers, Fullerton was genuinely impressed by the talent wearing Sox uniforms. But as Game One approached, Fullerton's confidence in his prediction of a White Sox victory would be undermined by a chance encounter with a former ballplayer.

Along with much of the Chicago sports press and a throng of Sox fans, Fullerton was on the train that carried the White Sox to Cincinnati on September 29. Once in town, Fullerton took lodgings in the Sinton Hotel, the spacious beaux arts accommodation where the Sox would be quartered. On the eve of Game One, the players put in a late-morning workout at the Cincinnati ballpark. Most then accompanied manager Gleason to nearby Latonia Race Track for a leisurely afternoon of improving the breed. In the meantime, the lobby of the Sinton was abuzz with Series-related gossip, rumor, and prediction, much of which was supplied by the sizable contingent of gamblers that had descended upon the hotel. One person looking to cash in on the Series was former major league pitcher Bill Burns. A talented but underachieving left-hander in his playing days, Burns was an interesting character. One popular baseball compendium describes him as "a crap-shooting, card playing gambler with good stuff but no ambition, known to read newspapers and doze on the bench during games."[10] The latter proclivity bestowed upon Burns the moniker "Sleepy Bill." Following his release by the Detroit Tigers in May 1912, Burns had spent his waning baseball years toiling in the Pacific Coast League, where his 1915 Los Angeles Angels teammates included White

Sox utilityman Fred McMullin. Since abandoning the diamond, Burns, a south Texas native, had made his living selling oil leases. But his true calling was plying games of chance.

On the afternoon before Game One, Burns encountered old acquaintance Hugh Fullerton in the hotel telegraph room and the two engaged in good-natured banter about the upcoming Series. Although Burns's tone was friendly, Fullerton was unsettled by the assurance that accompanied Sleepy Bill's advice that Fullerton get wise about the Series outcome. "The Reds are already in," confided Burns, knowingly.[11] Unsure of what to make of this intelligence but now made uneasy by possibilities of something untoward, Fullerton wired the newspapers carrying his column the following addendum to his next-day World Series copy: "Advise all not to bet on series. Ugly rumors afloat."[12] The following day, the still-shaken Fullerton enlisted the astute Christy Mathewson to assist him in assessing Series play. Years later, Fullerton would maintain that Mathewson, by then deceased, had also gotten wind of talk about a possible Series fix and that the two had charted 1919 Series action together in the press box, circling suspicious plays on their scorecards.[13] But whatever the degree of Fullerton's concern, few of his readers were made privy to it. Only two of the 40 newspapers that carried the scribe's Opening Game-day column included his Series betting advisory.[14] Oblivious to the rumors that troubled a few baseball insiders, the average fan was simply anxious for the White Sox–Reds battle to commence.

On October 1, 1919, Cincinnati's 30,000-seat Redland Field was jammed beyond capacity for the Series opener. The opposing starters were a study in contrast. Dutch Ruether, a tall 26-year-old left-hander, had won only three major league games prior to his breakout 19-win season for the 1919 Reds. Notwithstanding that impressive campaign, Ruether's résumé was no match for that of Chisox ace Eddie Cicotte. A 29-game winner in his thirteenth big league season, the stocky (5'9," 175 lb.) right-hander lacked overpowering stuff. Instead, Cicotte pitched with his head, mixing a serviceable fastball and curve with a wide array of trick pitches: spitter, screwball, emery ball, shine ball, and, most importantly, one of the first outstanding knuckleballs in baseball history. Remarkably, Cicotte wielded this eclectic arsenal with pinpoint control. During the 1919 regular season, he had surrendered a mere 1.24 walks per nine innings and had hit only two enemy batsmen in almost 307 innings pitched.

Right fielder Shano Collins got the Sox off smartly in the top of the first with a leadoff single, but a botched sacrifice attempt by Eddie Collins aborted any first-inning rally chance.[15] Cincinnati then broke the scoring seal with a tally in the bottom of the frame. After grooving a first-pitch fastball, Cicotte uncharacteristically hit Reds leadoff man Morrie Rath square in the back with his second pitch. Jake Daubert promptly singled Rath to third. A sacrifice fly by Heinie Groh then plated the Reds' run. But Cicotte escaped further difficulty, leaving the Sox trailing, 1–0, at the close of the first inning. Chicago immediately knotted the score in the second via a Reds error, a walk, and a two-out pop fly single by Chick Gandil. Over the next two innings, Cicotte and Ruether dispatched the opposition with little trouble. But with one down in the bottom of the fourth, the Sox faltered. With Reds outfielder Pat Duncan on first, Larry Kopf hit a comebacker to Cicotte. But what looked like a sure double play went unexecuted. First, Cicotte paused before making the throw to second. Then, Swede Risberg appeared to stumble over the bag, making a too-late toss to first. With the opportunity to close the inning having gone awry, Cicotte suddenly collapsed. Singles by outfielder Greasy Neale and backstop Ivey Wingo registered a run, putting the Reds ahead, 2–1. Pitcher Ruether then banged a triple off the left-center-field fence, driving in two more runs. Follow-up base hits by Rath and Daubert pushed the Reds margin to 6–1 before manager Gleason finally removed the beleaguered Cicotte from the hill. Late-inning insurance tallies off Sox relievers Roy Wilkinson and Grover Lowdermilk extended the final score to a crushing Cincinnati 9, Chicago 1.

Experts and fans alike were stunned by the one-sidedness of the Reds victory. As remarked by Pat Moran in his post-game commentary, Cincinnati had "outclassed the White Sox in every department of play."[16] Nor had the pummeling of Cicotte surprised the Reds skipper. While allowing that "Eddie is a remarkable pitcher," the Reds had "feasted" on his type of off-speed stuff all season. Moran confidently predicted that his "boys are going out ... to make it two in a row."[17] In his post-game commentary, Kid Gleason affected an unconcerned air, attributing the poor play of his team to complacency and overconfidence. In his mind, the lopsided Game One outcome had turned on a single play: the missed twin killing in the bottom of the fourth. Had the Sox successfully completed that play and gotten out of the inning unscathed, Cicotte "would have pitched the entire game and there's no telling what might have happened," said Gleason.[18] In any event, the Sox would have Lefty Williams "on the slab for the second game ... and a fighting gang behind him." That made Gleason feel "just the same now as I did at the start," certain of a White Sox Series victory.[19]

Game Two featured opposing southpaws, the Reds countering Williams with their own left-handed ace, Harry "Slim" Sallee, a 21-game winner during the regular season. After the teams had matched zeroes for three frames, Cincinnati broke through with a big inning, largely courtesy of Williams' abrupt loss of control. Two free passes followed by an Edd Roush single gave the Reds a 1–0 lead. After Roush was caught trying to steal, the third Williams walk of the inning and a triple by Kopf upped the Reds advantage to 3–0. Two innings later, Cincinnati tacked on another run, a two-out single by Neale driving in yet another walked Cincinnati baserunner. The Sox, meanwhile, were hitting Sallee regularly but squandering their scoring opportunities. Trailing by four, Chicago finally got on the scoreboard in the seventh. A single by Risberg and the mishandling of Ray Schalk's double into the right-field corner gave the Sox two unearned runs. But from there, Chicago could get no closer, dropping a 4–2 decision.

The Reds managed only four safeties off Williams but had been the beneficiaries of Lefty's wildness. Williams' half-dozen walks had created the baserunners who made the scoring difference. As noted by an appreciative Pat Moran, "Claude Williams was a great help to us today with those six base on balls. And we thank him."[20] Veteran Chicago sportswriter Irving Sanborn was less sanguine about the outcome, decrying "the almost criminal wild pitching of Lefty Williams." With Sox aces Cicotte and Williams both having been beaten by the Reds, "the Gleasons face the toughest proposition a ball club has ever went up against" in trying to capture the Series from two games behind, Sanborn opined.[21]

Back at home for Game Three but now in dire straits, the White Sox saw their Series hopes revived by Dickie Kerr. The little left-hander throttled the Reds on three hits, besting Ray Fisher, 3–0. The only runs that Kerr would need were supplied in the second via a two run single by Chick Gandil. A Risberg triple and an infield hit by Schalk plated the third Sox run in the fourth. After the game, the praise for Kerr was unanimous. A much relieved Kid Gleason exclaimed that "Kerr pitched one of the prettiest games I have ever looked at."[22] His opposite number was even more complimentary. "My hat is off to little Dick Kerr, for that boy pitched a brand of baseball never surpassed in a world's series clash," said Pat Moran.[23] The Sox Game Three win was just the tonic required for Gleason's embattled spirits. Now, all the Sox needed was another victory to tie the Series. And once they got even with the Reds, "the series is as good as over," proclaimed Kid.[24]

That bit of bombast set the stage for Game Four, the most controversial contest of the 1919 World Series. Eddie Cicotte returned to the mound for his second Series start, opposed by the Reds' hard-throwing right-hander Jimmy Ring. Both hurlers turned in superb, route-going performances. The outcome of the game, however, would not turn on pitching but on Cicotte's fielding. With the game scoreless in the top of the fifth inning, Cicotte muffed an easy comebacker hit by the slow-footed Pat Duncan. Still with time to make the play at first, Cicotte then threw wildly, sending Duncan all the way to second base. Kopf followed by drilling a single to left. With Joe Jackson firing an accurate bullet toward home plate, Duncan pulled up at third. But for reasons not readily apparent — Duncan was holding up and Kopf was not trying to advance an extra base, either — Cicotte did not let the throw go through to the plate. Instead, he attempted to cut the throw off, but succeeded only in deflecting the ball away from catcher Schalk. As the ball rolled off into foul territory, Duncan trotted home with the game's first run. Moments later, Greasy Neale doubled over Jackson's head, plating Kopf with the second and final run of Game Four.

In victory, Ring had been the equal of Kerr the day before, shutting out the opposition on three hits. The Cicotte pitching line was also splendid: two unearned runs on five hits allowed over nine innings. But Cicotte's fielding miscues had been the difference in a 2–0 Chisox loss that gave the Reds a commanding three-games-to-one lead in Series standings. A defiant Gleason, however, refused to concede the laurels. As he saw it, Series games thus far had been a matter of luck trumping skill. "Cincinnati has had all of it [luck]. We haven't had any," groused the Sox skipper. "If the rest of the series will only depend on ability, the Sox will win the next four straight and show that [Reds] bunch where they belong."[25]

On Sunday, October 5, 1919, the weather put temporary brakes on the Reds' momentum. Several driving rain showers rendered Comiskey Park unplayable and put Game Five over until the next day. With no game action to report but with copy still needing to be filed, the baseball press corps offered mid–Series assessments of developments to date. Apart from those working for Chicago newspapers, the notion that the Reds owed their two-game Series advantage to random chance was not widely shared in the Fourth Estate. To some, the difference lay with the two managers. In the opinion of sportswriter J.V. Fitz Gerald of the *Washington Post,* "Moran has outgeneraled, outmaneuvered, outguessed, and outsmarted Gleason. He has made the little leader of the Sox look like a bush league pilot. When the returns are in, the Sox will be able to lay much of their poor showing against the Reds largely at Gleason's door."[26] A non-bylined correspondent of the *New York Times* was another Gleason critic. His October 6 dispatch reported, "Many Chicago fans are criticizing the generalship of Gleason in the series. There is no question that he has been outgeneraled by Moran" (who, in turn, was praised for the Reds' aggressive, risk-taking style of play in the Series).[27] In truth, however, the gist of the Chicago problem was not unimaginative leadership by manager Gleason. It was anemic White Sox bats. In the first four Series games, the American League's best hitting team had managed only one earned run off Reds pitching. The other five Sox tallies were all tainted, leaving the Reds staff with a collective 0.34 ERA at the end of Game Four. The primary culprits in the Sox' lack of offensive output resided in the middle of the Chicago batting order. Despite a smattering of base hits, Buck Weaver, Joe Jackson, and Happy Felsch had not yet produced a single Series RBI. And things would only get worse in Game Five.

The fifth Cincinnati starter to make his debut in the 1919 World Series was a one-time White Sox prospect: shine ball artist Hod Eller. The butt of jokes and supposedly too dumb to benefit from Eddie Cicotte's tutelage on trick pitches, Eller had been cut by the Sox during 1916 spring training.[28] Now, the Indiana right-hander had the opportunity that he had been looking forward to ever since. The White Sox never had a chance. The motivated Eller was even more dominating than Jimmy Ring had been in Game Four, hurling the Reds to another three-hit shutout victory. In the process, Eller fanned nine Sox batters, including six in a row during the second and third innings.

Just as Eller had matched the pitching performance of Ring, Sox starter Lefty Williams replicated his own previous Series outing. As in Game Two, an otherwise stellar Williams performance was sabotaged by a lone big inning. For the first five frames, Williams was nearly untouchable, hurling one-hit shutout ball. Then without warning, he came undone. Eller, a good-hitting pitcher, started the Reds' decisive sixth-inning rally with a leadoff double. A single by Rath brought Eller in with the game's initial run. Following a sacrifice and a walk, Happy Felsch, previously touted by his manager as the best defensive center fielder in the AL, clumsily misplayed a Roush fly ball into a two-run triple. A sacrifice fly by Duncan then capped the Reds' four-run outburst. After that, Williams reverted to his earlier form, retiring the Reds without another baserunner through the eighth inning. But with Sox batters helpless against Eller, Game Five was irretrievably lost. An unearned Reds run in the ninth off Sox mop-up man Erskine Mayer produced a final score of Cincinnati 5, Chicago 0.

With the Reds needing only one more victory to secure the Series crown, the teams headed back to Cincinnati and the seemingly inevitable coronation of the home side. Back in Chicago, disheartened White Sox fans would find little comfort in the pre–Game Six comments of manager Gleason. "I don't know what's the matter but I do know something is wrong with my gang," moaned Gleason. "The bunch I had fighting in August for the pennant would have trimmed this Cincinnati bunch without a struggle. The bunch I have now couldn't beat a high school team."[29] Continuing in the same vein, Kid added, "I am convinced that I have the best ball club that ever was put together [but] I certainly have been disappointed in it in this series. It hasn't played baseball in a single game. There's only a bare chance they can win [the Series] now."[30] In the other dressing room, Pat Moran was all smiles. "We only need one game now," observed the Reds leader. "It doesn't make any difference whether it comes tomorrow, the next day, or the next. We are sure winners."[31]

Moran bestowed the first shot at clinching the Series upon Dutch Ruether, conqueror of the Sox in Game One. Last-ditch Chicago hopes rested with Dickie Kerr, thus far the White Sox' only winning pitcher in the Series. But ominously for Chicago, Kerr did not have his Game Three stuff. After missed scoring opportunities in their first two at-bats, the Reds broke through in the third inning to take a 2–0 lead. The key blow was a two-run double by Pat Duncan. In the fourth, a triple by Greasy Neale, a double by Ruether, and a Risberg throwing error garnered the Reds two more runs. Staked to a 4–0 advantage, Ruether mowed down the Sox just as he had in his previous start, until the Sox managed to scratch out a run in the fifth—snapping a 26-consecutive-inning scoreless streak in the process. Two walks, an infield hit by Kerr, and a sacrifice fly by Eddie Collins finally got the White Sox back in the run column. Down 4–1 in the sixth and with Series defeat now plainly in view, the Sox staged their first real post-season rally. It began when mis-communication between Reds shortstop Kopf and left fielder Duncan allowed a Weaver pop fly to fall safely for a leadoff double. Joe Jackson and Happy Felsch then capitalized on this break, registering their first RBI base hits of the Series. With the game now 4–3, manager Moran somewhat surprisingly yanked Ruether, summoning Jimmy Ring to the mound in relief. Two quick outs made the move look good, until a clutch single by Ray Schalk drove in Felsch with the score equalizer.

From that point on, Ring settled down, holding the Sox scoreless through the ninth. Kerr did the same, although not without difficulty. The situation in the bottom of the eighth was particularly perilous for Chicago. But with two men on base and two outs, Moran oddly permitted the weak-hitting Ring (lifetime BA .147) to bat. A meekly hit grounder produced an inning-ending force-out, preserving Sox chances for a win.[32] In the top of the tenth, Weaver led off with another bloop double. Jackson then bunted him to third. One out later, a Gandil bouncer escaped the infield, sending Weaver home for a 5–4 White Sox lead. In the bottom of the frame, the gritty Kerr preserved the edge, retiring the Reds in order. With Game Six in hand, the White Sox were now down four games to two and still alive in the Series, if only barely. Meanwhile, press box snipers focused their aim upon a new target: Reds manager Moran. Cited as failings were the quick hook applied to Ruether in the sixth inning and the non-use of veteran NL slugger and 1918 RBI champ Sherry Magee as a pinch-hitter for Ring in the eighth. Erstwhile Reds heroes

Kopf and Duncan were also chastised for letting the rally-starting Weaver pop fly fall between them.[33] On the other side, the comeback had resuscitated Kid Gleason's spirits. Everything now depended on an Eddie Cicotte victory in Game Seven. "If we can take that one," said Kid, "the next two will be easy.... We will go back to Chicago and win the series."[34]

Game Seven would prove to be the contest that Series pundits had anticipated at the outset — a comfortable Chicago win that featured timely White Sox hitting in support of a sterling pitching performance by the staff ace. RBI singles by Joe Jackson in the first and third innings produced an early 2–0 Sox lead. That margin was then doubled in the fourth via a two-run single by Happy Felsch. Meanwhile, Cicotte cruised, spacing seven hits and yielding only a harmless sixth-inning run. The end result was a complete game 4–1 victory and a degree of Series redemption for Eddie Cicotte. A clearly concerned Pat Moran was gracious in defeat: "The Sox won this afternoon because they deserved to win. They played a great game of ball."[35] Still, the Reds manager was optimistic that Hod Eller and "an even break in the luck of baseball" would produce a Series victory in the next game. Kid Gleason was equally confident of a White Sox triumph. Just as Cicotte had rebounded from two Series losses to hurl a gem, Gleason felt certain that Williams, "a wonderful pitcher," would do the same in Game Eight.[36] Already looking ahead to a Series-deciding Game Nine, Gleason had pitching bulwark Dickie Kerr in reserve for the clincher. But the change in Series fortunes had left the Sox skipper, once a 38-game winner himself, in such high spirits that he thought that "I could go in there and pitch myself and beat the Reds" in the Series finale.[37]

On October 9, 1919, the Cincinnati Reds required less than five minutes to bring Gleason back to reality. In the top of the first, Lefty Williams induced leadoff man Morrie Rath to fly out. He would not retire another Reds batter. Jake Daubert singled to right. So did Heinie Groh. Slumping Edd Roush then doubled down the right-field line, scoring Daubert. Pat Duncan followed with a double to left, giving Cincinnati a quick 3–0 lead. After Williams had dealt a first-pitch ball to Larry Kopf, Gleason had seen enough of his "wonderful pitcher." Enter hulking Sox reliever Bill James. But the Reds onslaught continued, with a single by catcher Bill Rariden upping the Reds' lead to 4–0 before James could stanch the rally. In the bottom of the first, a Nemo Liebold single and an Eddie Collins double had the Chicago faithful contemplating their own big inning. Sadly for the home crowd, it was not to be. Eller struck out Weaver, got Jackson on a foul pop up, and then fanned Felsch, preserving the Reds four-run lead intact. In the second, the Reds offense went back to work. An infield single by Groh and an opposite field double by Roush stretched the Cincinnati advantage to 5–0.

With two out in the bottom of the third, Joe Jackson belted a long home run into the right-field bleachers, the only round-tripper of the 1919 World Series. Thereafter, Eller returned to form, setting down Sox batters with little difficulty. In the visitors' fifth, a triple by Kopf and an RBI single by Neale restored the Reds' five-run edge. An inning later, Cincinnati seemingly put Game Eight and the World Series away with three more runs. The key blows were a two-run single by Roush and another RBI base hit by Duncan. Then in the eighth, the Reds stretched their lead to 10–1, via an RBI single by Rariden. Sox batsmen, meanwhile, remained punchless. Through seven innings, Hod Eller held Chicago to one run on five hits, striking out six. Finally, the AL champs stirred in the bottom of the eighth. Consecutive safeties by Weaver, Jackson, and Felsch trimmed the Reds' lead to 10–3. Misplayed fly ball base hits by Gandil and Risberg then plated two more Chicago runs, cutting the Reds margin to 10–5, before Eller got out of the inning.

Down to their last three outs, Chicago applied more pressure in the bottom of the ninth. With one out, a hit-batsman, an Eddie Collins single, and a stolen base put Chisox runners on second and third. But Eller would yield no further. He retired Weaver on a short fly to right for the second out, bringing Jackson to the plate with the Sox' very last chance. This time, baseball's peerless swing was good for no more than a routine grounder to Reds second baseman Rath. A short toss to first-sacker Daubert later, the 1919 World Series was history, the Cincinnati Reds having taken baseball's crown, five games to three.

After the game, Pat Moran was overjoyed. "The Reds are champions and I am the happiest man in the world tonight," he exclaimed. "I cannot praise my players high enough. They played a remarkable ball game, fought every minute to win, and there was never a time when they lost confidence."[38] In the Sox locker room, a disappointed Kid Gleason dutifully commended the victors. "There isn't anything to do but take your hat off to Pat Moran and his Reds. They are the World's Champions of baseball."[39] But the unexpected Series defeat was difficult for Gleason to swallow. "I tell you those Reds had no business beating a team like the White Sox. We played the worst baseball, in all but a few games, that we have played all year," lamented Kid. "I don't know what was the matter. Something was wrong."[40] Gleason then added a curious coda to his Series valedictory: "I didn't like the betting odds. I wish no one had ever bet a dollar on the team."[41]

From a statistical standpoint, the White Sox had not posted the kind of numbers that had made them the class of the American League during the regular season. The AL's best-hitting team had posted a paltry .224 team batting average in the Series and had gone a stupefying 26 consecutive innings —

from midway in Game Three to the middle of Game Six—without scoring a single run. The Sox pitching had been spotty (a 3.42 ERA that was mediocre by the standards of the period), and its defense worse, committing 12 errors in eight games. Individual performances were mixed. His bat coming alive in the later games, Joe Jackson had paced all Series batters with a .375 BA, and had driven in a team-leading six runs. Buck Weaver (.324) and Ray Schalk (.304) had also posted solid batting marks. At the other end of the spectrum were disappointing performances by Eddie Collins (.226) and Happy Felsch (.192), and dreadful ones by Swede Risberg (.080, plus four fielding errors) and Nemo Leibold (.056). The performance of Sox hurlers also ran the gamut, from the clutch complete game victories of Dickie Kerr (2–0, 1.42 ERA) to the futility of Lefty Williams (0–3, 6.61 ERA), with Eddie Cicotte (1–2, 2.91 ERA) somewhere in the middle. With the Reds only marginally better at the plate (.253 team BA), the difference had been the Cincinnati pitching staff and its sparkling 1.63 ERA for the Series.

In their post-mortems, baseball pundits were generous in their praise of the new champions. Yet the experts differed on whether the outcome of the 1919 World Series was testament to the superiority of the Reds or the product of underperformance by the White Sox. In the view of sportswriter James Isaminger of the *Philadelphia North American,* "the Reds won the title because they were a better ball team than the White Sox."[42] To Joe Vila of the *New York Sun,* however, the Sox "were caught napping. They were over-confident. They underrated the Reds."[43] But within hours of the final Series out, another factor—sinister and disturbing—was introduced into the debate about the result of the 1919 Fall Classic: the possible corruption of White Sox players.

Notes

1. Although the columns were doubtless ghostwritten for the busy skippers, the copy contained daily quotations from Gleason and Moran that may be presumed genuine.
2. As quoted in the *Washington Post,* September 28, 1919, and elsewhere.
3. *Ibid.*
4. As per the *Washington Post,* September 29, 1919. Third to first, the A's quartet consisted of Frank "Home Run" Baker, Jack Barry, the same Eddie Collins, and Stuffy McInnis.
5. *Ibid.*
6. As per the *Washington Post,* September 30, 1919.
7. As per the *Washington Post,* September 28, 1919.
8. *Ibid.*
9. As quoted in the *Washington Post,* September 30, 1919.
10. See Mike Shatzkin, editor, *The Ballplayers: Baseball's Ultimate Biographical Reference* (New York: Arbor House, 1990), 136.
11. As per the Fullerton testimony at the trial of Joe Jackson's breach-of-contract suit against the White Sox in February 1924. See Jackson Trial Transcript (hereafter JTT), pp. 1064–1065.

12. As later maintained by Fullerton in *The Sporting News,* October 17, 1935.
13. *Ibid.*
14. *Ibid.*
15. For a batter-by-batter reconstruction of 1919 World Series games, see William A. Cook, *The 1919 World Series: What Really Happened* (Jefferson, NC: McFarland, 2001).
16. As per the *Washington Post,* October 2, 1919.
17. *Ibid.*
18. As quoted in the *Washington Post,* October 2, 1919.
19. *Ibid.*
20. As per the *Washington Post,* October 3, 1919.
21. *Chicago Tribune,* October 3, 1919.
22. As quoted in the *Washington Post,* October 4, 1919.
23. *Ibid.*
24. *Ibid.*
25. As per the *Washington Post,* October 5, 1919.
26. *Washington Post,* October 6, 1919.
27. *New York Times,* October 6, 1919.
28. As per Chicago sportswriter James Crusinberry in the *Chicago Tribune,* October 7, 1919.
29. As per the *Washington Post,* October 7, 1919.
30. *Ibid.*
31. *Ibid.*
32. Moran's eighth-inning strategy was perplexing. With the potential Series-clinching run on base and unused Dolf Luque available to pitch the ninth and beyond, Moran bypassed capable pinch-hitters like Sherry Magee and Rube Bressler and let the weak-hitting Ring bat.
33. See the *Cincinnati Post,* October 8 and 9, 1919.
34. As quoted in the *Washington Post,* October 8, 1919.
35. As per the *Washington Post,* October 9, 1919.
36. *Ibid.*
37. *Ibid.* As a major league pitcher, Gleason had gone 138–131 before his arm gave out in 1895. He then played another dozen years, primarily as second baseman.
38. As per the *New York Times,* October 10, 1919.
39. As quoted in the *Washington Post,* October 10, 1919.
40. As quoted in the *Chicago Tribune,* October 10, 1919.
41. *Ibid.*
42. As per an Isaminger column in *The Sporting News,* October 16, 1919.
43. As per a Vila column in *The Sporting News,* October 16, 1919.

3

Rumblings of Scandal

On October 10, 1919, unease about the integrity of the Series performance of the White Sox made its way into newsprint via a Hugh Fullerton column in the *Chicago Herald Examiner.* In addition to voicing concern about the legitimacy of the Series outcome, Fullerton also made the startling assertion that seven unnamed Sox players would not return to the team in 1920.[1] The insinuation that the 1919 World Series had not been on the level was poorly received by most in the sporting press. Cubs beat writer Oscar Reichow dismissed the Fullerton column as sour grapes by an embarrassed expert who had predicted an easy Sox victory.[2] The response of Boston sportswriter James C. O'Leary was even harsher: "It is inconceivable that baseball writers should have dignified these [fix] reports — lies made out of whole cloth — by printing them and even for a moment put a lot of honest ballplayers under the lens of suspicion. It is a shame."[3]

More substantive refutation of the Fullerton column emanated from an unlikely source: Christy Mathewson. In a post–Series opinion piece entitled "Baseball Not Crooked in Spite of Big Betting," Fullerton's expert on 1919 World Series play stated, "The rumors and utterings about the honesty of the series are ridiculous to me."[4] Listed as "irrefutable arguments" against a fix even being attempted were: (1) the inherent honesty of ballplayers; (2) the large number of players needed for a fix to succeed; (3) the quick removal of any corrupted pitcher by his manager; (4) the prohibitive cost, and (5) the reaction of honest teammates. In Mathewson's view, "if ballplayers on a World Series team found their fellows trying to toss one off, they would kill the guilty ones."[5] Thus, Mathewson concluded, "baseball is honest and will stay honest in spite of the abuse that it has taken from time to time."[6]

Two days after Mathewson had exonerated the 1919 Series, *Collyer's Eye,* a weekly horse racing trade sheet, published explicit but little-noticed accusations of World Series corruption. According to investigative reporter Frank

O. Klein, the Series had been fixed, with Abe Attell being named as chief fix promoter.[7] Attell, former world featherweight boxing champ and sometime bodyguard of New York underworld financier Arnold Rothstein, had a well-earned reputation as a hustler not averse to participation in well-paying sports scams.[8] Soon thereafter, New York sportswriters Bill MacBeth and Bill Farnsworth publicly joined the ranks of Series skeptics.[9] Then, on November 14, a call for inquiry into the outcome of the 1919 Series was made by respected sports columnist Harry A. Williams of the *Los Angeles Times.*[10] The following day, *Collyer's Eye* struck again, citing Eddie Cicotte, Chick Gandil, Lefty Williams, Swede Risberg, Joe Jackson, Happy Felsch, and Fred McMullin as being under suspicion for corrupt Series play.[11] One month later, Fullerton returned to the controversy with a syndicated column that bore the provocative title, "Is Big League Baseball Being Run for Gamblers, With Players in the Deal?"[12] Follow-up Fullerton postings on baseball's corruption problems were then published into early January 1920.[13]

Syndicated sportswriter Hugh Fullerton was the first scribe to publicly express skepticism about the integrity of Sox play in the 1919 World Series.

Major league baseball offered little official response, leaving disparagement of Fullerton and his allies to friendly organs like *The Sporting News* and *Baseball Magazine.* In the short run, the strategy worked. The burgeoning scandal lost traction with a fandom eager for a new season to begin and soon faded from public consciousness. When Spring 1920 arrived, the sporting public quickly became engrossed in the action, particularly the slugging exploits of New York Yankees pitcher-turned-outfielder Babe Ruth, embarking on the season that would change the very way the game was played. In his first full season as an everyday player, Ruth would hit .376, with 54 home runs and 137 RBIs. He also walked 148 times, scored 158 runs, and posted a .530 OBP and a .847 slugging percentage. Major league baseball had never seen a performance like it.[14] The defending AL champions, however, would supply formidable opposition to Ruth and his Yankees. Apart from Chick Gandil, suspended by club owner Comiskey after refusing to sign a 1920 contract that included no raise, the Sox lineup was intact. And with Shano Collins filling in capably at first base and Red Faber (23 wins) returning to form, Gandil's absence would hardly be noticed by Chicago faithful. The AL pennant chase became a tight three-way race between the Chicago, New York, and Cleveland clubs, all of which would set new franchise attendance records, with the Yankees topping the 1 million home fans mark.[15]

Notwithstanding the diversion of the new pennant campaigns, baseball was unable to clear itself entirely of controversy about the game's integrity. The 1920 season would be dogged by a number of nagging distractions. The first of these took the form of Lee Magee, a one-season Federal League star who seemed to wear out his welcome quickly wherever he went in baseball. In February 1920, Magee was given his unconditional release by the Chicago Cubs, notwithstanding solid statistics for the previous season. Acquired from Brooklyn early in the 1919 season, Magee (born Leopold Christopher Hoernschemeyer) had been a useful pickup for Chicago, playing three infield positions as well as the outfield, while batting a solid .292. When no other team made an offer for his services, Magee, sensing a blacklist, began making noises about corruption in baseball. "If I am barred," said Magee, "I'll take quite a few people with me. I'll show up some people for tricks turned since 1906."[16] Then Magee took a fateful step. He instituted a lawsuit for damages against the Cubs in the Court of Common Pleas, Hamilton County (Cincinnati).

Filed on April 14, 1920, and subsequently removed to federal court on diversity of citizenship grounds by Cubs lawyers,[17] the action would prove a disaster for plaintiff Magee. On May 20, the Cubs moved for dismissal, informing U.S. District Court Judge John W. Peck that Magee had privately admitted trying to throw a July 1918 game while a member of the Cincinnati Reds and was, therefore, unfit for continued employment by a major league baseball team. The game in question was a July 25, 1918, contest between Cincinnati and the Boston Braves, played while the peripatetic Magee was a Reds teammate of reputed fix master Hal Chase. Despite the worst efforts of the pair, the Reds won, 4–2, in 13 innings, with Magee reluctantly scoring the go-ahead run on a long triple by Edd Roush. According to the moving papers, Magee had confessed his involvement in the plan to dump the game to NL President John Heydler and Cubs President William L. Veeck, Sr., during a recent meeting held at the Congress Hotel in Chicago.[18]

The dismissal motion was denied but when the suit went to trial, additional evidence of Magee's perfidy was exposed. Particularly illuminating was the testimony of Boston bookmaker James Costello, who revealed that after the July 1918 game fix effort had failed, Magee reneged on his bet by stopping payment on the $500 check that he had given to Costello as guarantee of a Reds loss. When his turn on the witness stand came, the best that Magee could muster in response was the limp claim that he had intended his bet to be on the Reds to win, but had been secretly double-crossed by teammate Hal Chase, the fix instigator.[19] The jury was unimpressed, deliberating for only 44 minutes before finding in favor of the Cubs. Magee's baseball career was over.[20]

Apart from some temporary embarrassment, major league baseball weathered the Magee storm handily. Attendance at ballparks continued to soar, with fans energized by exciting pennant races, particularly in the AL. Then in mid-summer, a scandal that would have far more serious Black Sox repercussions erupted on the West Coast. On August 3, 1920, Pacific Coast League President William H. McCarthy announced that an investigation into gambling allegations had prompted the release of the league's leading batter, outfielder Harl Maggert of the Salt Lake City Bees, and the banning of just-released major league star Hal Chase from PCL ballparks. Vernon Tigers team captain Babe Borton was also under suspicion, indefinitely suspended pending the outcome of a bribery probe.[21] Soon, news reports revealed that Maggert was suspected of accepting a $300 bribe from Borton to "lay down" during a crucial late–1919 season series between Salt Lake City and Vernon. Californian Chase, then playing intermittently for San Jose in the outlaw Mission League, was accused of attempting to bribe Salt Lake City pitcher Spider Baum earlier in 1920.[22] Within days, the scandal mushroomed, enveloping more players and ultimately calling into question the legitimacy of Vernon's 1919 PCL crown.[23] In due course, the matter would be brought to the attention of a Los Angeles County grand jury, as will be discussed in Chapter 8. But by that time, the focus of baseball scandal followers had been diverted to a more momentous venue: Chicago.

As noted in the Preface, the inquiry that exposed the Black Sox scandal initially had nothing to do with the 1919 World Series. It centered on an inconsequential August 31, 1920, game between the Cubs and the Philadelphia Phillies. With both clubs languishing deep in the second division, the contest was without meaning in the 1920 NL pennant race. Even so, the game seemed to be attracting inordinate interest in baseball betting circles. Shortly before game time, Cubs President William L. Veeck, Sr., was disturbed by telegrams and long-distance telephone calls that implied that the Cubs would dump the game. According to wires from men identified as W.H. Brown, Bart Tanner, Mitchell B. Stevens, Tommy Ryan, "friend Harry," and H. Stevens, and long-distance telephone calls by G.R. Allen and J.H. Clinton, all reputedly of Detroit, the fix was in.[24] Acting quickly, Veeck contacted Cubs manager Fred Mitchell who then replaced scheduled starter Claude Hendrix with staff ace Grover Cleveland Alexander. Promised a healthy bonus for a winning performance, Alex pitched well but dropped a 3–0 decision to the Phillies' Lee Meadows.

After several days of rumination, Veeck chose to go public, a decision probably occasioned by the unhappy experience of trying to resolve the Lee Magee problem confidentially. Veeck was also doubtless concerned about the reaction of his boss, Cubs owner William Wrigley, a vocal proponent of punitive justice in the PCL scandal. Wrigley was livid at the prospect that the Los Angeles Angels, which he also owned, might have been cheated out of the previous season's PCL crown and had loudly demanded the expulsion of corrupted players. "The crooks and gamblers in baseball must go," Wrigley had declared. "Baseball is the greatest American sport and it must not be made less attractive with the public by the presence of dishonest players in the ranks."[25] On September 4, 1920, Veeck summoned the press to inform them that he had retained the Burns Detective Agency to investigate both the playing and the betting on the Cubs-Phillies game of August 31. Veeck simultaneously pledged the Chicago franchise's full cooperation with any inquiry that might be undertaken by NL President John Heydler. Veeck also invited local sports scribes to conduct their own probe of the situation. National Base Ball Writers Association of America President Irving Sanborn promptly took up the invitation, appointing BBWAA/Chicago members a committee of the whole, with *Chicago Herald Examiner* sports editor Sam Hall to serve as chairman.[26] But before the above inquiries had made much headway, a new force assumed control of the investigation, namely Judge Charles A. McDonald and the Cook County grand jury.

Notes

1. *Chicago Herald Examiner,* October 10, 1919.
2. As per a Reichow column in *The Sporting News,* October 16, 1919.
3. As per an O'Leary column in *The Sporting News,* October 16, 1919.
4. Published in the *New York Times,* October 16, 1919.
5. *Ibid.*
6. *Ibid.*
7. *Collyer's Eye,* October 18, 1919.
8. Attell, a truly great fighter in his prime, had been world featherweight (then 122 lb.) champion from 1903 to 1912. But throughout his career, and particularly toward its

end, the Little Champ was suspected of ring deceptions. After he finally hung up the gloves, Attell was always on the lookout for a quick score. An engaging if incorrigible hustler his entire life, Abe Attell (1883–1970) has been enshrined in various boxing halls of fame, his dubious reputation notwithstanding.

9. See *New York Tribune,* October 18, 1919 (MacBeth); *New York American,* October 18, 1919 (Farnsworth).

10. *Los Angeles Times,* November 14, 1919.

11. *Collyer's Eye,* November 15, 1919.

12. Published in the *New York Evening World,* December 15, 1919.

13. Published in the *New York Evening World,* December 17, 18 and 20, 1919, and January 2, 1920.

14. Ruth's 54 homers were more than the total hit by any other major league team in 1920. The game would soon undergo change as players attempted to emulate the long-ball hitting style of the Babe. But it would take another dozen seasons before another ballplayer besides Babe (Jimmie Foxx in 1932) would top Ruth's 1920 home run output.

15. While the 1920 New York Yankees' 1,289,422 home attendance figure made it the first franchise to go over the 1 million mark, New York was not that far ahead of the attendance figures of Cleveland (912,832) and Chicago (833,492).

16. As quoted in the *New York Times,* March 24, 1920, and *The Sporting News,* April 1, 1920.

17. As reported in the *New York Times,* January 10, 1920, and elsewhere. As a non-resident of Ohio, the Chicago Cubs had automatic grounds to have the case transferred to a federal forum.

18. Following the meeting, Chase, by then with the Giants, was quietly declared persona non grata and dropped from the New York roster. For more on Chase's banishment, see Donald Dewey and Nicholas Acocella, *The Black Prince of Baseball: Hal Chase and the Mythology of the Game* (Toronto: Sport Classic Books, 2004), 282–307.

19. As per the *Chicago Tribune and Washington Post,* June 9, 1920.

20. For a fuller account of the Magee lawsuit, see Martin Donell Kohout, *Hal Chase: The Defiant Life and Turbulent Times of Baseball's Biggest Crook* (Jefferson, NC: McFarland, 2001), 227–233.

21. For a comprehensive account of the PCL scandal, see Larry R. Gerlach, "The Bad News Bees: Salt Lake City and the 1919 Pacific Coast League Scandal," *Base Ball: A Journal of the Early Game,* Vol. 6, No. 1, Spring 2012, 35–74.

22. As reported in the *Chicago Tribune* and *Los Angeles Times,* August 4, 1920, and elsewhere.

23. To follow the public unfolding of the PCL scandal, see the *Los Angeles Times,* August 5 to 18, 1920.

24. As reported in the *Chicago Evening Post* and *Chicago Herald Examiner,* September 4, 1920. To no surprise, all the names provided by fix informants proved fictitious.

25. As quoted in the *Los Angeles Times,* August 13, 1920.

26. As reported in all the Chicago daily newspapers and elsewhere.

4

A Grand Jury Is Convened

As already mentioned, the judicial aspects of the Black Sox scandal—grand jury, criminal trial, and civil litigation—involve distinct, and very different, types of legal proceedings. Of the three, the grand jury hearing is the least understood. This is a product of unfamiliarity, as few readers of this work are likely to have set foot in a grand jury room. And in the case of the Black Sox, the problem is compounded by the highly unconventional manner in which the proceedings were conducted. To convey an appreciation of the latter, a short primer on grand jury law and practice is necessary.

The grand jury is a venerable institution that dates from 12th-century England and remains to this day the primary means by which those accused of crime in this country are brought to trial.[1] A grand jury normally consists of 16 to 23 citizens who reside in that jurisdiction. Grand jurors serve for a fixed period of time, during which they consider evidence of crime gathered against those who have been charged with lawbreaking by the police. Grand jurors do not determine guilt or innocence, but simply decide whether the continued prosecution of the accused is warranted. Although a staple of the criminal justice system, grand jury proceedings are not uniformly conducted. They are variable in nature, governed by the statutes, court rules, and local practices indigenous to the locale where the offense occurred. But regardless of where conducted, a hallmark of grand jury proceedings is secrecy. Neither the public nor the press may attend a grand jury session. Nor is the accused or his attorney allowed to be present. As the grand jury is an arm of the court, a judge may preside over the proceedings but this is not the norm. Generally, a member of the prosecutor's office is in charge. The only persons privy to the grand jury process are the grand jurors, the grand jury stenographer, grand jury clerical personnel, and the prosecutor, all of whom take an oath to keep the proceedings secret. The secrecy mandate, however, does not extend to the subject matter of the inquiry or to the identity of grand jury witnesses. Such witnesses, moreover, are free to divulge their testimony to the press or public, if they so choose, after their appearance.

The proceedings themselves are entirely one-sided, as the grand jury hears only evidence presented by the government. Grand jurors are at liberty to pose questions but the bulk of witness examination is customarily left to the prosecutor. Proof may take any form as rules of evidence do not apply and the grand jury routinely receives hearsay, questionably seized evidence, and other forms of information that may not be admissible at trial. At the conclusion of the evidence presentation, the grand jury is instructed on the applicable law by the prosecutor and potential charges are outlined. During its deliberations, the grand jury, again, does not decide the question of guilt or innocence. It only evaluates whether there is probable cause[2] to believe: (1) that a serious criminal offense (typically called a felony) occurred within its territorial limits, and (2) that the accused participated in its commission. If at least a majority of the panel as fully constituted (i.e., 12 of a 23-member grand jury) is persuaded that the charging standard has been met — in reality, the determination rendered in the vast majority of cases presented — the accused stands indicted.[3] A formal statement of charges, known as a true bill, is drafted by the prosecutor, endorsed by the grand jury foreperson, and then made public by its return to a designated judge in open court.

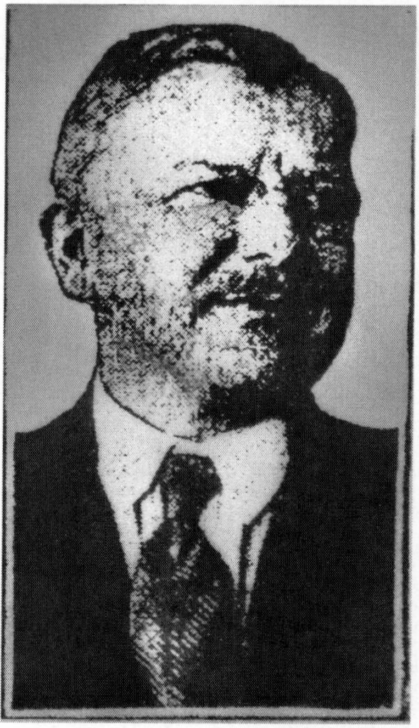

An avid Chicago baseball fan, Judge Charles A. McDonald initiated the Cook County grand jury investigation that led to the exposure of the Series fix.

Finally, preliminary note should be taken of the singular nature of the proceedings conducted in the Black Sox case. Midway through the grand jury hearings, it was reported that "officials of Chief Justice McDonald's court, desirous of giving the national game the benefit of publicity in its purging, lifted the curtain on the grand jury proceedings."[4] But such a bland pronouncement does not do the proceedings adequate justice. For what transpired in and about the Cook County grand jury room in the fall of 1920 was remarkable for many things, not the least of which was the total disregard of the principle of grand jury secrecy by those involved. Not a day went by without wholesale disclosure of grand jury proceedings, with witness testimony often reprinted verbatim in the news. All of this was entirely unlawful, for the principle of grand jury secrecy was not optional, a matter that could be relaxed in the name of some putative public interest. It was black letter law and ironclad. Only shortly after the Black Sox grand jury hearings concluded, the Illinois Supreme Court reaffirmed this precept, reiterating that "in furtherance of justice and upon grounds of public policy, the law requires that grand jury proceedings shall be regarded as privileged communications and the secrets of the grand jury room shall not be revealed."[5]

Aside from disregard of that dictum in the Black Sox proceedings, the daily leak of grand jury testimony was oft-times accompanied by another extra-legal phenomenon: public commentary about the probe or its targets by the grand jury prosecutor, the panel foreman, and even, on occasion, the presiding judge. These commentaries were also completely inappropriate, if not unlawful, as public statements about matters likely to end up in litigation could not properly be uttered by officers of the court, even in 1920 Chicago. Because out-of-court public statements about trial-bound cases were deemed inherently prejudicial to a fair trial, they were expressly prohibited by the Illinois canons of legal ethics. More particularly, those canons banned "newspaper publications by a lawyer as to pending or anticipated litigation."[6] A similar prohibition on public comment extended to Illinois judges and those, such as grand jury members and court attendants, subject to judicial supervision.[7] But in the Black Sox matter, the siren call of media attention proved irresistible to its principal actors. Even the grand jury panelists were swept up, happily posing for group photos taken by the Chicago press corps.[8] Little if any notice, however, was taken of the rampant breach of grand jury law, ethical prescription, or legal decorum that attended the Black Sox hearings. In hindsight, perhaps the most remarkable aspect of the grand jury proceedings in the Black Sox case was the reaction to its unorthodox modus operandi. There was none.

The proceedings themselves involved some of Chicago's most formidable personalities. Arguably more than any other force, the exposure of the Black Sox scandal can be attributed to the zeal of Cook County Circuit Judge Charles A. McDonald. A veteran jurist first elected to the bench in 1910, McDonald was an avid baseball fan and a longtime acquaintance of AL president Ban Johnson, White Sox owner Charles Comiskey, and other dignitaries of the game. Only recently, Johnson had endorsed McDonald as a "good man" to succeed Garry Herrmann as chairman of the National Commission.[9] But in September 1920, the judge was focused on his position as newly installed chief justice of the Cook County criminal courts. According to Landis biographer David Pietrusza, a private meeting between Judge McDonald and league presidents Johnson and Heydler was held shortly after Veeck's disclosures about the suspicious Cubs-Phillies game.[10] On September 7, 1920—in his first official act as chief justice—McDonald brought this game to the attention of a newly empanelled Cook County grand jury. He began his instructions by acknowledging "press accounts of the recent baseball scandal" and denouncing the "coterie of unscrupulous gamblers" that was alleged to have approached Cubs players about throwing the contest.[11] After a heartfelt tribute to baseball as "our national sport" and the source of "healthful, wholesome exercise" for the country's youth, McDonald warned that the future of the game was imperiled if its integrity was subject to doubt. This being so, it was

> a matter of public importance which is the duty of the grand jury to investigate thoroughly ... so that everyone implicated in the infamous conspiracy to bring the national game of baseball into disrepute and to injure the business of the respective club owners and their individual players should be brought to speedy justice and exposed to public scorn.[12]

The judge concluded his charge by urging the grand jurors to "wipe out" the "pernicious business" of pool selling on baseball via indictment of the racket's "prompters."[13] Conspicuous by its absence was any mention of the 1919 World Series in the instructions given to the grand jury.

A ringing, if windy, public endorsement was bestowed on the grand jury's investigation by Chicago's chief prosecutor, Cook County State's Attorney Maclay Hoyne, who pledged,

> Every resource of the State's Attorneys Office [SAO] will be used, if necessary, to uncover and bring to justice the ring of professional gamblers whose operations threaten to besmirch the one great American sport which so long has been run upon highly honest and unquestionably straight lines.... The baseball gambler is the greatest peril of professional baseball today, and all that this office can do will be done to put him where he belongs.[14]

Like the instructions of Judge McDonald, the remarks of State's Attorney Hoyne made no reference to the previous season's World Series. And the resources that Hoyne's office would bring to the baseball gambling probe would not include the participation of Hoyne himself, then locked in a bitter primary fight for re-nomination by local Democrats. Although a highly visible two-term incumbent, Hoyne had antagonized factions of the party establishment by waging an independent campaign to become Chicago mayor in 1918. Political payback came in the form of multiple Democrat challengers for Hoyne's state's attorney post, including Michael Igoe, the minority leader in the Illinois House of Representatives and a former federal prosecutor. Hoyne's administration of his office was also taking fire from the leading Republican candidate, Circuit Court Judge Robert E. Crowe. Crowe remained on the bench while he campaigned, alternating criticism of President Woodrow Wilson's foreign policy[15] with judicial rulings sharply critical of the SAO.[16] With Hoyne thus needing to busy himself on the hustings, appearance before the grand jury in the baseball probe would be left to his subordinates, at first Assistant State's Attorneys (ASA) John Foster and Hartley Replogle, and thereafter Replogle and ASA Ota P. Lightfoot.[17]

Notwithstanding the fanfare, the grand jury inquiry got off to a slow start. Apart from a September 8 cameo by Cubs President Veeck, who "promised all the cooperation he could bring to their aid,"[18] the panel conducted no baseball-related work for the next two weeks. This lull in the proceedings gave the probe-opposed editorial page of *The Sporting News* the opening needed to cast a pall on the investigation, dismissing the rumored fix of the Cubs-Phillies game as a hoax concocted by "a bunch of blackleg gamblers ... [acting] with the obvious purpose of getting suckers to bite and plunge, or with spiteful intention of besmirching baseball for purposes best known to themselves."[19] The investigation, however, was not so easily discouraged and, over time, began to pick up momentum.

The rumors of October 1919 were revived by *New York Sun* sportswriter Joe Vila, who penned a syndicated column that alleged that five unnamed White Sox players had conspired to throw the World Series, a charge that prompted Chisox treasurer Lou Comiskey to issue Vila a public invitation to present his evidence to the Cook County grand jury.[20] Vila, however, expressed regret that the "press of recent business assignments" obliged him to decline a Chicago trip.[21] Judge McDonald, meanwhile, expanded the grand jury's writ to embrace matters well beyond the suspect Cubs-Phillies game. "You have been called together to consider baseball gambling in all its ramifications," he explained. "A stain has been placed on the great national American game and you and the public will want to know all about it."[22] Chicago police were also stirred to action, arresting a number of previously unmolested baseball pool operators. "I will instruct all captains to get busy and root out all the baseball pools operating in their districts," declared Chicago Police Chief John J. Garrity following the arrests.[23]

On September 15, 1920, insurgent candidate Michael Igoe scored a decisive victory in the Democratic Party primary for the Cook County State's Attorney post. An embittered Hoyne thereupon decamped for an extended family vacation in New York, leaving the baseball gambling investigation to his subordinates.[24] The following day, the BBWAA probe was declared stillborn, chairman Hall having been too busy to convene a meeting of his investigative committee. And, unbeknownst to press or public, the renowned Pinkerton Detective Agency had just declined a confidential request for an investigation of the 1919 World Series made by AL President Johnson.[25]

Yet, such setbacks proved brief. Renewed impetus was supplied to the investigation by the publication of a letter to the *Chicago Tribune* by prominent baseball fan Fred Loomis. Citing the "perfectly good grand jury located in this county," Loomis pressed for inquiry into the by-now widespread report that the play of the 1919 World Series had been contaminated by "an alleged conspiracy between certain unnamed members of the Chicago White Sox and certain gamblers."[26] And Ban Johnson, reportedly in private communication with Judge McDonald, was determined to see Series scandal allegations probed.[27] Shortly thereafter, grand jury subpoenas were issued for MLB executives Johnson, Heydler, Comiskey, and Veeck, and for an assortment of Chicago sports journalists, including Bert Collyer and Frank O. Klein of *Collyer's Eye*.[28] It was also reported that the grand jury would be making inquiry into why Comiskey had withheld 1919 World Series checks from eight of his players.[29]

On the eve of substantive grand jury proceedings, federal authorities suddenly swung into action. Chicago Internal Revenue Service Chief Harry W. Mager publicly initiated "a move to collect hundreds of thousands" of dollars in excise taxes evaded by baseball pool operators.[30] Also targeted was one J.L. McDaniel, reputed head of the Indianapolis firm that printed the pool slips, an estimated 100,000 of which were being shipped to Chicago each week.[31] In the midst of a late-season road trip, meanwhile, the Chicago Cubs strangely depleted their playing roster by sending home hurler Claude Hendrix, the originally scheduled starter in the suspect game of August 31, as well as infield regulars Buck Herzog and Fred Merkle, and reliever Paul Carter. When called upon to explain, Manager Fred Mitchell maintained, somewhat improbably, that the move had no connection to the imminent grand jury probe into game-fixing allegations.[32] The players simply were not needed for the road trip. Nor would their services be required in future, as the major league careers of this quartet — for whatever reason — had effectively been brought to a close.[33]

Notes

1. In its pertinent part, the Fifth Amendment of the United States Constitution provides, "No person shall be held to answer for a capital, or otherwise infamous crime, unless on presentment or indictment of a Grand Jury." Although constitutionally acceptable alternatives to the grand jury process have been adopted in various states, most jurisdictions, including Illinois, retain the grand jury system as the instrument through which serious crimes are charged.

2. Probable cause is an amorphous concept, not susceptible to precise definition. But generally speaking, it is "more than bare suspicion but less than the quantum of evidence [i.e., proof beyond a reasonable doubt] required to sustain a conviction." See *Black's Law Dictionary,* 9th edition, Bryan A. Garner, editor (St. Paul: West, 2009), 1321.

3. In the ten years that the author spent as grand jury section chief in the Middlesex County (NJ) Prosecutor's Office, the grand jury returned true bills in approximately 90% of the cases presented. Evidentially shaky or otherwise problematic criminal cases were usually resolved by means other than the grand jury process.

4. As reported in the *Atlanta Constitution* and *Los Angeles Times,* September 29, 1920, and elsewhere.

5. *People v. Goldberg,* 302 *Ill.* 559, 135 *N.E.* 84 (Sup. Ct. 1922).

6. In Illinois, public comment by an attorney on a pending court matter was proscribed by Canon 20, Illinois State Bar Association Canons of Professional Ethics, adopted June 24, 1910.

7. The current version of this ethical mandate is Illinois Code of Judicial Conduct, Canon 3A4(b)(6), adopted August 6, 1983.

8. Group photos of the grand jurors were published in the *Chicago Daily News* and *Chicago Evening Post,* September 23, 1920, and *Chicago Tribune,* September 24, 1920.

9. *Washington Post,* August 4, 1920. See also the *Chicago Evening Post,* September 7, 1920. In an interview years later, McDonald stated that Herrmann once offered him "the job later given to Judge Landis" but McDonald had declined because "I initiated the [Black Sox] probe," as per the *Chicago Tribune,* December 17, 1944.

10. The meeting place has been fixed as Chicago's Edgewater Golf Club. See David Pietrusza, *Judge and Jury: The Life and Times of Judge Kenesaw Mountain Landis* (South Bend, Ind.: Diamond Communications, 1998), 164.

11. The text of Judge McDonald's instructions to the grand jury was published complete and verbatim in the *Chicago Daily Journal, Chicago Daily News* and *Chicago Evening Post,* September 7, 1920.

12. *Ibid.* The court's assignment reportedly elicited a cheer from the grand jurors, as per the *Chicago Herald Examiner* and *Chicago Tribune,* September 8, 1920.

13. It was estimated that baseball pools netted $40,000 per day in the city alone. See *Chicago Daily Journal,* September 9, 1920.

14. As reported in the *Chicago Daily Journal,* September 7, 1920, *Chicago Herald Examiner,* September 8, 1920, and elsewhere.

15. See e.g., *Chicago Tribune,* August 16, 1920.

16. See e.g., *Chicago Tribune,* August 19, 1920, regarding the dismissal of three election fraud prosecutions wherein Crowe found that the SAO "was not acting in good faith." Hoyne's demand that Judge Crowe recuse himself from SAO cases until after the election fell on deaf ears. Today, Crowe would have been obliged to resign from the bench the moment that he declared his candidacy for a non-judicial office. See Illinois Code of Judicial Conduct, Canon 7(B)(2).

17. The grand jury performance of Foster attracted unspecified criticism and he was supplanted early in the probe by ASA Lightfoot. ASA Ernest Stanley was also assigned to the matter.

18. As per the *Chicago Daily Journal,* September 8, 1920, and the *Chicago Herald Examiner,* September 10, 1920.

19. *The Sporting News* editorial, published September 9, 1920.

20. See the *New York Sun,* September 13, 1920 (Vila), and *Chicago Herald Examiner,* September 15, 1920 (Lou Comiskey).

21. As reported in the *Chicago Tribune,* September 17, 1920.

22. As reported in the *Chicago Daily Journal,* September 10, 1920.

23. As quoted in the *Chicago Daily Journal,* September 11, 1920.

24. Notwithstanding the sting of Judge Crowe's rulings against his office, Democrat Hoyne and his staff would openly support the Republican candidate over Democrat Igoe, a "venomous little fool" whom Hoyne detested. See the *Chicago Tribune,* October 15, 1920.

25. As reflected in correspondence preserved in the Black Sox file at the Giamatti Research Center, National Baseball Hall of Fame and Museum, Cooperstown, New York. During the Series, Johnson apparently had the Cal Crim Detective Agency of Cincinnati monitoring events, as related in Susan Dellinger, *Red Legs and Black Sox: Edd Roush and the Untold Story of the 1919 World Series* (Cincinnati: Emmis Books, 2006), 243–251, 256–273.

26. Published September 19, 1920, the Loomis letter was actually ghostwritten by *Tribune* sportswriter James Crusinberry, who himself would become a significant witness in the grand jury probe. Crusinberry would reveal his authorship of the Loomis letter in a late-life article published in *Sports Illustrated,* September 17, 1956.

27. According to Eliot Asinof, *Eight Men Out: The Black Sox and the 1919 World Series* (New York: Henry Holt, 1963), 155.

28. As reported in the *Chicago Evening Post* and *Chicago Herald Examiner,* September 21, 1920.

29. *Ibid.*

30. As reported in the *Chicago Daily Journal,* September 22, 1920.

31. As per the *Chicago Evening Post,* September 21, 1920.

32. As per the *Chicago Evening American* and *Chicago Tribune,* September 24, 1920.

33. Hendrix, Herzog, and Carter would never appear in another major league game. Apart from a handful of appearances for the 1925–1926 Yankees, the big league career of the ill-starred Merkle was over as well.

5

Early Grand Jury Proceedings

The grand jury proceedings in the Black Sox case began in earnest on September 22, 1920. In what would become a pattern, the action inside the grand jury room was accompanied by official pronouncement outside of it. Judge McDonald inaugurated the practice with the public assurance that "we are trying to help, not injure, baseball. If anyone is guilty of fixing games, the public ought to know it. It is time for a show-up for the benefit of the public as well as the sport. We are after all forms of gambling, the betting rings by big professional gamblers and the little baseball pools."[1] Also making his speaking debut was Henry H. Brigham, an automobile company president who had been appointed grand jury foreman. Following an extended private conference with ASA Replogle, Brigham announced, "All the members of the grand jury are keen to learn if there is crookedness in the playing of major league baseball. We are going to sift thoroughly the stories that have been circulated, and this investigation will probably decide whether the great American sport has been debauched to make a gamblers' holiday."[2]

Author Note: Because only fragments of the actual grand jury record survive, an unimpeachable account of the testimony taken by the grand jury cannot be rendered. The following exposition has been stitched together from official record fragments, contemporaneous newspaper reportage, and, occasionally, Black Sox literature.

The evidence-gathering phase of the grand jury proceedings commenced with the testimony of White Sox owner Charles A. Comiskey, accompanied into the grand jury room by his son Lou and team secretary Harry Grabiner.[3] During his 45-minute appearance, the "Old Roman" acknowledged that he had had suspicions about his team's play in the 1919 Series and had withheld the Series checks of eight Chisox players afterwards. To resolve the issue,

After a slow start, the courthouse appearance of White Sox owner Charles A. Comiskey and Cubs President William L. Veeck, Sr., signaled that the grand jury probe had begun in earnest.

Comiskey had offered a $10,000 reward for information about the alleged bribing of the players and had retained private detectives to investigate the matter. Those detectives, however, had "found nothing to substantiate the rumors" of crooked Series play by White Sox players. His testimony concluded, Comiskey was excused from the witness stand to the reported applause of the panel.[4] During the testimony of Cubs President William L. Veeck, Sr., the grand jury was provided with telegrams, correspondence, and an "armful" of investigative reports pertaining to the August 31 Cubs-Phillies game.[5] But "no tangible information" upon which the prosecution of any player could be based had been unearthed by Veeck's detectives.[6] *Chicago Herald Examiner* sports editor Sam Hall, chairman of the aborted BBWAA probe, offered the grand jury his opinion that only two corrupt players were required to fix a game. As for the 1919 World Series, Hall asserted that "the better team lost last year but, of course, that does not prove that the series was crooked. I have no positive knowledge of that."[7]

American League President Ban Johnson was the behind-the-scenes force driving the inquiry into the bona fides of the 1919 World Series.

While it received no immediate press attention, the testimony of *Chicago Tribune* sportswriter James Crusinberry was easily the most significant presented to the panel at the hearing's initial proof-gathering session. Provided were the first purported details of the fix of the 1919 World Series.[8] According to Crusinberry, Hal Chase had conceived the plot, partnering with White Sox first baseman Chick Gandil on the selection of the players to be corrupted. New York underworld financier Arnold Rothstein bankrolled the scheme. Well after the Series was over, Crusinberry had obtained firsthand confirmation of the fix. On July 17, 1920, he and fellow sportswriter Ring Lardner had eavesdropped on a New York City barroom conversation between White Sox manager Kid Gleason and an inebriated Abe Attell. During the encounter with Gleason, Attell acknowledged that the 1919 Series had been fixed, expressing a sort of surly regret for his own involvement in the deed.[9] Before departing the stand, Crusinberry also identified ardent Sox fan and serious World Series betting loser Sam Pass as a potential source of fix information for the grand jury. The final grand jury witness of September 22 was AL President Ban Johnson, who created a stir outside the hearing room by informing assembled reporters that games during the 1919 season had been fixed.[10] But whether Johnson was referring specifically to the 1919 World Series was not made clear and his actual grand jury testimony did not address the subject, being confined to platitudes about baseball's support for the panel's work and the like.[11] Substantive testimony would have to await subsequent grand jury appearances by the witness.

The proceedings of September 23 were more eventful. Even before the grand jury reassembled, readers of the *Chicago Daily Journal* were regaled with "Rube Benton's Own Story" by the day's featured witness.[12] The Benton exposé focused upon an August 1919 bribe supposedly offered the New York Giants southpaw in a Chicago café by Cubs infielder Buck Herzog and Hal Chase, by then a member of the Giants. After Benton had refused the bribe and posted a 6–3 victory over the Cubs, Giants third baseman Heinie Zimmerman showed his contempt for Benton with the comment, "You poor fish. Didn't you know there was $400 waiting for you to lose the game today?"[13] Months after the fact, Benton reported the incident to Giants coach Art Fletcher. Manager John McGraw was notified of the matter by Benton the following spring. Benton concluded his account by relating, "I don't know anything about the rumor of crookedness among other clubs, and I don't know if they are true or not. That is all I have to tell the grand jury. That is the end of my story."[14]

But once before the grand jury, Benton had a lot more to tell. In addition to repeating his newspaper accounts of Giants-related skullduggery, Benton provided information about the 1919 World Series fix. In particular, Benton maintained that while the Giants were on a post-1919 season barnstorming trip, Chase received wires from ex-major league pitcher Bill Burns.[15] As a result, Chase made $40,000 through "wise bets" placed on the Series. Giants pitcher Jean Dubuc had also been in communication with Burns, receiving a telegram from Sleepy Bill during the Series that advised him to "bet on Cincinnati tomorrow." Benton further testified that he later learned that the Series had been fixed from Philip Hahn, a Cincinnati betting commissioner. A gambling syndicate in Pittsburgh was said to be behind the scheme.[16]

Reaction to publication of the Benton grand jury testimony was furious. An angry Buck Herzog branded Benton's account of the café bribe offer "a lie. Benton's been telling that mess of trash a long time."[17] Herzog also disclosed that Benton's allegations against him were not new, having been quietly investigated and deemed groundless during confidential proceedings conducted by NL President Heydler.[18] Herzog then unveiled affidavits recently secured from Boston Braves teammates Art Wilson and Tony Boeckel, each of which averred that Benton himself had admitted to profiting from advance knowledge of the Series fix. Benton, it was alleged, had won $3,800 betting on tips supplied by Chase.[19] As soon as the Herzog accusations were printed, Benton responded in kind, publicly labeling the claim that he had won big betting on the 1919 Series "all pure hot air." Benton's wagering had been confined to friendly $20 bets with Giants teammate Larry Doyle, such small stakes gambling having had the tacit approval of manager McGraw.[20]

Back inside the grand jury room, the September 23 session concluded with the recall of Cubs President Veeck for brief testimony that did not garner press notice and the appearance of Samuel W. Pass, best man at the wedding of White Sox catcher Ray Schalk and an intimate of many on the Chicago roster. A natural raconteur, Pass spent most of his time on the stand entertaining the grand jurors with baseball stories. Regarding the 1919 World Series, Pass had bet on the White Sox and lost, much to his surprise. The die-hard Sox supporter estimated his total betting deficit at $3,200, a good part of it lost to ex-featherweight boxing champ Abe Attell.[21] After the Series was over, Pass initiated his own personal inquiry into the legitimacy of the outcome but had uncovered only unsubstantiated rumor and hearsay, including reports of gamblers meeting with White Sox players at the Warner Hotel during the Series.[22] On this point and others, Pass thought that more solid information might be gleaned by the grand jury via interrogation of Henrietta Kelley, in-season boarding house landlady of various White Sox players. The bombshell revelation of the day, however, came not from the witness stand, but from ASA Replogle. Speaking to a press assemblage at session's end, Replogle declared, "The last World Series between the Chicago White Sox and the Cincinnati Reds was not on the square. From five to seven players on the White Sox are involved."[23] Almost simultaneously, AL President Johnson voiced the claim that the White Sox would not dare win the 1920 pennant for fear that "the gambling syndicate would tell what they knew of the conduct of certain players in the Cincinnati-Sox world's championship of 1919."[24] Johnson also publicly identified Eddie Cicotte, Chick Gandil, and Fred McMullin as three of the Sox players whose Series checks had been withheld by Comiskey.[25]

The most significant scandal-related development of the following day was widespread publication of a *cri de coeur* from a wounded Comiskey.[26] It began with a brief outline of his lifelong connection to baseball during which "at all times [I have] endeavored to be honest with the public, fair with my ball players and in turn I believe my reward has been the confidence the people have shown in my integrity and honesty."[27] As for the 1919 World Series, Comiskey had heard rumors "that some of my ball players had been fixed" immediately upon his arrival in Cincinnati for the Series opener. On the morning of Game Two, furthermore, Comiskey had instructed manager Gleason "to take out any ball player who did not appear to be doing his best." Comiskey had also conveyed his concerns about Chisox play directly to NL President Heydler, bypassing his own league president "because I had no confidence in Johnson."[28] After the Sox had lost the Series, Comiskey offered a $10,000 reward "for proof of the fixing of any of my ball players." On his own initiative, Comiskey also retained private detectives who had cost him $4,000 "to run down every clew [clue] imaginable but could get nothing tangible." In addition, Comiskey had dispatched Gleason to interview a bitter East St. Louis gambler who "would tell the story of the alleged frame up if he could get his $5,000 [lost betting] back."[29] All to no avail. Comiskey ended his defense with a denunciation of Johnson and the National Commission for a lack of cooperation with his efforts and by pledging to fire "any of my players who are not honest ... no matter who they are, even if doing so resulted in clos[ing] the gates of the park that I've spent a lifetime to build and in which in the declining years of my life I take the greatest measure of pride and pleasure."[30]

Back at the courthouse, Benton had retaken the witness stand to amplify his earlier testimony. As he had the previous evening in the press, Benton denied that he had ever won big money wagering on the 1919 Series. He also related that betting commissioner Hahn had told him that Eddie Cicotte, Chick Gandil, Lefty Williams, Happy Felsch, and a fifth player whose name Benton could not now recall had been corrupted by the Pittsburgh syndicate.[31] Meanwhile, Benton adversaries resumed the counterattack. Buck Herzog weighed in again, publicly alleging that Benton had admitted winning $1,500 on the Series during confidential hearings conducted into the Magee/Chase game-fixing incident.[32] NL President Heydler openly disparaged Benton as well, stating that if published reports of his grand jury testimony were accurate, Benton had either perjured himself before the grand jury or perjured himself at the Heydler hearing.[33] Heinie Zimmerman also branded Benton "a liar." Zimmerman said that he had been suspended from the Giants and banished back to New York on the morning that the Chicago café bribe offer was supposedly made.[34] And Philip Hahn, newly arrived in Chicago and armed with affidavits, directly contradicted the leaked Benton testimony. Hahn confirmed that he had been on a post-season hunting trip with Benton but maintained that the two had never discussed the fix of the 1919 World Series, of which Hahn had utterly no knowledge.[35] Nor was Hahn acquainted with Cicotte, Gandil, or the other Chicago players reportedly implicated in the fix.[36]

At the conclusion of the September 24 proceedings, Judge McDonald huddled with grand jury personnel. Jury foreman Brigham then issued a lengthy public statement that read, in part,

> We have evidence that crooked work was done but we believe it has been confined to comparatively few players, and was a result of the pollution of the players by an unscrupulous gang of professional gamblers, the same gang that has crucified horse racing and the kind that has killed the boxing game.[37]

Vacationing lame-duck SA Hoyne also chimed in from New York, asserting that he had "no doubt the 1919 World Series was crooked and that at least one Chicago player was crooked."[38] Hoyne, however, assured the public that "everything will be done to get to the bottom of the thing in order that justice may be done to baseball and that gambling be eradicated."[39]

Predictable headlines blazed across the mastheads of the next day's newspapers. "Proof of Baseball Bribery Found, Says Grand Jury Foreman," declared the *Chicago Daily News,* while the *Los Angeles Times* enticed readers with the caption: "Did Gamblers Fix Games? Grand Jury Finds Convincing Evidence."[40] Purported details of the fix were also published. The *Chicago Tribune,* for example, identified Hal Chase and Abe Attell as the masterminds and placed a $100,000 price tag on the fix[41] while the *New York Times* cast Attell and Chick Gandil in the leads, with Bill Burns in a supporting role.[42] The eight White Sox players believed targeted by the grand jury — Gandil, Eddie Cicotte, Lefty Williams, Happy Felsch, Swede Risberg, Joe Jackson, Fred McMullin, and Buck Weaver — were publicly identified and deemed likely to be indicted on conspiracy to defraud charges.[43] The speculation intensified the following day with publication of the grand jury testimony of former Cubs owner and racetrack regular Charles Weeghman. "Lucky Charlie" revealed that while attending Saratoga Racetrack in the summer of 1919, he had been informed that the upcoming World Series would be fixed. Weeghman's informant was Chicago high roller and horse racing odds-maker Mont Tennes, who confided that seven White Sox players had been bribed by Arnold Rothstein, using associates like Nat Evans, Nicky Arnstein, Abe Attell, and Max Blumenthal as his intermediaries.[44] Weeghman, however, was dubious that Rothstein was involved in such an enterprise. Said Weeghman, "I know Rothstein would bet his shirt if he thought he was right. He has a lot of money and bets freely but I doubt that he would permit himself to be mixed up in an affair like this. I think that he is on the square."[45]

As the grand jury recessed pending the availability of subpoenaed White Sox players, scandal reportage turned to speculation about the testimony expected from Chisox landlady Henrietta Kelley and Dr. Raymond Prettyman, the Weaver family dentist. Reportedly, Mrs. Kelley had overheard incriminating remarks made during the Series by star boarder Eddie Cicotte,[46] while Prettyman had supposedly been made privy to an attempt by Fred McMullin to deliver a package believed to contain "a large sum of currency" to the Weaver residence.[47] Both Kelley (who may have been Eddie Cicotte's sister) and Prettyman were less than pleased by their portrayal as important witnesses against the grand jury targets. Said Kelley, "I am an ardent baseball fan and several families of baseball stars live in my apartments. However, I don't know any information that I could give the grand jury that would be of value to them."[48] Prettyman went even further. While refusing to divulge the substance of his testimony, the dentist was sorely put out by the insinuation that he might incriminate Weaver, his friend and patient. About his grand jury appearance, Prettyman told the press that whatever he had to reveal, "I can assure you that it will be a vindication of Buck Weaver."[49] McMullin, meanwhile, flatly denied ever delivering a package to the Weaver house.[50] Denial of a different sort was issued by Mont Tennes. Although he had talked baseball with Weeghman in Saratoga, Tennes had never said anything about fixed World Series games. Tennes knew nothing about that and had no complaints about the Series outcome. Tennes declared that he "had bet on the White Sox. I lost my bet and made no claim of fraud," all of which he would willingly repeat for the grand jury if called to testify.[51]

Publication of the Weeghman testimony also elicited a response in New York, where the Rothstein public relations apparatus swung into action. Friendly *New York American* sportswriter Bill Farnsworth rose to Rothstein's defense, disclosing that Rothstein had refused to finance the World Series fix when approached by Bill Burns in the grill room of the Astor Hotel. Rothstein had called Burns a "skunk" and warned Burns never to speak to him again.[52] Despite this, Rothstein had been ensnared in fix rumors because the likes of Abe Attell and Curley Bennett had dropped his name in their effort to co-opt the Burns fix proposition.[53] Farnsworth, however, remained "confident that Rothstein had nothing to do with the fixing," noting that Rothstein had bet $70,000 on the White Sox to win the Series.[54] Shortly after the Farnsworth testimonial had been syndicated nationwide, celebrity New York private eye Val O'Farrell released more sensational scuttlebutt attesting to Rothstein's innocence. In addition to spurning Burns, Rothstein had turned down a different Series fix proposition broached by a Long Island gambler called "Orby" and Giants outfielder Benny Kauff. O'Farrell, moreover, claimed to have proof (which he did not exhibit) that a fix-related telegram bearing the initials *AR*—reportedly received by Attell in Cincinnati — had been sent by Curley Bennett, not Rothstein.[55]

Swelling the pro–Rothstein chorus was none other than Ban Johnson, recently returned from a private audience with the gambler in Manhattan. Based on that encounter, Johnson pronounced himself "convinced that Rothstein had no hand in the fixing of the series."[56] Johnson displayed a far less charitable attitude toward former friend Comiskey. Trashing the published Comiskey statement without mentioning the Sox owner by name, Johnson declared that he stood "squarely behind the grand jury and the authorities in the responsibility they have assumed and will not enter into further discussion of personal matters that only tend to mislead and nauseate the public."[57] Far more damaging to the Comiskey image were public remarks by Clyde Elliott, president of the Chicago-based Greater Stars Production Company and an avid Sox fan. Through his theatrical connections, Elliott knew East St. Louis theater owner/gambler Harry Redmon and had served as liaison for White Sox officials seeking information from Redmon and his associates during their post–Series trip to St. Louis. That trip had yielded fix information dividends but no action by club officials. More explicitly, Elliott charged that only days after the Series conclusion, Comiskey and other team officials had been provided with evidence that seven White Sox players had been bought by New York gamblers for $100,000 and that the 1919 Series had been deliberately lost. Yet nothing had been done by Comiskey and company to rectify the situation.[58]

With NL President Heydler waiting in the wings, the grand jury seemed poised to return its attention to allegations related to the senior circuit. Heydler warmed up for his appearance by publicly disclosing that his own investigation had uncovered no evidence that the Cubs-Phillies game of August 31— the original subject of the grand jury probe — had been fixed.[59] Nor did Heydler find credible the bribe allegations made by Rube Benton against Buck Herzog. "I don't know what to think about Benton," mused Heydler. "He told many stories [and] his reputation in our league is not the best."[60] Fireworks were predicted in the now almost daily bulletin of grand jury foreman Brigham. As the panel made ready to resume its work, Brigham stated,

> A number of Chicagoans are going to find themselves involved in this mess. They face indictment. ... Chicago and the baseball world will be amazed at the facts that we have uncovered in connection with crooked gambling in baseball. I think the first bomb will be exploded early next week.[61]

In the form of a personage entirely unknown to Brigham, his words were about to become prophetic. For miles distant, a figure from baseball's margins was giving the interview that would blow open the Black Sox scandal.

Notes

1. As reported in the *Chicago Evening Post,* September 22, 1920.
2. As quoted in the *Chicago Daily Journal,* September 22, 1920.
3. *Ibid.* A singular provision in Illinois law permitted a grand jury witness to have his attorney in attendance — but only as an observer, not as a participant in the proceedings. The fact that two non-attorneys were permitted to attend Comiskey is but a small indicator of the disregard for grand jury protocol that pervaded the Black Sox proceedings.
4. As reported in the *Chicago Daily Journal,* September 22, 1920.
5. As reported in the *Chicago Daily Journal* and *Chicago Daily News,* September 22, 1920.
6. *Ibid.*
7. As quoted in the *Chicago Daily News,* September 22, 1920.
8. The Crusinberry testimony is recounted in a syndicated column by sportswriter James L. Kilgallen, published in the *Atlanta Constitution,* October 31, 1920, and by Crusinberry himself decades later in his *Sports Illustrated* piece. A more accessible source for the Crusinbery testimony is Carney, 103–104.
9. See *Atlanta Constitution,* October 31, 1920.
10. As reported in the *Chicago Daily Journal,* September 22, 1920, and the *Chicago Evening American* and *Los Angeles Times,* September 23, 1920.

11. As per the *Chicago Daily News,* September 23, 1920.

12. See the *Chicago Daily Journal,* September 23, 1920. A story about crooked baseball with a Rube Benton byline appeared that same date in the *Chicago Evening American.* The expected testimony of Sox manager Gleason, as well as that of Chicago sportswriters Harvey Woodruff and Irving Sanborn, was deferred to permit them to attend crucial late-season White Sox games. Bert Collyer and Frank O. Klein, also subpoenaed for September 22, were not called to testify on that date and apparently never appeared before the grand jury. A lengthy, if incomplete, handwritten list of grand jury witnesses preserved at the Chicago History Museum does not include the names of Collyer or Klein. See Chicago History Museum (CHM), Black Sox file, Box 1, Folder 5. The witness list does include the name of former *Chicago Tribune* reporter William Birch, another witness subpoenaed for September 22, but no published mention of his testimony was found by the author.

13. As per the *Chicago Daily Journal,* September 23, 1920.

14. *Ibid.*

15. As per the *Chicago Daily News,* September 23, 1920. During the 1919 World Series, the Giants played a string of exhibition games in upstate New York and New England. Although nagged by injuries, Chase accompanied the team and remained a New York Giant in good standing until February 1920, when his involvement in the Lee Magee affair was uncovered. See Dewey and Acocella, 292–307.

16. As reported in the *Chicago Daily News,* September 23, 1920, and elsewhere.

17. As quoted in the *Chicago Daily News,* September 23, 1920.

18. *Ibid.*

19. The Wilson and Boeckel affidavits were published verbatim in the *Chicago Daily News* and *Chicago Evening Post,* September 24, 1920, and elsewhere.

20. As per the *Chicago Daily Journal,* September 23, 1920, and *Chicago Daily News,* September 24, 1920.

21. See the *Boston Globe, Chicago Daily Journal* and *Chicago Tribune,* September 24, 1920.

22. *Ibid.*

23. As reported in the *Chicago Tribune,* September 23, 1920, and elsewhere.

24. As reported in the *Chicago Daily Journal,* September 23, 1920. See also the *Chicago Herald Examiner,* September 23, 1920.

25. *Chicago Daily Journal,* September 23, 1920.

26. Published as a formal statement by "Charles A. Comiskey, Owner of the White Sox" in the *Chicago Daily Journal, Chicago Daily News* and *Chicago Evening Post,* September 24, 1920.

27. *Ibid.*

28. *Ibid.*

29. *Ibid.*

30. *Ibid.* The disgruntled gambler is presumably Harry Redmon.

31. See Carney, 113, and the *Boston Globe,* September 25, 1920.

32. As reported by James Crusinberry in the *Chicago Tribune,* September 24, 1920.

33. As reported in the *Chicago Evening Post,* September 24, 1920.

34. As per the *Chicago Evening American,* September 25, 1920.

35. As reported in the *Chicago Evening Post,* September 24, 1920, and *The Sporting News,* September 30, 1920. A letter from National Commission chairman/Reds President Garry Herrmann to AL President Johnson attesting to Hahn's character and offering to arrange for his appearance before the grand jury is contained in the Black Sox file at the Giamatti Research Center. Hahn never testified, but so strong were his public protests against Benton's claims that there was speculation that Benton had confused Hahn with Lee Heine, "a king gambling operator in Cincinnati whose place is a hangout for players," as per the *Chicago Evening Post,* September 24, 1920.

36. *Chicago Evening Post,* September 24, 1920.
37. As quoted in the *Chicago Daily Journal, Chicago Daily News* and *Chicago Evening Post,* September 24, 1920, and elsewhere.
38. As per the *Chicago Tribune* and *New York Times,* September 24, 1920.
39. *Ibid.*
40. *Chicago Daily News* and *Los Angeles Times,* September 25, 1920.
41. *Chicago Tribune,* September 25, 1920.
42. *New York Times,* September 25, 1920.
43. See e.g., *Boston Globe* and *Chicago Tribune,* September 25, 1920.
44. As reported in the *Chicago Daily News* and *Chicago Tribune,* September 26, 1920. For an informative profile of Jacob "Mont" Tennes, the Chicago counterpart of Manhattan's Arnold Rothstein, see *Mont Tennes, King of Gamblers* at *http://chicagocrimescenes.blogspot.com/2009/04/mont-tennes-king-of-gamblers.html.*
45. As quoted in the *Chicago Daily News,* September 26, 1920.
46. Reportedly, Cicotte had said something to his brother Jack along the lines of "What do I care? I got mine." See the *Chicago Daily Journal* and *Chicago Daily News,* September 28, 1920.
47. Prettyman was allegedly informed of the matter by a Mrs. Cook, Weaver's mother-in-law. Various accounts of the incident had a heated argument ensuing between McMullin and Weaver, after which either McMullin retrieved the package (*Chicago Daily Journal,* September 25, 1920) or Weaver reluctantly kept it (*Chicago Tribune,* September 26, 1920). That the package contained "a large sum of currency" is a description of its contents attributed to McMullin by Mrs. Cook in reportage of Prettyman's subsequent grand jury testimony. See *New York Times,* October 2, 1920.
48. As quoted in the *Chicago Daily Journal,* September 25, 1920.
49. *Ibid.*
50. As per the *Chicago Tribune,* September 27, 1920. Weaver, likewise, publicly denied that the incident had ever occurred, as reported in the *Boston Globe,* September 27, 1920.
51. As reported in the *Chicago Tribune,* September 27, 1920. See also, the *Chicago Evening Post,* September 27, 1920. Tennes had reportedly lost $80,000 betting on the hometown Sox during the Series.
52. As published in the *New York American,* September 26, 1920, and syndicated nationwide immediately thereafter. See e.g., the *Chicago Herald Examiner,* September 27, 1920.
53. Farnsworth presumably refers to the real-life Joseph "Curley" Bennett, a thuggish Tammany Hall foot soldier and, like Attell, a part-time Rothstein bodyguard (and not to Des Moines gambler David Zelcer, the Black Sox defendant accused of posing as "Bennett" at the Sinton Hotel in Cincinnati).
54. As per the *New York American,* September 26, 1920.
55. As reported in the *Los Angeles Times,* September 30, 1920.
56. As reported in the *Chicago Evening Post,* September 25, 1920.
57. As quoted in the *Chicago Daily Journal* and *Chicago Evening American,* September 27, 1920.
58. As reported in the *Chicago Herald Examiner,* September 26, 1920.
59. As reported in the *Chicago Evening Post* and *Chicago Tribune,* September 27, 1920.
60. As quoted in the *Chicago Evening Post,* September 27, 1920.
61. As quoted in the *Boston Globe,* September 26, 1920.

6

The Scandal Explodes

On September 27, 1920, sportswriter James Isaminger provided readers of the *Philadelphia North American* with the first detailed account of the fixing of the 1919 World Series. Isaminger's source was fix insider Billy Maharg, a figure fairly well known to Philly fight fans but an enigma to many Black Sox commentators, a number of whom embrace the peculiar but persistent notion that Maharg's real name was Graham — Maharg spelled backwards. To clarify the matter, William Joseph Maharg was the second of three children born to laborer George Alexander Maharg and his Irish immigrant wife Kate (nee Carney).[1] Short (5'4½") but tough and athletic, Billy Maharg began a six-year career as a local club fighter while still a teenager. By the time he hung the gloves up in early 1907, Maharg, a durable but soft-punching lightweight, had gone the distance 74 times, mostly in six-rounders.[2] A lifelong bachelor, Maharg subsequently worked as a common laborer but remained close to the local sports scene. In May 1912, he was one of the area athletes pressed into service by Detroit management for a game against the A's after Tigers regulars had struck in solidarity with a suspended Ty Cobb. Four years later, Maharg, a boarding house friend of Phillies ace Grover Alexander and a team go-fer, made another major league appearance, pinch-hitting and then playing one inning in the outfield during a meaningless season-ending Phillies game. As for the fix of the 1919 World Series, Maharg had been enlisted in the plot by his friend Bill Burns. According to Maharg, the White Sox had deliberately lost Game One, Game Two, and Game Eight of the Series.[3]

Among the highlights of the Maharg interview was the assertion that the fix had been instigated by White Sox hurler Eddie Cicotte, not gamblers. In mid–September 1919, Cicotte had approached Burns at a New York hotel, informing Burns that eight Sox players were prepared to dump the Series in exchange for $100,000. Maharg recounted that Arnold Rothstein had declined to finance the fix — Rothstein did not think that fixing the World Series was possible — but that the fix proposition was subsequently revived by Abe Attell, posing as Rothstein's agent. Once the fix was in place, Attell reneged on a $20,000 payment due the players after the Sox lost Game One. Then, Attell short-changed the players by half after the Sox defeat in Game Two. The players promptly retaliated by posting an unscripted victory in Game Three, wiping out the heavily betting Burns and Maharg in the process. Following his return to Philadelphia, Maharg heard that Attell and Midwestern gamblers had revived the fix, intimidating Sox starter Lefty Williams into his dreadful Game 8 performance. As summed up by Maharg, "Burns and I lost every cent we had in our clothes. The whole upshot of the matter was that Attell and his gang cleaned up a fortune and the Sox players were double crossed out of $90,000 that was coming to them."[4]

Fix insider Billy Maharg's late September 1920 newspaper interview blew the simmering Series scandal wide open.

The Maharg story was immediately circulated nationwide by the Associated Press and other wire services, to swift and stunning effect. A dismayed Charles Comiskey promptly telegrammed Maharg, urging him to appear before the grand jury and promising Maharg the advertised $10,000 reward, if his account proved true.[5] Maharg would never appear before the panel[6] but that proved of little moment. The scandal dominoes had been set in motion. Within 48 hours, four White Sox players would admit their roles in the fix.

To varying degrees, the recitals of the Maharg story were confirmed by implicated Sox players. But the accounts of Eddie Cicotte, Joe Jackson, Lefty Williams, and Happy Felsch were far from uniform. Differences, some of them significant, resided in the players' description of events. Taken together, however, the Cicotte/Jackson/Williams/Felsch admissions left little doubt that the Series had been corrupted. The first Sox player to confess involvement in the fix was stress-ridden Eddie Cicotte, summoned to the office of White Sox attorney Alfred Austrain on the morning of September 28.[7] Confronted by ASA Replogle and Austrian, Cicotte quickly broke down and admitted involvement in the fix. According to Cicotte, talk about throwing the World Series had first begun among the White Sox during a late-season train ride. Envious of the $10,000 rumored to have been paid Cubs players to throw the 1918 Series, the Chisox group agreed to do the same if they could get that kind of money.[8] Cicotte himself agreed to participate in the fix for an individual $10,000 payoff. Sometime later, "some men came to the Warner [Hotel] and left this money in my room." Cicotte did not know if the other players had received any money but identified "the men who were in the deal [as] McMullin, Gandil, Weaver, Williams, Jackson, Felsch, and myself."[9] Shortly thereafter, Cicotte was whisked to the Cook County courthouse where he was briefly interviewed in chambers by Judge McDonald. Cicotte then appeared before the grand jury.

Author Note: Unlike that of Joe Jackson and Lefty Williams, the grand jury testimony of Eddie Cicotte has not survived intact. The best sources currently extant are a synopsis of the Cicotte testimony created by an unidentified ASA in attendance during the grand jury session[10] and excerpts of the grand jury record incorporated into the January 14, 1924, deposition of Cicotte for the Jackson breach-of-contract suit against the White Sox.[11] Newspaper accounts of the Cicotte grand jury testimony must be approached with particular caution, as the tearful, abjectly confessing figure portrayed in typical scandal reportage contrasts sharply with the guarded, often less-than-forthcoming witness reflected in the surviving parts of the official record. At junctures where the conflict between official record excerpts and the reportage is pronounced — such as passages pertaining to what Cicotte said about his intent and performance in Game One and Game Four — the ensuing text will favor the record, with differing newspaper versions of the matter recounted via endnote.

As with any potential target of grand jury action, the Cicotte appearance commenced with recitation of the legal rights relinquished by the witness and Cicotte's voluntary waiver of these rights.[12] After providing some personal/professional background, Cicotte testified that the World Series fix was first discussed at a players meeting conducted at the Ansonia Hotel in New York around September 10 or 12, 1919. Present at the meeting were Lefty Williams, Joe Jackson, Chick Gandil, Buck Weaver, Swede Risberg, Fred McMullin, and Cicotte.[13] The idea of dumping the upcoming Series was promoted by Gandil and McMullin, one of whom said, "We ain't getting a divil [*sic*] of a lot of money and it looks like we could make a big thing if we threw these games to Cincinnati."[14] Asked his price privately by Gandil and McMullin after the meeting, Cicotte said, "I would not do anything like that for less than $10,000," to which the pair replied, "We can get that together and we can fix it up."[15] Cicotte did not inquire how many other Sox had committed to the fix.

A second fix meeting was held three days prior to the start of the Series at the Warner Hotel in Chicago. Present at this conference were Gandil, Felsch, Weaver, McMullin, and perhaps Williams[16] as well as Cicotte, who announced that "there is so much double crossing stuff, if I went in [on] the series [fix] I wanted the money put in my hand." And Cicotte would have to have that money in his hand before the team departed for Cincinnati.[17] After Gandil replied, "Okay," Cicotte left the meeting to socialize with non-conspiring teammates. When he returned to his hotel room several hours later, Cicotte found $10,000 under his bed pillow.[18] Regarding his performance in Game One, Cicotte testified that "I tried to walk [Reds leadoff batter] Rath and I hit him." From there, Cicotte claimed to have undergone a reformation. He now wanted to win but "tried too hard."[19] Cicotte pitched good ball but the Reds just "made clean base hits."[20] After Game One was over, Cicotte did not speak to Gandil or McMullin and was "sick all night" in his hotel room, telling bunkmate Felsch, "Happy, it will never be done again."[21]

Cicotte was suspicious of Williams' wildness in Game Two but did not speak to Lefty after the loss.[22] When the team returned to Chicago, Cicotte abandoned his room at the Warner Hotel, taking up lodgings at Henrietta Kelley's boarding house.[23] His brother Jack and other family members were also staying there during the Series but Cicotte said nothing about the fix to them.[24] Cicotte was not concerned when Dickie Kerr pitched Chicago to a 3–0 victory in Game Three as the Sox did not have to lose every game, just the Series.[25] As for his own performance in Game Four, Cicotte testified, somewhat paradoxically, that he too had pitched to win. "I tried to make good but I made two errors. I was very anxious to get the ball but [we] didn't make any runs. If we could make four or five runs, I would have won that game."[26] As for the potential consequences of such a victory, Cicotte asserted, "I didn't care whether I got shot out there the next minute. I was going to win the ball game and the series."[27]

Cicotte was not particularly enlightening about the gamblers who had financed the fix. He did not know who had furnished the bribe money but supposed that "some gamblers" had made money on the Sox' performance.[28] As for his purported change of heart during the Series, Cicotte "was going to take a chance. I wanted to win. I could give [the $10,000] back with interest, if they would only let me win the game that day."[29] But Cicotte conceded that he never offered to return the bribe money as "I couldn't very well do that." Instead, Cicotte had kept the money, using it to pay off the mortgage on farm property and to buy supplies.[30]

At the conclusion of the Cicotte testimony, courthouse officials went into huddle. At approximately 2:00 P.M., grand jury foreman Brigham "sent for the newspapermen and in the presence of the jury announced the voting of [true] bills and the names of the players [charged]."[31] Indicted were Cicotte, Gandil, Risberg, Jackson, Felsch, Williams, Weaver, and McMullin, the eight men soon to be branded the Black Sox. The immediate charge was the generic "conspiracy to commit an illegal act." More specific charges would be drafted in due course.[32] The grand jury's intentions were then discussed by ASA Replogle:

> This is just the beginning. We will have more indictments within a few days and before we get through we will have purged organized baseball of everything crooked and dishonest.... We are going after the gamblers now. There will be indictments within a few days against men in Philadelphia, Indianapolis, St. Louis, Des Moines, Pittsburgh, Cincinnati and other cities. We've got the goods on these men and we are going to the limit.[33]

Shortly after Replogle's remarks, Henrietta Kelley took the stand but the admissions of Cicotte had rendered her appearance largely superfluous. Her testimony was little reported and Kelley herself dismissed the notion that she was an important witness. "I don't know anything," Kelley declared. "I never overheard any conversations ... that would in any way help this investigation.[34]

This cleared the way for the courthouse arrival of Joe Jackson, who had been biding his time in the Austrian office. Earlier in the day, Jackson had announced his intention to face down the allegations swirling around him, stating, "I am willing to go before anyone at any time, any place to testify to what I know. I know little except rumors. I know I have never been approached with any gambling propositions. If anyone ever does approach me, I'll knock his block off."[35] After a brief meeting with Judge McDonald in chambers, Jackson entered the grand jury room where, following the rights waiver ritual, he rendered the testimony that remains a source of Black Sox controversy to this day. Reduced to its essence, the Jackson testimony contains two assertions that are difficult to reconcile. One the one hand, Jackson admitted joining the plot to throw the 1919 World Series and accepting payment for his role in the fix. On the other, Jackson asserted that he had done nothing on the field to earn that payment, having played every Series game to win.[36]

On the damning side of the ledger, Jackson provided a fairly detailed account of the fix from his perspective. Contradicting Eddie Cicotte, Jackson testified that he had not attended the player conference at the Ansonia Hotel where the fix was first proposed.[37] Nor had he been present at the follow-up meeting held at the Warner Hotel, although Lefty Williams had told Jackson about it.[38] Rather, Jackson was propositioned privately by Chick Gandil.[39]

The arrangement reached was the subject of the following grand jury exchange:

> ASA REPLOGLE: How much did he promise you?
> JACKSON: $20,000 if I would take part.
> ASA REPLOGLE: And you said you would?
> JACKSON: Yes, sir.
> ASA REPLOGLE: When did he promise to give you the $20,000?
> JACKSON: It would be paid after each game.
> ASA REPLOGLE: How much?
> JACKSON: Split up some way. I didn't know just how much it amounted to, but during the series it would amount to $20,000.[40]

When he went unpaid after the White Sox lost Game One, Jackson asked Gandil, "What's the trouble?" but Gandil assured him that "everything is all right," Gandil had the money. Then, Jackson testified, "We went ahead and threw the second game," only to be unpaid again. Jackson now asked Gandil, "What are you going to do?" and Gandil replied, "Everything is all right" once more.[41] When no money was forthcoming after Game Three, Jackson told Gandil that "somebody is getting a nice little jazz, everything is crossed." But Gandil responded that the fault lay with Abe Attell and Bill Burns. They had crossed him.[42]

On the evening before the White Sox were to return to Cincinnati, Lefty Williams entered Jackson's room at the Lexington Hotel and threw $5,000 down onto the bed. At that, Jackson asked, "What the hell had come off here?"[43] Williams replied that Gandil "said we got the screw through Abe Attell. He got the money and refused to turn it over to him [Gandil]."[44] But Jackson suspected that Gandil actually had the money and had "kept the majority of it for himself."[45] When Jackson complained, Gandil told him that Attell "gave him a jazzing" and that Jackson could either "take that [$5,000] or leave it alone."[46] When Jackson told his wife that evening that he had "got $5,000 for helping to throw [Series] games," Katie Jackson told Joe that "she thought it was an awful thing to do."[47] Jackson put the $5,000, "some hundreds, mostly fifties" in denomination, in his pocket and took it with him to Cincinnati.[48] Regarding the other conspirators, Cicotte had told Jackson that he received $10,000 up front and scolded Joe as "a God damn fool" for not getting paid the same way.[49] Risberg and Williams told Jackson that they had received $5,000 each but Jackson did not believe them. He suspected that Gandil, Risberg, McMullin, Cicotte, and Williams had cut up the bribe money "to suit themselves."[50] Jackson understood from "the boys" that Felsch had also received $5,000[51] but had no knowledge of any payoffs made to Weaver. All that Jackson knew about Buck was that Gandil had told him that Weaver "was in on the deal."[52]

Lead grand jury prosecutor Hartley Replogle and a wary-looking Joe Jackson pose for the press after Jackson's revelatory grand jury appearance.

While incriminating, the impact of these admissions is somewhat diminished by Jackson's testimony about his World Series play. Jackson insisted that he had played to win throughout the Series. When asked in particular about the controversial Game Four, Jackson stated that he had batted to win, fielded to win, and run the bases to win.[53] While Jackson saw some questionable play, particularly by Cicotte and Williams, he himself had not done anything to throw Series games.[54] Jackson had "tried to win all the time."[55] Jackson was ashamed of himself for accepting the $5,000 and had offered to reveal everything that he knew about the fix to White Sox management in the fall of 1919. But team brass had not brought him in.[56] Jackson was also suspicious of late 1920 season performances by Cicotte and Williams, but declared himself anxious to win the pennant and then capture the World Series.[57] This led to a poignant exchange near the end of Jackson's testimony:

> ASA REPLOGLE: You didn't want to do that last year, did you?
> JACKSON: Well, down in my heart, I did. Yes.[58]

Moments later, the grand jury proceedings were recessed for the day.[59]

Like every other facet of the grand jury proceedings, news of the charges

The eight indicted White Sox players drew the scorn of *The Sporting News*.

leaked immediately. Player sidekick Sam Pass spread the word to the Clean Sox and touched off a celebration that extended into the wee hours. Among those toasting the indictments were Eddie Collins, Ray Schalk, Shano Collins, Nemo Leibold, Amos Strunk, Eddie Murphy, and former Chisox players Zeb Terry and Tom Daly.[60] That morning, the indictments were headlined in newspapers across the country. Also contained in most news accounts was an official notice from Comiskey, often reprinted verbatim, which informed the eight charged players of their immediate and indefinite suspensions pending the outcome of the proceedings.[61] Although club leadership put a brave face on the situation — Kid Gleason said that he was "glad that the thing had come to a head" and that the Sox would carry on with "the honest [team] members we have left"[62] — the gutting of the roster doomed Chicago's chances to prevail over Cleveland and New York in the tight three-way AL pennant chase of 1920. A bittersweet public statement issued by Comiskey extolled Judge McDonald, grand jury foreman Brigham, and the panel members "who so diligently strove to save and make America's great game the clean sport it is and are to be commended, in no uncertainness, by all sports followers, in spite of what happened today."[63]

Far less newspaper space was devoted to protestation of innocence. Only brief mention, for example, was afforded Buck Weaver's denial of involvement in the fix. Pointing to his .333 Series batting average (actually .324), Weaver exclaimed, "That ought to be a good enough alibi."[64] Fred McMullin was equally indignant, calling the allegation that he had delivered fix money to the Weaver home "a joke. I have nothing to fear and don't understand how things got this far."[65] A similar reaction to the charges was registered by Happy Felsch: "It's all bunk as far as I'm concerned. I've always been on the square. All I want is a chance to face the grand jury."[66] Less forthcoming was a sullen Lefty Williams, who informed an inquiring reporter that "if I've got anything to say, I'll say it to the grand jury. My word is as good as Jackson's."[67]

Unfortunately for the accused, far greater print space was accorded to an extended post-grand jury interview given by Joe Jackson.[68] In the interview, Jackson related that following telephone calls placed from the Austrian office to an unsympathetic Judge McDonald, he had gone to the jurist's chambers, where

> I said I got $5,000 and they promised me $20,000. All I got was the $5,000 that Lefty Williams handed me in a dirty envelope. I never got the other $15,000. I told that to Judge McDonald. He said he didn't care what I got.... I don't think the judge likes me. I never got the $15,000 that was coming me.[69]

Jackson further explained that his revelations were prompted by the attitude of Gandil, Risberg, and McMullin. When he threatened to expose the fix unless paid in full, Jackson was brushed off.

> They said to me, "You poor simp, go ahead and squawk.... Every honest ballplayer in the world will say you're a liar. You're out of luck. Some of the boys were promised a lot more than you and got less." That's why I went down and told Judge McDonald and told the grand jury what I knew about the frame up.[70]

To make his situation seemingly irretrievable, Jackson then added,

> And I'm going to give you a tip. A lot of these sporting writers that have been roasting me have been talking about the third game of the World's Series being square. Let

> me tell you something. The eight of us did our best to kick it and little Dick Kerr won the game by his pitching. Because he won it, those gamblers double crossed us because we double crossed them.[71]

Jackson's reported remarks concluded with expressions of concern for his own safety, citing threats by Risberg that Jackson took seriously. Said Jackson, "Swede's a hard guy."[72]

The signal grand jury event of September 29, 1920, was the appearance of Lefty Williams. His arrival was preceded by a trip to the Austrian office, where Williams gave the White Sox counsel a formal sworn statement admitting complicity in the fix.[73] According to Williams, the idea of throwing the 1919 World Series was first broached to him by Chick Gandil outside the Ansonia Hotel. Williams later attended a meeting with Gandil, Eddie Cicotte, Buck Weaver, and Happy Felsch at the Warner Hotel in Chicago where the players were introduced to Sullivan and Brown from New York, the gamblers fixing the Series or their front men, Williams was not sure which.[74] After the meeting, Williams informed Gandil that, regarding the proposed Series fix, "anything that they did would be agreeable to me, if it was going to happen anyway. That I had no money, I may as well get all I could."[75] Williams then revealed that "I was supposed to get $10,000 after the second game when we got back to Chicago, but I did not get this until after the fourth game. And then he [Gandil] said that the gamble[rs] had called it off. And I figured there was a double cross someplace."[76] Eddie Cicotte was of the same mind and thereafter he and Williams had pitched to win.[77]

Williams also informed Austrian that there had been a second plot to fix the Series. Before the first game in Cincinnati, Gandil advised Williams, Cicotte, Weaver, and Felsch that Abe Attell and Bill Burns were engineering a "fixing where we would get $100,000, making $20,000 more that I never received."[78] Gandil stated that Attell and Burns would make $20,000 payments after each lost game but Williams did not know if Gandil ever got the money. Williams never spoke to Gandil about it. Nor did Weaver or Felsch ever tell Williams "whether they got a penny or not."[79]

It has widely been supposed that Williams' subsequent grand jury appearance was confined to recital of the statement that he had given in the Austrian office. This is incorrect. During his time on the witness stand, Williams expanded significantly on the revelations of his formal statement.[80] Upon entering the grand jury room, Williams was notified by ASA Replogle that he had already been indicted and that anything that Williams testified about could later be used against him in court. Replogle also reminded Williams of advice just given him privately by Judge McDonald, namely that if Williams "comes in here and helps the State clean up matters, that might be taken into consideration and probably would be taken into consideration if he was found guilty and there was punishment to be meted out."[81] After Williams indicated his understanding, Replogle read aloud the formal waiver of rights that must precede testimony by a grand jury target. Williams again indicated that he understood and signed the waiver form.[82]

In his testimony, Williams stated that Risberg and McMullin did not attend the meeting at the Warner Hotel where gamblers Sullivan and Brown were introduced to the players,[83] but asserted that "eight of them were supposed to be in on the fixing," naming for the record "Cicotte, Gandil, Weaver, Felsch, Risberg, McMullin, Jackson and myself."[84] After the Warner Hotel meeting, Williams had walked the streets with Weaver and Felsch discussing how Series games might be thrown. To that purpose, Williams suggested, "If it becomes necessary to strike out in a pinch or anything, if a crucial moment arrives, strike out. Boot the ball. Do anything."[85] Regarding the pre–Game One meeting in Cincinnati between Gandil, Cicotte, Weaver, Felsch, and Williams and the second fix tandem of Attell and Burns, Williams testified that Burns told the players that Attell would produce the promised $100,000. Williams was disposed to dealing with the pair because "we went so far, we might as well get all we can get."[86]

Notwithstanding his admitted agreement to the World Series fix, Williams insisted that he had done nothing intentional to throw Game Two. Said Williams, "I was a little nervous, naturally, and there was the three bases made by the shortstop [i.e., the fourth inning triple hit by the Reds' Larry Kopf]" but Williams had not pitched to lose. "I didn't have to. I just pitched naturally and walked the fellows after that they made base hits."[87] As maintained in his statement to Austrian, Williams testified that he was not paid off until after Game Four when he received a telephone call from Gandil and then collected the $10,000 from Chick. Williams then returned to the Lexington Hotel, throwing a $5,000 share on the bed and telling Jackson, "That's all we got. We have been double crossed some way."[88] As for that payoff, Williams stated that he and Jackson "took the money and counted it, and we went to Cincinnati and came back and it wasn't out of our possession for a minute."[89] Once back in Chicago, a ballpark security officer informed Jackson that the Lexington Hotel was not safe, being the site of frequent room burglaries. Upon receiving this news, Jackson and Williams collected their wives and moved to the Warner Hotel.[90] When she found out, Lyria Williams was angry with Lefty for agreeing to the fix — until he showed her the $5,000. Then she said, "You have done it. What can I say now? ... Let it go and just get the best of it."[91] Williams denied that he had placed bets on the World Series. Nor had his wife, "to my knowledge."[92] Whether other Sox players had wagered on the Series was unknown to Williams.[93] As with Game Two, Williams claimed that he had done nothing deliberately to lose Game Five. To the contrary, Williams had "pitched as hard in that game as I ever pitched in my life."[94] And before his dismal start in Game Eight, Williams had told Jackson on the way to the ballpark that "if we have been double crossed, I am going to pitch to win this game if I can possibly win it."[95]

At the conclusion of the Williams testimony, the grand jury voted indictments against Joseph "Sport" Sullivan and Brown, the otherwise unidentified gambler from New York.[96] The remainder of the session was then consumed by testimony from NL President Heydler and Giants manager McGraw about the handling of the Chase, Magee, and Zimmerman controversies.[97] In the process, Heydler supported Buck Herzog in his dispute with Rube Benton, informing the panel that the NL's internal probe of the Café bribe allegations had culminated in the exoneration of Herzog.[98] At that moment, Herzog was about to be in need of good news. At the conclusion of a Cubs exhibition game in Joliet on the next afternoon, a scandal-incensed fan, perhaps confusing Buck Herzog with the just indicted Buck Weaver, attacked Herzog with a knife. Fortunately, Herzog survived the assault with only superficial slash wounds, while his assailant escaped altogether, drifting back into the crowd before he could be identified and taken into custody.[99] That exhibition game, however, would mark the last time that Herzog would ever wear the uniform of a major league baseball team.

The final admission of World Series bribe-taking by a White Sox player appeared in the press. Featured in the September 30, 1920, edition of the *Chicago Evening American* was an interview with Happy Felsch conducted the previous day by reporter Harry Reutlinger. It began with Felsch lamenting,

> Well, the beans are all spilled and I think that I am through with baseball. I got my $5,000 and I suppose the others got theirs, too. If you say anything about me, don't make it appear that I am trying to alibi. I'm not. I'm as guilty as the rest of them. We are all in it alike.[100]

After denying allegations that the White Sox had thrown games during the 1920 season as "bunk,"[101] Felsch confirmed Cicotte's now widely published admissions about the fix of the 1919 World Series:

> Cicotte's story is true in every detail. I don't blame him for telling.... I was ready to confess myself yesterday, but I didn't have the courage to be the first to tell. I never knew where my $5,000 came from. It was left in my locker at the clubhouse and there was always a good deal of mystery about the way it was dealt out. That was one of the reasons why we never knew who double crossed us on the split of the $100,000. It was supposed to be an even split but we never got it.[102]

Regarding who was responsible for the shortchange, Felsch suspected Gandil "because he was the wisest of the lot and had enough sense to get out of baseball before the crash came.[103] But I have heard since that it was Attell. Maybe it was Attell. I don't know him, but I had heard that he was mixed up with the gamblers who were backing us to lose."[104]

When asked about how Cicotte had obtained $10,000, Felsch replied, "because he was wise enough to stand pat for it, that's all. Cicotte had brains. The rest of us roundheads just took their word for the proposition that we were going to get an even split on the $100,000."[105] Like the other admitted bribe-takers, Felsch denied making any deliberate misplays during the Series. "I'm not saying that I double crossed the gamblers," Felsch explained. "The breaks just came so I was not given a chance to do anything toward throwing a game."[106] This included his butchering of Edd Roush's fly ball triple in Game Five, a misplay so egregious that fellow Black Sox later chastised Felsch for putting on a "clown act." Not deliberate, insisted Felsch. He had genuinely lost the ball in the sun.[107] The article ended with Felsch's forlorn observation,

> I got $5,000. I could have got just about that much by being on the level if the Sox had won the series. And now, I'm out of baseball — the only profession I knew anything about, and a lot of gamblers have gotten rich. The joke seems to be on us.[108]

Coinciding with the publication of the Felsch interview was a pennant-clinching September 30 victory by the Cleveland Indians. Despite a makeshift last-week lineup, the Chisox had battled to the wire, finishing the 1920 campaign in second place with a fine 96–58 record, two games behind the flag winners. Ironically, that record was largely attributable to the performance of players now suspended. Joe Jackson had had an outstanding year, batting .382, and setting career-high marks in home runs (12) and RBIs (121). He had also led the AL with 20 triples. Happy Felsch had enjoyed a breakout year (.338/14/115), posting personal bests in virtually every offensive category. The same was true of Buck Weaver, whose 208 hits, 74 RBIs, and .331 batting average were all new personal highs. Notwithstanding the suddenly high-octane offenses of the 1920 season, Eddie Cicotte (21–10) and Lefty Williams (22–14) had remained stalwart, combining with Red Faber (23–13) and Dickie Kerr (21–9) to accord the 1920 White Sox the rare distinction of having four 20-game winners on the same pitching staff. Factoring in Eddie Collins (.372), Shano Collins (.303), and Cooperstown-bound backstop Ray Schalk, the Chicago White Sox franchise should have been poised for dynasty. But these men would never again be in uniform together, and White Sox fans were fated to endure mediocrity and worse for the next four decades.

Notes

1. Billy Maharg was named for his grandfather William J. Maharg, a shoe maker-turned-coal miner born in western Pennsylvania in June 1829. For a more complete rendition of the Maharg lineage, see the author's profile of Billy Maharg on the SABR BioProject website.

2. Including unofficial newspaper decisions, Billy Maharg posted a 45–11–4 ring record, with 14 no decisions. Of his victories, only two came by knockout, as per *http://www.boxrec.com*.

3. As reported in the *Philadelphia North American,* September 27, 1920, and republished immediately thereafter in newspapers nationwide.

4. *Ibid.*

5. As reported in the *New York Times,* September 28, 1920, and elsewhere.

6. There were conflicting reports regarding Maharg's intentions. According to an Associated Press dispatch, Maharg accepted Comiskey's offer, wiring instructions that a certified check for $10,000 be deposited with *Chicago Tribune* sports editor Woodruff for collection by Maharg after he testified. See e.g., *Los Angeles Times,* September 29, 1920. See also, *Chicago Evening Post,* September 29, 1920. Other reports had Maharg refusing the Comiskey reward, Maharg declaring, "I don't want it. I didn't tell the truth for money," as reported in the *Washington Post,* September 30, 1920. In any event, Maharg did not testify during the grand jury proceedings.

7. The exact circumstances that brought Cicotte to the Austrian office are unclear. For a survey of various scenarios, see Carney, 117–119.

8. As per the notes of the Cicotte admissions at the Austrian office taken by ASA Replogle, preserved in CHM, Black Sox file, Box 1, Folder 2.

9. *Ibid.* There was apparently no mention of Swede Risberg by Cicotte during the interrogation in the Austrian office.

10. Preserved in CHM, Black Sox file, Box 1, Folder 7.

11. Memorialized in the trial transcript of the Jackson civil suit, reviewed by the author at the temporary offices of the Chicago Baseball Museum (CBM) at Rush University Medical Center in Chicago.

12. Grand Jury Synopsis (Hereafter GJS), para. 1. The formal waiver form signed by Cicotte memorialized his relinquishment of the constitutional right to remain silent. Cicotte also ceded the immunity from prosecution that might have attended placement of an unheeded target before the grand jury. Facsimiles of the immunity waiver forms of Cicotte, Jackson and Williams are contained in the Black Sox file at the Chicago History Museum.

13. Cicotte grand jury testimony as embedded in the record of the Jackson civil trial at JTT, p. 1214, et seq. See also, GJS, para. 3.

14. JTT, p. 1214.

15. *Ibid.*

16. JTT, p. 1227; GJS, para. 6.

17. JTT, pp. 1231–1232; GJS, para. 8.

18. JTT, p. 1236; GJS, para. 8.

19. JTT, pp. 1274–1275; 1294–1295. Note: In taking notes on the CBM transcript of the Jackson civil trial, the author at times neglected to take down the precise page. Hence, certain of the transcript citations provided herein are approximations or page ranges.

20. JTT, pp. 1274–1275; GJS, para. 10. Press accounts portray Cicotte's testimony about his Game One pitching performance in an entirely different light. According to the Associated Press, Cicotte said, "I wasn't putting anything on the ball. You could read the trademark on it when I lobbed the ball up to the plate," as published in the *Los Angeles Times,* September 29, 1920, and elsewhere.

21. JTT, pp. 1245–1247; GJS, para. 11.

22. JTT, p. 1247; GJS, para. 14.

23. The relationship between Cicotte and Kelley is unclear. GJS, para. 17, summarizes the Cicotte testimony about events after Game Two as follows: "I didn't talk to Williams after the second game, but went to bed on the train and when we arrived in Chicago went to my sister's house at 3909 Grand Boulevard. Her name is Henrietta D. Kelly [*sic*]. My brother and oldest girl were there." But Cicotte's impersonal identification of Kelley during his January 1924 deposition for the Jackson civil suit belies a familial relationship between the two. And U.S. census data do not reveal a Cicotte sister named Henrietta.

24. JTT, pp. 1238, 1274; GJS, para. 17 to 19.

25. JTT, p. 1274.

26. JTT, p. 1276; GJS, para. 21. Again, the Associated Press reported the Cicotte testimony very differently. Regarding Game Four, Cicotte is quoted as saying that "all the runs scored against me [i.e., two] were due to my own deliberate errors. I did not try to win the game," as per the AP night wire and reprinted in September 29, 1920 papers ranging from the *Los Angeles Times* to the *Bradford (Pa.) Era.* See also, *Atlanta Constitution,* September 29, 1920: "The fourth game, played at Chicago, was deliberately thrown away, according to courtroom officials who heard Cicotte's testimony to the grand jury."

27. JTT, pp. 1274–1275.

28. JTT, p. 1262.

29. JTT, pp. 1298–1299.

30. JTT, pp. 1236–1238; GJS, para. 8.

31. As reported in the *Chicago Daily News,* September 28, 1920. The publication of charges prior to completion of the grand jury probe was unorthodox and ran counter to ASA Replogle's previously stated preference that "all indictments ... be returned in a bunch after the inquiry" was concluded, as reported in the *Chicago Evening Post,* September 28, 1920.

32. As reported in the *Los Angeles Times,* September 29, 1920, and elsewhere. In due course, formal indictments would be drafted by First Assistant State's Attorney Edwin J. Raber, the SAO resident expert on indictments, as per the *Chicago Herald Examiner,* September 28, 1920.

33. As quoted in the *Los Angeles Times,* September 29, 1920.

34. As reported in the *Chicago Evening Post,* September 28, 1920. The *Chicago Evening American*, proud of its self-proclaimed scoop on Kelley's existence, persisted in its portrayal of her as an important witness. According to the *Evening American,* Kelley had, in fact, testified to overhearing Cicotte say to brother Jack, "To hell with 'em. I got mine," as reported in its September 29 edition.

35. As quoted in the *Chicago Evening Post,* September 28, 1920.

36. The transcript of the Jackson testimony is one of the few grand jury artifacts that survive intact to this day. Long out of public view, the transcript resurfaced in October 1988 when the successors to the Austrian law firm made a copy available to the Chicago Historical Society. The transcript was subsequently appended to a popular Jackson biography. See Harvey Frommer, *Shoeless Joe and Ragtime Baseball* (Dallas: Taylor Publishing Co., 1992), appendix at 192–215. It is now readily available on the Internet. See e.g., *http://www.1919blacksox.com/transcripts1.htm.*

37. Jackson Grand Jury transcript (hereafter JGJ), page 4, lines 6 to 8.

38. JGJ5–21 to JGJ6–8.

39. JGJ6–13 to 16.

40. JGJ6–17 to 24. Jackson subsequently testified that he had previously rejected fix overtures from Gandil, first in Boston when Jackson was offered $10,000 and then later in Chicago when Gandil upped the fix offer to $20,000. But the Jackson testimony regarding the second fix offer is cryptically worded and can just as easily be interpreted as a

Jackson acceptance. See JGJ19–8 to 25. Given that, it is unclear whether Jackson agreed to the fix during his second private meeting with Gandil or at some later time.

41. JGJ9–4 to 13.
42. JGJ9–14 to 18.
43. JGJ4–14 to 21.
44. JGJ6–25 to JGJ7–5.
45. JGJ7–5 to 9.
46. JGJ7–10 to 12.
47. JGJ4–20 to JGJ5–3.
48. JGJ12–5 to 10.
49. JGJ16–21 to JGJ17–12.
50. JGJ17–23 to JGJ19–6.
51. JGJ16–9 to 14.
52. JGJ20–3 to 7.
53. JGJ11–11 to 24. From the transcript it appears that Jackson construed the question as relating to Game One and then couched his answer in terms applicable to the entire Series.
54. JGJ12–20 to JGJ13–24.
55. JGJ14–3. Like Cicotte, Jackson was victimized by specious accounts of his testimony circulated by the Associated Press. Among other things, newspapers that subscribed to AP claimed that "Jackson said that throughout the series he either struck out or hit easy balls when hits would have meant runs." See e.g., *Los Angeles Times,* September 29, 1920.
56. JGJ14–18 to 19; JGJ12–13 to 16.
57. JGJ22–11 to JGJ23–3; JGJ23–16 to JGJ24–5.
58. JGJ24–6 to 7.
59. Because this work tries to avoid taking sides, a forensic dissection of Joe Jackson's grand jury testimony will not be attempted. But certain non-judgmental points can fairly be made. To the extent, for example, that assessments can be made from a dry, ninety-year-old record, there appears to be no evidence that Jackson was intoxicated or otherwise impaired while testifying. His answers were almost invariably responsive to the question and coherent. Nor is there any proof that Jackson's testimony was implanted in his mind by Alfred Austrian or some other White Sox agent, assuming, of course, that anyone outside the fix was even conversant with its details on September 28, 1920. In this regard, Jackson's employment of the word *instigator* (JGJ12–14) betrays no outside influence. For Jackson was an uneducated man, not a stupid one. At the time, Jackson was a well-traveled 32-year-old adult, a savvy small businessman, and a veteran of the vaudeville stage. And his speech, while occasionally colloquial, was by no means unsophisticated or monosyllabic. In the end, the conundrum of the Jackson grand jury testimony — inconsistent or irreconcilable answers on a core issue — does not readily lend itself to faraway armchair analysis. Suffice it to say that contradictory testimony by a witness on a crucial point is not an unheard of event in the courthouse.
60. As per Rick Huhn, *Eddie Collins,* 177–178.
61. See, e.g., *Chicago Tribune* and *New York Times,* September 29, 1920.
62. As quoted in the *Chicago Tribune,* September 29, 1920.
63. As reported in the *Chicago Herald Examiner,* September 29, 1920.
64. As reported in the *Boston Globe* and *New York Times,* September 29, 1920. The *Chicago Evening Post* also took passing notice of Weaver's assertion of innocence.
65. As quoted in the *Chicago Daily Journal,* September 29, 1920.
66. As per the *Chicago Evening Post,* September 29, 1920. See also, *Chicago Herald Examiner,* September 29, 1920, for like statements by Felsch.
67. As quoted in the *Chicago Evening Post,* September 29, 1920.
68. Initially printed in the *Chicago Tribune,* September 29, 1920, and then circulated

nationwide via the AP wire service. See, e.g., *Steubenville* (Ohio) *Herald-Star,* September 29, 1920. Unlike the more famous "Say it ain't so, Joe" anecdote, the authenticity of this interview has not been credibly challenged.

69. Per the *Chicago Tribune,* September 29, 1920.

70. *Ibid.*

71. *Ibid.*

72. *Ibid.* The line was later employed in the Nelson Algren poem *A Silver-Colored Yesterday,* as per Carney, 276.

73. The Williams statement was reprinted verbatim in the *Chicago Daily Journal* and *Chicago Daily News,* September 29, 1920, and widely excerpted elsewhere. The statement can now be accessed on-line via *http://www.1919blacksox.com/transcripts4.htm.*

74. As published in the *Chicago Daily Journal,* September 29, 1920.

75. *Ibid.*

76. *Ibid.*

77. *Ibid.*

78. *Ibid.*

79. *Ibid.*

80. A transcript of the Williams grand jury testimony was among the long-missing Black Sox documents acquired in December 2007 by the Chicago History Museum and is currently stored in CHM, Black Sox file, Box 1, Folder 2.

81. Transcript of Williams grand jury testimony (hereafter WGJ) 23–11 to 21. Note: The numbering on the CHM transcript of the Williams testimony begins at 23.

82. WGJ23–22 to WGJ24–7.

83. WGJ25–25 to WGJ26–7; WGJ26–20 to 22; WGJ28–19 to WGJ29–6.

84. WGJ30–20 to 24.

85. WGJ29–27 to WGJ30–7.

86. WGJ26–29 to WGJ27–3. Williams also testified that he never heard Hal Chase's name mentioned during fix meetings. Nor had he heard anything connecting Heinie Zimmerman or Joe Gedeon to the fix, although Gedeon was a friend of McMullin. WGJ35–10 to 19.

87. WGJ32–22 to WGJ33–2.

88. WGJ27–7 to 22.

89. WGJ27–23 to 25.

90. WGJ27–26 to WGJ28–7.

91. WGJ36–1 to 6; WGJ37–2 to 4.

92. WGJ35–26 to 29. In the days prior to Williams' grand jury appearance, it had been reported that Lyria Williams had placed Series bets against the White Sox. See *Boston Globe* and *Chicago Tribune,* September 26, 1920.

93. WGJ37–6 to 10.

94. WGJ33–11 to 20.

95. WGJ34–15 to 26.

96. As reported in the *Chicago Daily News,* September 29, 1920, and newspapers nationwide. As Sullivan was a prominent Boston bookmaker whose name had already been mentioned in scandal reportage (See e.g., *Washington Post,* September 20, 1920; *Chicago Evening Post,* September 24, 1920), identifying him as one of the two fixers mentioned by Williams was not difficult. But the true identity of Brown would remain a mystery to Cook County officials.

97. See *Chicago Tribune* and *New York Times,* September 30, 1920. As a county grand jury sitting in Illinois would have no legal jurisdiction to return criminal charges on extra-territorial matters, the Heydler and McGraw testimony mostly served only informational purposes. Many of the events in question, moreover, fell beyond the general two-year statute of limitations for the bringing of criminal charges in Illinois.

98. As per the *Chicago Tribune,* September 30, 1920.

99. As reported in the *Chicago Evening American* and *Chicago Herald Examiner,* October 1, 1920, and *Boston Globe*, October 2, 1920.

100. Published in the *Chicago Evening American,* September 30, 1920, and viewable on-line at *http://www.1919blacksox.com/transcripts3.htm.*

101. *Chicago Evening American,* September 30, 1920. More than forty years later, Felsch would admit that, under pressure from gamblers, the Black Sox had thrown games during the 1920 season as well. Said Felsch, "Playing rotten, it ain't that hard to do once you get the hang of it. It ain't hard to hit a pop-up while you take what looks like a good cut at the ball," as quoted in Eliot Asinof, *Bleeding Between the Lines* (New York: Holt, Rinehart & Winston, 1979), 117.

102. *Chicago Evening American,* September 30, 1920.

103. Gandil had rejected Comiskey's raise-less $4,000 contract offer for the 1920 season and spent the season on the suspended list. Game Eight of the 1919 World Series was the last time that Gandil would play anywhere in organized baseball.

104. *Chicago Evening American,* September 30, 1920.

105. *Ibid.*

106. *Ibid.*

107. *Ibid.*

7

The Grand Jury Probe Continues

Whether to horn in on the publicity bonanza or to achieve genuine law enforcement objectives, investigations into major league baseball by various prosecutorial agencies quickly mushroomed. In short order, probes of the playing of the 1919 World Series were announced by U.S. Attorney Thomas H. Morrow of Cincinnati, Special Prosecutor Charles Whitman of New York, and District Attorneys Harry H. Rowland (Pittsburgh), Louis Capelle (Hamilton County/Cincinnati), and Edward Swann (Manhattan). Simultaneously, U.S. Attorney Charles F. Clyne of Chicago launched an investigation into baseball pools, while Brooklyn DA Harry K. Lewis started a probe of alleged plans to rig the upcoming Brooklyn-Cleveland World Series. Even the IRS got into the act, promising audits of the indicted players for failure to report their bribe income.[1] Instituted with varying degrees of fanfare, all of these investigations would come to nothing.

Back at the Cook County courthouse, the grand jury's one-month term of service was about to expire, with much Black Sox-related work yet to be completed. Accordingly, Judge McDonald reconstituted the body into a specially designated investigative panel and extended its term indefinitely.[2] In so doing, the court stated that the "ballplayers and all others involved in crooked work will be indicted, prosecuted and punished."[3] Then, unexpectedly, the validity of the grand jury proceedings was called into question via a stunning communiqué issued by SA Hoyne, one which coincidentally exposed seething dissension in SAO ranks. Still vacationing in New York, Hoyne voiced strong displeasure with the staff attorneys conducting the grand jury probe, ostensibly for thwarting efforts to keep him abreast of developments.[4] Hoyne had intended for office secretary George Kenney to superintend the proceedings in his absence. But ASAs Replogle and Lightfoot deeply mistrusted Kenney (and perhaps Hoyne, as well), refusing him access to probe evidence and otherwise keeping him in the dark about the investigation's progress.[5] The two grand jury prosecutors had also countermanded Kenney's order that Lt. Thomas Sheehan, head of the SAO Detective Bureau, brief Chicago Police Chief Garrity on the investigation, an action that resulted in Sheehan's immediate firing when Hoyne found out.[6] But far more troubling than the exposure of antagonism within the SAO, Hoyne's remarks also publicly impugned the legality of the criminal charges reportedly voted by the grand jury. From Hoyne's vantage point, the only viable criminal charges in the case were gambling-related misdemeanors, not the felony offenses returned by the panel.[7] To rectify the situation, Hoyne directed that the grand jury proceedings be suspended until he returned to Chicago.[8]

Publication of the Hoyne comments generated a firestorm. Judge McDonald immediately rebuked Hoyne, informing him publicly that the probe would proceed — with or without the assistance of the Cook County State's Attorneys Office.[9] "The investigation will continue without interruption," thundered McDonald. "The White Sox players against whom indictments have been voted can and will be prosecuted in this jurisdiction."[10] Grand jury foreman Brigham and a number of individual panel members also declared their intention to proceed,[11] while the scholarly Alfred Austrian embarrassed Hoyne via a widely published tutorial on the applicable Illinois statutes and the legal precedent that supported the felony charges returned by the grand jury.[12]

Outgoing Cook County State's Attorney Maclay Hoyne steered an erratic course between promoting and obstructing the grand jury probe.

An abashed Hoyne quickly capitulated. Complaining that he had been misquoted in the press, Hoyne proclaimed, "I want to deny statements attributed to me that I doubted the [grand jury's] jurisdiction in returning indictments against the eight White Sox players and the gamblers involved in the

1919 series conspiracy."[13] Hoyne continued, "I made no demand that the investigation be halted. I simply asked the grand jury not to take any action until I get the chance to go over the evidence and check up on some [evidence] that I expect to get [here in New York]."[14] Regarding reportage of his remarks, Hoyne insisted that what he had actually said was that "there was not sufficient evidence to warrant indictments when I left Chicago," hastening to add that that was "no longer true given the new evidence produced after my departure."[15] Meanwhile in Chicago, Judge McDonald, mollified by Hoyle's backtracking, stated that he had assumed all along that Hoyne must have been misquoted. The court, moreover, was agreeable to deferring the formal unveiling of the grand jury indictments until Hoyne had returned to the office.[16]

The grand jury hearing of October 1 proceeded as originally scheduled, punctuated by a surprise appearance by Hoyne himself. After spending an hour closeted with the panel, Hoyne publicly endorsed the true bills previously voted by the grand jury.[17] He also revealed that just after the 1919 World Series was over, Sox owner Comiskey had come to Hoyne, "not as an official but as a friend," and asked him to conduct an investigation of his team's play. Hoyne had agreed, with Comiskey footing the expenses of a SAO detective who had shadowed the Sox during 1920 spring training. The exercise, however, had been "unable to uncover conclusive evidence of a [Series] fix."[18] More ominously, Hoyne further disclosed that "while in New York, I gathered loose threads of a 1920 scandal in baseball that would far surpass that of last season." Hoyne had not yet had the opportunity "to run it down to a certainty but I will venture to say that there is a more and bigger scandal coming in baseball."[19]

Boston bookmaker Joseph "Sport" Sullivan loudly protested his indictment, vowing not to be made the "goat" for Series fix profiteers.

Back inside the grand jury room, the panel heard from National Commission chairman/Cincinnati Reds President Garry Herrmann, who testified about the NL inquiry into Hal Chase's alleged attempts to fix games during the 1918 season. During the Herrmann appearance, the grand jury was provided with affidavits collected during the league's probe from managers Mathewson (Reds) and McGraw (Giants) and various players.[20] Next, an impromptu appearance was put in by an unexpectedly available Ban Johnson, who supplied the panel with a brief update on his investigation of the Series scandal, the details of which were not published.[21] The proceedings then concluded with supplemental testimony by Cubs President Veeck, who revealed that the team's investigation of fix allegations about the August 31 Cubs-Phillies game had determined that the rumors were just a ruse designed to affect the betting odds on the contest.[22]

Press reports of the succeeding day's grand jury action had to compete for space with denials of guilt from many quarters. At a joint press conference with Risberg and McMullin, Buck Weaver professed his innocence. "They have nothing on me," asserted Buck. "I am going to hire the best lawyer in Chicago to defend me, and I'm going to be cleared."[23] Similar sentiments were offered by the other two, with a miffed Risberg adding that "I made Jackson apologize for the story he spread about me. I never threatened him."[24] From a hospital bed in Lufkin, Texas, where he was recovering from a recent appendectomy, Chick Gandil chimed in, denying participation in any World Series fix and expressing disbelief at the published grand jury testimony of Joe Jackson and Lefty Williams.[25] An even bigger splash was made by Sport Sullivan in New York. Emerging from seclusion with Boston lawyer William J. Kelly in tow, Sullivan declared,

> They have indicted me and made me the goat, and I'm not going to stand for it. I know the whole story of the deal from beginning to end. I know the big man whose money it was that paid off the Sox players — and I'm going to name him.[26]

Sullivan further stated that "he knew the names of all, or nearly all, of the big gamblers who had won large sums by having advance information on the result of the series." But he declined to divulge any of those names "in advance of his talk to the Chicago officials."[27] The Sullivan announcement coincided with an angry outburst from Abe Attell, who blamed Arnold Rothstein for connecting Attell's name to the fix story. Like Sullivan, Attell had retained legal counsel and promised in a few days to "shoot the [scandal] lid sky high."[28] But not all of the day's news emanated from those implicated in the scandal on the defense side. SA Hoyne was back before the press, this time expanding on his claims about crooked 1920 play. According to Hoyne, "at least six 1920 major league games" had been fixed by the same clique of gamblers who had rigged the previous World Series.[29] Almost simultaneously, Chisox bench-warmers Harvey McClellan and Byrd Lynn made a like charge.[30] Lynn was particularly outspoken, asserting that "we lost the [1920] pennant because certain players — they are among the eight indicted by the Cook County grand jury — didn't want to win."[31]

At the courthouse, proceedings continued with testimony by Clyde Elliott about his post–Series trip to St. Louis with White Sox manager Gleason and club employee Norris O'Neill. Dr. Raymond Prettyman, the Weaver family dentist, also put in an appearance. But only sparse details of either the Elliott or Prettyman testimony reached newspaper readers.[32] More space was devoted to an interim report by the grand jury accepting continued service as a special panel in order to complete "our inquiries and investigations relative to these dishonesties and to these criminal practices in our great national game." The panel promised "a full and detailed report ... at the conclusion of our work."[33] The interim report continued,

> The jury expresses its esteem and appreciation for the competent services rendered by ASAs Replogle, Lightfoot and Hodges.[34] Mr. Replogle is especially commended for his persistent diligence and his competence in handling the baseball matter and in view of the prospect of this jury's being impaneled as a special grand jury, we recommend his retention as principal counsel for the special grand jury.[35]

Before standing in recess while the 1920 World Series was played, the grand jury conducted a scattershot session on October 5. The hearing was preceded by official announcement that a clean bill of health had been extended to the 1920 World Series. "Every man on the Brooklyn and Cleveland team is as innocent as a newborn babe and in no way implicated in any baseball scandal past or present," ASA Replogle informed the press.[36] The bulk of the day's witnesses — Giants owner Charles Stoneham, manager John McGraw, former coach Art Fletcher, Giants trainer J.L. Mackall, and players Fred Toney, Larry Doyle, and Benny Kauff— were summoned to testify about NL-related matters. Insight into the gambling situation in Detroit, locus of the original Cubs-Phillies game fix reports, was sought from Tigers manager Hugh Jennings, but he proved of little help. Evidence about the 1919 World Series investigation was supplied by former Giants pitcher Jean Dubuc who revealed that he had discussed fix rumors with Bill Burns prior to the start of the Series. Thereafter, Burns wired Dubuc, advising him to bet on the Reds, with the actual Burns telegrams received in evidence by the grand jury.[37] Aspects of the White Sox internal probe of the Series were elicited from Kid Gleason and Norris O'Neill, both of whom were also quizzed about Chisox play during the 1920 season. Although he had no definite proof, Gleason conceded his suspicions about his team's play, particularly during a crucial late-season series in Boston.[38] Meanwhile from Greenville, South Carolina, came word that Joe Jackson and Lefty Williams were consulting a local attorney. Complete with an exquisitely garbled metaphor, the pair subsequently issued the following statement about the grand jury probe: "If investigators probe thoroughly, they may find men higher up in baseball at the bottom of the scandal."[39]

Even while the proceedings were in recess, strategic maneuvers continued. Sullivan's attorney contacted the SAO on behalf of his client, but what he wanted was not disclosed.[40] Days later, Abe Attell was located in Montreal, with no immediate plans for returning south of the border. "When I am ready, I will go back of my own free will and tell them all I know," said Abe, betraying little enthusiasm for meeting with authorities, a condition perhaps occasioned by outstanding subpoenas issued for the Little Champ by Manhattan DA Swann and Nassau County DA Charles Weeks, both of whom were probing Rothstein casino operations.[41] A more cooperative attitude was anticipated from East St. Louis theater owner and World Series betting loser Harry Redmon and his St. Louis gambling pals Joe Pesch and Thomas Kearney, all of whom had been subpoenaed to appear before the grand jury.[42] Meanwhile in a private communication, AL President Johnson directed the attention of ASA Replogle toward a new potential grand jury target: Des Moines gambler Ben Levi, reportedly a major winner in high stakes wagering on the 1919 World Series.[43]

Grand jury proceedings resumed after the completion of the 1920 series, but they got off slowly when the call for the St. Louis-area witnesses went unanswered in the grand jury waiting room.[44] Their secret sponsor, a chagrined Ban Johnson, quickly sent the grand jury word that Redmon had taken ill, Pesch had been suddenly called to California, and Kearney would be unable to appear until the following week.[45] In their absence, Cubs manager Fred Mitchell and club secretary John O. Seys made brief appearances related to the August 31 Cubs-Phillies game.[46] A few minutes of testimony by Brooklyn team owner Charles Ebbets yielded no trace of 1920 World Series corruption, while Boston magnates George Grant (Braves) and Harry Frazee (Red Sox) were excused before reaching the witness stand.[47] The remainder of day's the hearing was then devoted to testimony about the operation of baseball pools,[48] but was not entirely uneventful. Pool operator Charles Blagen managed to get himself arrested for some unspecified transgression during his grand jury appearance.[49]

On October 22, 1920, Ban Johnson returned to the stand to brief the grand jury on the AL's probe of the 1919 World Series. Among those interviewed during a Johnson trip to St. Louis was Browns infielder Joe Gedeon, who thus became a person of interest to the panel.[50] Testimony by Harry Long, a clerk at the Chicago Board of Trade, helped quantify the extent of Sport Sullivan's betting on the Series. According to Long, he personally had placed $29,000 in wagers on the Reds for Sullivan.[51] The grand jury also heard more testimony regarding the operation of baseball pools in the greater Chicago area, with newspaper reportage emphasizing the hard-luck story of streetcar conductor Roy Slawson, stiffed on the advertised $10,000 prize for holding a winning $1 ticket.[52] At the conclusion of their day's labors, the grand jurors handed down superseding indictments against the eight White Sox players already charged and added Abe Attell, Hal Chase, and Bill Burns to the roster of gamblers indicted. The new indictments were reportedly prompted by the need to rectify "technical defects" in the original charges.[53] In announcing the new charges, officials at the SAO designated Chase as "the chief instigator of the game selling."[54]

The last major probe witnesses appeared before the grand jury on October 26, 1920. After waiving his right to remain silent, Joe Gedeon testified that he had been informed of the Series fix beforehand by a White Sox player whom he was not pressed to identify (but who was presumed to be either Swede Risberg or Fred McMullin, both friends of Gedeon). Sport Sullivan and "R. Brown of New York" were named by Gedeon as the handlers of gambler interests.[55] With his advanced knowledge of the fix, Gedeon had placed Series bets through St. Louis gamblers Carl Zork and Ben Franklin and won $600.[56] Of far greater significance, Gedeon testified that there had been a meeting of gamblers at the Sherman Hotel in Chicago after the White Sox had unexpectedly won Game Three. Present at the meeting were Zork, Franklin, Abe Attell, Bill Burns, Harry Redmon, and Joe Pesch, the latter two refusing to contribute $10,000 shares to a gamblers' fund being collected to get rebellious Sox players to return to the fix.[57]

The Gedeon account of the Sherman Hotel conclave was largely corroborated by Harry Redmon when he took the witness stand. Redmon further revealed that after attending the first two Series games in Cincinnati, he had traveled to Chicago with St. Louis gambler Joe Pesch and Sid Keener, sports editor of the *St. Louis Times.* While he and Pesch were in the city, Pesch learned of the fix from the Levi brothers, Ben and Lou. According to the Levis, seven White Sox regulars and sub McMullin had been corrupted. When Redmon later encountered Zork at the Morrison Hotel, a beaming Zork claimed credit for organizing the Series fix. Redmon was skeptical that Zork was the fix mastermind, but was aware that Zork had put $50,000 on the Reds prior to leaving St. Louis. Redmon had also observed Sport Sullivan in action in and around Chicago hotels.[58] As for his own Series wagering, Redmon had backed the White Sox in the first two Series games, losing approximately \$3,500. He then switched to the Reds for Game Three and dropped another \$3,500. Still, Redmon refused to be a contributor to the fund being gathered by Zork and Franklin to reinstate the fix after the Game Three upset.[59]

New York underworld financier Arnold Rothstein indignantly proclaimed his innocence both inside and out the grand jury hearing room.

Redmon also testified that he had informed manager Gleason and the others of the fix when the Sox entourage had made its discreet post–Series visit to St. Louis.[60] That winter, moreover, he and Pesch had traveled to Chicago, where they repeated what they knew to club owner Comiskey and various club officials. As Redmon recalled, Sox lawyer Alfred Austrian did most of the talking on the other side, with Comiskey doing little more than grumbling that Joe Jackson had cost him \$70,000-\$80,000. Redmon had made no claim on the Comiskey reward money and was angered that club officials had taken no corrective action after the briefing.[61] The ensuing publication of the Redmon account of his meeting with White Sox officials touched off a public relations skirmish, with Clyde Elliott vocally supporting Redmon, "a gentleman of impeccable integrity,"[62] while Chisox secretary Harry Grabiner defended the club's disinclination to act upon "the hard luck yarn of a loser."[63]

The celebrity highlight of the grand jury proceedings was doubtless the appearance of Arnold Rothstein, who had arrived in Chicago bristling with well-rehearsed indignation over the connection of his name to the scandal.[64] Why uncouth local newspaperman had greeted him at the train station as if he were a common criminal, the New York underworld kingpin complained.[65] Once before the panel, Rothstein smoothly related his now familiar story about rejecting the fix overtures of Bill Burns at the Astor Hotel. Rothstein had promptly informed John McGraw of the plot, urging him to pass along a warning to Sox manager Gleason. But McGraw had declined, telling Rothstein that Gleason already had enough to worry about.[66] The witness had thereafter been victimized by Abe Attell and others who had used Rothstein's name without his permission or knowledge in their efforts to corrupt Sox players. As for his stake in the 1919 Series, Rothstein had bet on the White Sox and lost $6,000.[67]

Following the Rothstein performance, his claims of innocence were supported by Alfred Austrian. Not only had Rothstein not had a hand in the corruption of the 1919 World Series, "he has done everything he could to prevent the fixing," announced Austrian.[68] Rothstein "has told me, as counsel for the White Sox, everything he knows about the fixing," continued Austrian. "He has proved himself guiltless."[69] Not to be outdone, Ban Johnson then declared himself satisfied that Joe Gedeon was "entirely innocent," as well.[70] Of more immediate consequence to the probe's two spotlight witnesses, the SAO publicly exonerated Rothstein and Gedeon of complicity in the World Series fix, adding that their testimony had "materially strengthened the case against some of the men already indicted."[71] The grand jury session concluded with little-noted testimony by *Sporting News* executives J.G. Taylor Spink and Al Herr, both of whom had no first-hand knowledge of the scandal but had assisted AL President Johnson in his inquiries in St. Louis.[72] The panel also heard from more baseball pool witnesses before adjourning for the day.

The final bit of noteworthy grand jury testimony was given on October 29 by Johnson, reappearing before the panel to provide additional information on the now mostly forgotten Cubs-Phillies game. Citing information furnished by *Kansas City Post* sports editor Otto Floto, Johnson testified that Cubs hurler Claude Hendrix had wired Kansas City gambler H.A. "Frock" Thompson, telling him to bet $5,000 on the Phillies. Thompson had also received similar directives from Hal Chase and former Phillies pitcher Gene Packard.[73] Upon being informed of the Johnson testimony, Thompson issued a swift public denial, maintaining that he did not even know Hendrix.[74] In any event, the matter received no further attention from the grand jury. Its final witnesses were Chicago Police Chief John J. Garrity, testifying about the extent of baseball pool operations in the city, and yet more pool operators and their dissatisfied customers.[75]

At the conclusion of the October 29 session, the grand jury formally returned indictments charging Edward V. Cicotte, Claude Williams, Joe Jackson, Fred McMullin, Arnold Gandil, George Weaver, Oscar Felsch, Charles Risberg, William Burns, Hal Chase, Joseph J. Sullivan, Rachael Brown,[76] and Abe Attell with five counts of conspiracy to obtain money by false pretenses and/or a confidence game.[77] Simultaneously, indictments for the unlawful sale of lottery tickets were returned against baseball pool operators Martin Carlin of Universal Baseball Pool; Frederick C. Walters of the American-National Pool, and William Chellius/Great Western Pool of South Chicago.[78]

On November 6, 1920, the panel released a six-page report on its inquiry.

The report praised Judge McDonald for "ordering this investigation and [he] will have rendered the American public a great service if the inquiry has the effect of preventing baseball players of the future from being contaminated and corrupted by unscrupulous swindlers and gamblers."[79] The report also lauded ASA Replogle and recommended that he be retained as special prosecutor for the case by the incoming SAO administration.[80] There was also praise for "the spirit shown by the officials of baseball during the course of the investigation." The panel felt confident that baseball's leadership "may henceforth be relied upon to eliminate any players they strongly suspect."[81] Although the evidence presented had necessitated the indictment of eight players, the report observed,

> Considering the magnitude of the enterprise and the great number of ball players engaged, we believe a comparatively small number of the players have been dishonest. We were gratified to find players who immediately reported to their managers the suggestions of "fixing" and likewise managers who immediately discontinued players who were implicated in any way in attempts to corrupt the game. The adoption of this practice as a fixed policy, no matter at what cost, will make impossible the repetition of the present troubles.[82]

The report had also scathing words for the operation of baseball pools, asserting that the "unsuspecting people of Chicago and other cities are fleeced out of hundreds of thousands of dollars weekly during the baseball season. The pools are, almost without exception, conducted by irresponsible persons who operate without definite system and without regularity of practice."[83] To drive home the point, indictments were returned against three additional pool operators: Peter Hansen and Ralph Hansen of the Chicago Heights Baseball Pool and Charles Haas of the Blue Island Baseball Pool.[84]

In his final meeting with the panel, Judge McDonald complimented the grand jury on exposing "conditions of bribery and crookedness in organized baseball that shocked the conscience of the clean, sport-loving American public." The panel's probe had been "the only effective way by which the baneful influence of a coterie of crooks and plug-uglies could have been thwarted and the national game purified and restored to the confidence of the public."[85] The court then discharged the special baseball gambling panel from service and brought the Black Sox scandal grand jury proceedings to a close. Or so it seemed at the time.

Notes

1. As reported in the *Chicago Tribune* and *New York Times,* September 30, 1920, *Boston Globe,* October 1 and 3, 1920, and elsewhere.

2. As reported in the *Chicago Evening Post* and *Chicago Tribune,* September 30, 1920, and elsewhere.

3. As per the *Boston Globe,* September 30, 1920, quoting Judge McDonald.
4. As reported in the *Chicago Daily Journal,* September 30, 1920.
5. As reported in the *Chicago Tribune,* September 30, 1920.
6. As per the *Chicago Daily Journal,* September 30, 1920
7. As reported in the *Chicago Daily Journal* and *Chicago Daily News,* September 30, 1920. If Hoyne were correct, the Black Sox scandal would not have fallen under the charging purview of the grand jury (which does not ordinarily take action on misdemeanors and other non-felony offenses), thus placing a cloud over the proceedings in their entirety.
8. As per the *Chicago Tribune,* September 30, 1920.
9. As reported in the *Chicago Tribune* and *New York Times,* September 30, 1920. As the grand jury is an arm of the judicial, rather than executive branch, Judge McDonald had absolute and unfettered control of the proceedings and did not legally require the cooperation of the State's Attorneys Office. Although probably impractical in the Black Sox hearings, McDonald could simply have appointed a special counsel to take charge of the probe, if he had so desired.
10. As quoted in the *Chicago Daily Journal* and *Chicago Evening Post,* September 30, 1920.
11. As reported in the *Chicago Daily Journal,* September 30, 1920, and *Chicago Herald Examiner,* October 1, 1920.
12. As published in the *Chicago Tribune* and *New York Times,* October 1, 1920, and elsewhere.
13. As quoted in the *Chicago Herald Examiner,* October 2, 1920.
14. As quoted in the *Chicago Evening Post,* October 1, 1920.
15. As per the *Chicago Herald Examiner,* October 2, 1920.
16. As reported in the *New York Times,* October 1, 1920. This face-saving pronouncement followed a closed-door meeting between Judge McDonald and SAO senior staff attorneys, including 1st ASA Raber and ASA Marvin P. Barnhart, as per the *Chicago Evening Post,* September 30, 1920.
17. As per the *Chicago Herald Examiner,* October 1, 1920.
18. As per the *Chicago Daily Journal,* October 1, 1920. Similar quotes appeared in the *Los Angeles Times,* October 2, 1920.
19. As quoted in the *Chicago Evening Post,* October 1, 1920, which also reported the reply of a somewhat vexed Brooklyn DA Lewis: "My investigations have not disclosed a single suspicion that there has been an attempt to fix the upcoming series" between the Robins and Cleveland.
20. As reported in the *New York Times,* October 1, 1920, and *Chicago Tribune,* October 2, 1920.
21. Johnson's grand jury appearance was noted with no details provided in the *Chicago Evening Post,* October 1, 1920.
22. As reported in the *Los Angeles Times,* October 1, 1920.
23. As quoted in the *Chicago Herald Examiner,* October 2, 1920, True to his word, Weaver promptly retained Thomas D. Nash, an experienced and politically connected criminal defense attorney, as reported by the *Chicago Daily Journal,* October 2, 1920.
24. As per the *Chicago Herald Examiner,* October 2, 1920, and *Atlanta Constitution,* October 5, 1920. Left unreported was just how Risberg had extracted Jackson's purported apology.
25. As reported in the *Los Angeles Times* and *New York Times,* October 1, 1920.
26. As quoted in the *Boston Globe,* October 2, 1920. See also the *Chicago Evening Post,* October 2, 1920.
27. As per the *Boston Globe,* October 2, 1920. The following day, lawyer Kelly would be issuing denials that Sullivan had threatened to expose Series fixers. See *Washington Post,* October 3, 1920.

28. As reported by the *Chicago Tribune* and *Los Angeles Times,* September 29, 1920. A day later, Attell asserted that ten unnamed gamblers had made at least $250,000 on the fix, as reported in the *Chicago Daily Journal* and *Chicago Daily News,* September 30, 1920. Meanwhile, new Attell lawyer William J. Fallon, the gifted but unscrupulous star of the NYC criminal defense bar, declared that Attell had had "absolutely nothing" to do with the fix of the Series, as per the *Los Angeles Times,* September 30, 1920.

29. As reported in the *Chicago Herald Examiner,* October 2, 1920.

30. As reported in the *Chicago Evening Post,* October 2, 1920, *Boston Globe,* October 4, 1920, and elsewhere.

31. *Ibid.* See also, *New York Times,* October 4, 1920. Chisox captain Eddie Collins had reportedly taken complaints about suspicious play during a crucial late-season series with the Boston Red Sox directly to Comiskey, but no action was taken by club management. Later, Collins pointedly accused Buck Weaver and Eddie Cicotte of crooked play during the 1920 season, stating that "if gamblers didn't have Weaver and Cicotte in their pocket, then I don't know anything about baseball," as quoted in *Collyer's Eye,* October 30, 1920.

32. An intriguing divergence emerges, however, regarding the Prettyman testimony. To the extent that it garnered coverage, the now familiar hearsay about the McMullin visit to the Weaver residence was generally attributed to Prettyman. See e.g., *New York Times,* October 2, 1920, and *The Sporting News,* October 7, 1920. But an altogether different account of anticipated Prettyman testimony had been ferreted out by the *Chicago Daily Journal.* According to the *Journal,* Prettyman had advised ASA Lightfoot of fix-related information that he had received from a fellow dentist, Dr. P.P. Barnhart. As per Prettyman, Barnhart had been told that the Series had been fixed and that the plot had been instigated by a White Sox player who resided at the Warner Hotel (implicitly Eddie Cicotte). Barnhart's informant was one Clark Estes, a stockyard dealer who had bet on the Series with Barnhart. When subsequently contacted by the *Journal,* Barnhart confirmed the story but Estes denied it. See *Chicago Daily Journal,* September 30, 1920. But whether or not this tale was the subject of Prettyman's actual grand jury testimony is unknown.

33. As reported in the *Chicago Daily Journal* and *Chicago Evening Post,* October 2, 1920, and elsewhere. Unlike a regular grand jury, whose job is simply to indict or not indict, an investigative grand jury oft-times issues a report, commonly called a presentment, in addition to returning charges. Such presentments recount the factual findings of the panel's probe, demand remedial action by government officials, and/or otherwise elucidate the problem that the grand jury was impaneled to investigate.

34. *Ibid.* The acknowledgment of ASA Ernest Hodges, an SAO staff attorney unconnected to the baseball probe, reflects the fact that the normal regimen of criminal cases was not neglected by the panel. Once reconstituted as a specially designated investigative body, however, the panel had the luxury of concentrating exclusively on baseball, leaving the regular calendar of cases to the new incoming October grand jury.

35. As reprinted in the *Chicago Daily Journal* and *Chicago Evening Post,* October 2, 1920.

36. As quoted in the *Chicago Evening Post,* October 5, 1920. The 1920 Fall Classic would, however, produce a minor embarrassment. Robins hurler Rube Marquard was arrested for scalping his Series tickets, as reported in the *Chicago Evening Post,* October 9, 1920, and elsewhere. For more on the Marquard arrest — he was convicted and paid a nominal fine — see Larry D. Mansch, *Rube Marquard: The Life and Times of a Baseball Hall of Famer* (Jefferson, NC: McFarland, 1998), 183–187.

37. As reported in the *Chicago Evening Post* and *New York Times,* October 5, 1920, and *Boston Globe,* October 6, 1920.

38. As reported in the *Boston Globe,* October 6, 1920. See also, *Chicago Herald Examiner,* October 4, 1920, forecasting the Gleason/O'Neill testimony.

39. As reported in the *Chicago Evening Post* and *Chicago Tribune,* October 6, 1920.

40. See *Chicago Evening Post,* October 7, 1920, and *Chicago Tribune,* October 8, 1920.

41. As quoted in the *Boston Globe,* October 16, 1920.

42. As reported in the *Chicago Herald Examiner* and *Washington Post,* October 16, 1920. Press reports regarding subpoenas were somewhat misleading, as the Cook County grand jury had no power to compel out-of-state witnesses to appear before it. All the grand jury could do regarding non–Illinois residents was issue unenforceable invitations to appear and testify before the panel.

43. As memorialized in a letter dated October 19, 1920, preserved in the Black Sox file at the Giamatti Research Center.

44. As per the *Chicago Tribune* and *New York Times,* October 20, 1920.

45. As reported by the *Chicago Herald Examiner,* October 22, 1920.

46. As reported in the *New York Times,* October 20, 1920. A year later at trial, Seys would testify that he had served as a stakeholder for bets placed on the Reds by Abe Attell for Game One and Game Two but brief press report of the Seys grand jury testimony made no mention of this unseemly event.

47. As per the *New York Times,* October 20, 1920.

48. See generally, *Chicago Tribune,* October 19 and 20, 1920. Testimony about baseball pool operations was provided by sundry elected and police officials, as well as a number of pool operators, one of whom (Joe Lloyd) described his business as an "indoor sport," rather than a gambling enterprise, as related in the *Chicago Herald Examiner,* October 22, 1920.

49. As reported in the *New York Times,* October 20, 1920, which presumed non-cooperation by Blagen.

50. As per the *New York Times,* October 22, 1920.

51. As reported in the *Chicago Herald Examiner,* October 22, 1920. The *Boston Globe* and *New York Times,* October 23, 1920, placed the figure at $27,000, while an AP wire dispatch gave $37,000 as the amount bet by Long on Sullivan's behalf. See e.g., *Los Angeles Times,* October 23, 1920.

52. The *Chicago Tribune,* October 23, 1920, reported that pool operators had offered $20 when Slawson tried to redeem his ticket. The *Chicago Herald Examiner,* October 22, 1920, upped the settlement offer to $500, while the *Chicago Daily Journal,* October 28, 1920, reported that Slawson ultimately settled with the pool operators for $2,100.

53. As reported in the *Boston Globe* and *Chicago Tribune,* October 23, 1920, and elsewhere.

54. As per the *Boston Globe,* October 23, 1920.

55. As reported in the *Kansas City Times, Los Angeles Times* and *Washington Post,* October 27, 1920.

56. As per the *Chicago Herald Examiner* and *Washington Post,* October 27, 1920.

57. As reported in the *Chicago Herald Examiner* and *Kansas City Times,* October 27, 1920, and *The Sporting News,* November 4, 1920.

58. As per transcript excerpts of the sometimes convoluted grand jury testimony of Harry Redmon, preserved in CHM, Black Sox file, Box 1, Folder 2.

59. *Ibid.* Redmon testified that the Zork/Franklin group had solicited a $5,000 contribution from him, not the $10,000 specified by Joe Gedeon.

60. This presumably reinforced the little-reported testimony that the grand jury had received earlier from Clyde Elliott.

61. As per the Redmon grand jury testimony transcript. See also *The Sporting News,* November 4, 1920, which, in recounting the testimony, described Redmon as "a successful businessman with sporting inclinations, square as a die and his word is his bond."

62. As quoted in the *Chicago Daily Journal,* October 28, 1920.

63. As reported in the *Chicago Tribune,* October 28, 1920, and elsewhere.

64. Orchestration of the Rothstein performance is usually credited to attorney William J. Fallon, as per Gene Fowler, *The Great Mouthpiece: A Life Story of William J. Fallon* (New York: Covici, Friede, 1931), 276–277. It should be noted that Fallon was never counsel of record for Rothstein during the Black Sox scandal, or at any other time, for that matter. While in Chicago, Rothstein was represented by attorney Meier Steinbrink (*Chicago Tribune,* October 26, 1920) and/or attorney Hyman Turchin, as per the *Chicago Evening American,* October 27, 1920.

65. As reported in the *Chicago Tribune,* October 26, 1920.

66. As reported in the *Chicago Tribune,* October 27, 1920, and *The Sporting News,* November 4, 1920. McGraw heatedly denied the claim, calling Rothstein "several kinds of liar," according to the Ban Johnson career retrospective interview published in the *Chicago Tribune,* March 10, 1929.

67. As reported in the *Chicago Herald Examiner* and *Chicago Tribune,* October 27, 1920, and elsewhere.

68. As quoted in the *Los Angeles Times* and *Washington Post,* October 27, 1920.

69. As per the *Boston Globe* and *New York Times,* October 27, 1920.

70. As reported in the *Boston Globe* and *Washington Post,* October 27, 1920.

71. As per the *Boston Globe* and *New York Times,* October 27, 1920.

72. As per the *Boston Globe,* October 28, 1920.

73. As reported in the *Chicago Evening American* and *Chicago Herald Examiner,* October 30, 1920, and *The Sporting News,* November 4, 1920. Note that Harry Grabiner's famously lost diary reputedly cited Packard as a 1918 World Series fixer, as per Bill Veeck, Jr., with Ed Linn, *The Hustler's Handbook* (New York: Fireside Books, 1965), 296.

74. As per *The Sporting News,* November 4, 1920. Hendrix, a local product, maintained his off-season home in the Kansas City area.

75. As noted in the *Chicago Evening American* and *Chicago Tribune,* October 29, 1920.

76. Earlier in the month, the SAO had decided that the first name of the mysterious defendant Brown was *Raphael,* as reported in the *Boston Globe,* October 6, 1920. The basis for the amendment of the Brown first name to *Rachael* was not announced by prosecutors and the SAO was never able to figure out who defendant Brown really was. For more on this minor scandal puzzler, see William F. Lamb, "A Black Sox Mystery: The Identity of Defendant Rachael Brown," *Base Ball, A Journal of the Early Game,* Vol. 4, No. 2, Fall 2010, 5–11.

77. As reported in the *Chicago Herald Examiner* and *Chicago Tribune,* October 30, 1920, and elsewhere. Returning an indictment is a perfunctory ritual performed in open court during which the grand jury formally presents a document (indictment) wherein the charges against the accused are specified in writing. In the ordinary case, the return of an indictment provides the first public notice of a criminal charge preferred by a grand jury. But in the Black Sox case, grand jury action against the accused was already a matter of common knowledge. The original indictments were drafted by 1st ASA Edwin J. Raber, as reported by the *Chicago Tribune,* October 28, 1920, and are now viewable online at http://www.cookcountyclerkofcourt.org.

78. As reported in the *Boston Globe* and *New York Times,* October 30, 1920.

79. As excerpted in the *Chicago Daily News,* November 6, 1920, and *Chicago Tribune,* November 7, 1920.

80. As per the *Chicago Tribune,* November 7, 1920.

81. *Ibid.*

82. *Ibid.*

83. As reported in the *Chicago Daily News,* November 6, 1920.

84. As reported in the *Chicago Daily News* and *Chicago Evening Post,* November 6, 1920.

85. As quoted in the *Chicago Tribune,* November 7, 1920.

8

POST-INDICTMENT TURMOIL

While the Cook County probe of the 1919 World Series was in progress, the ultimate outcome of the Black Sox scandal was being foreshadowed by events unfolding on the West Coast. On October 15, 1920, a Los Angeles County grand jury commenced inquiry into alleged corruption of Pacific Coast League play.[1] Among other things, the panel focused on an all-purpose slush fund purportedly maintained by the Vernon Tigers; the alleged bribery of Salt Lake City players by Vernon team captain Babe Borton; and the legitimacy of Vernon's 1919 PCL title.[2] As in Chicago, the proceedings featured testimony by numerous league officials and players, including grand jury targets Borton, Harl Maggert, and Bill Rumler. The latter two, both Salt Lake City stalwarts, were accused of accepting bribes from Borton to throw a crucial October 1919 series to Vernon. Former Salt Lake City pitcher Gene Dale, then playing in the Texas League, was also suspected of taking a payoff from Borton. The mastermind and financier of the fix was reputed to be West Coast gambler Nate Raymond. According to investigators, Raymond had invested $10,000 in arranging the fix and then won $50,000 betting on Vernon.[3]

On December 11, 1920, the grand jury returned indictments that charged Borton, Maggert, Rumler, and Raymond with various conspiracy-related offenses.[4] More particularly, the accused were charged with (1) conspiracy to defraud the 1919 runner-up Los Angeles Angels of $3,985 in fan-generated bonus money that was awarded to the PCL pennant winner; (2) conspiracy to defraud the corporate owners of the Vernon, Salt Lake City, and Los Angeles clubs of their right to have PCL games decided "honestly and fairly"; and (3) conspiracy to defraud the "admission paying witnesses" to the rigged Vernon/Salt Lake City series.[5] The indictments further alleged that "had defendants Maggert and Rumler used their best efforts to win baseball games for Salt Lake City, the Los Angeles baseball team" would have been the 1919 PCL pennant winner.[6]

Unveiled with considerable fanfare, the charges would be short-lived. Two weeks later, Los Angeles County Superior Court Judge Frank R. Willis granted a defense application to dismiss the indictments.[7] In the court's view, the conduct alleged, while reprehensible, was not criminal in nature. Specifically, Judge Willis ruled,

> There is nothing in the penal code of California providing for prosecution of the offenses named in the indictment. The conspiracy if it existed, and if it was carried out, constituted a violation of contract. The remedy for that is in civil courts. The contract broken provided that the men should play to the best of their ability.[8]

In California, therefore, it was not a crime for players and gamblers to work together to throw professional baseball games. Such conduct was merely a breach of the player's contract with his ball club and the only legal remedy was to seek monetary damages in civil court. And because the court's ruling was premised not on disputed issues of fact, but upon binding construction of California statutes, the charges could not be re-presented to the grand jury for further action. Rather, criminal charges in the PCL scandal were barred as a matter of law. The accused were, therefore, permanently off the hook, at least as far as the California criminal justice system was concerned.[9]

Victorious in the November 1920 election, incoming State's Attorney Robert E. Crowe inherited the Black Sox prosecution from the Hoyne administration.

The reaction to the Willis ruling by PCL officials was swift and punitive, a harbinger of the course that would later be followed in the Black Sox case. PCL President William H. McCarthy stated his position on the matter bluntly, proclaiming that "even if these players may not be punished criminally, Borton, Rumler, and Maggert stand indicted and convicted in the eyes of the Coast League baseball public. If the law cannot punish them, it remains for baseball to do its share anyway and at least to keep them from participating in the professional ranks."[10] Official action along the lines proposed by McCarthy was not long in coming. Only weeks later, Babe Borton, Harl

Maggert, Bill Rumler, and Gene Dale were expelled from organized baseball.[11]

Back in Chicago, attention had been diverted from the baseball scandals by the November 1920 elections. Little note, for example, was taken of the retention of former ASA Henry Berger as local counsel by the Attell defense.[12] Berger, a skilled legal infighter with close ties to the Hoyne administration, would prove a major figure in Black Sox case developments, both inside the courtroom and out.[13] Another pivotal character entered the lists on November 3, 1920, when the Republican electoral landslide swept Judge Robert E. Crowe to victory in the Cook County State's Attorneys race. Upon being sworn into office a month later, prosecution of the Black Sox indictments would become Crowe's responsibility.

On November 5, 1920, Buck Weaver and Fred McMullin posted $10,000 bond and were allowed to remain at liberty pending the disposition of the case. "The charges aren't true and we can prove it," said Weaver. "All we ask is that the baseball public withhold its judgment until we have had the chance to appear in court."[14] The cry of innocence was echoed the following week by McMullin, now back home in California. McMullin also disclosed that Happy Felsch was challenging the authenticity of his published interview in the *Chicago Evening American*. As relayed to the press by McMullin, Felsch was contending that "the confession claimed to have been made by him to a newspaper was given on the telephone, and that he was not on the other end of the line. In other words, he [Felsch] claims the confession was a 'phoney.'"[15] Days later, Joe Jackson joined in, maintaining that "I never confessed to throwing a ball game in my life, and I never will."[16] This evidently proved too much for Judge McDonald, who promptly informed the press that "Jackson's testimony was made under oath before the grand jury. If he denies that testimony when he is brought to trial, he will be guilty of perjury and could be prosecuted under that charge."[17]

Amid the dueling pre-trial statements of Black Sox actors an event of more lasting significance occurred: the appointment of Chicago federal district court judge Kenesaw Mountain Landis to the newly created position of commissioner of major league baseball. Back on the scandal front, plea negotiations between the SAO and Cicotte defense counsel Daniel P. Cassidy were widely reported.[18] But Cassidy put a damper on press speculation that a deal had been reached by denying that Cicotte would turn state's evidence.[19] Another uncooperative defendant was Hal Chase, who made plain that he would not appear voluntarily in a Chicago courtroom. "If they want me, let 'em extradite me," snarled Chase from California.[20] Meanwhile, Abe Attell surfaced in New York, reporting to the Manhattan District Attorney's Office but refusing to answer questions about anything.[21] Prospects for a speedy resolution of the Black Sox case were dealt another blow by an SAO insider. In a syndicated article penned by sportswriter James L. Kilgallen, George Kenney, secretary for outgoing SA Hoyne, was quoted as saying that it was unlikely that "the trial will be held before next summer."[22] Reasons for the delay anticipated by Kenney included the trial calendar priority that had to be accorded Chicago's multitude of incarcerated defendants, the oncoming change in SAO administration and personnel, and the sentiment "in some quarters ... that the indicted players have been punished enough."[23] Among those departing the SAO was Black Sox grand jury prosecutor Hartley Replogle[24] who, along with Hoyne and Kenney, was about to become the focus of grand jury inquiry himself.

During the post-indictment period, concerns were raised about the security of the evidence amassed by the grand jury during the Black Sox investigation. Shortly before he was scheduled to leave office, SA Hoyne directed Kenney to collect the documentary evidence from ASA Replogle. Replogle refused to relinquish it and notified Judge McDonald of Hoyne's demand for delivery of the evidence. The news incensed McDonald, who immediately ordered that the grand jury record be impounded by the clerk of the court. But he was too late, for Kenney had somehow managed to procure the Black Sox documents, which he then turned over to Louise Burch, Hoyne's private stenographer.[25]

When called to account, Hoyne's justification was weak. "As outgoing State's Attorney, I was responsible for all the papers" in possession of the office, Hoyne explained lamely. Given the prominence of the Black Sox case, Hoyne wanted to ensure that the grand jury record was secure and intact for his successor. "There was no scandal and no wrongdoing," insisted Hoyne.[26] McDonald was skeptical. So were Commissioner-elect Landis and AL President Johnson. Following a conference between the two, Landis, still a sitting federal judge, threatening to initiate a federal probe of the matter if any of the grand jury records had been "tampered with or were missing."[27] The worst fears of baseball and judicial officials were realized weeks later when managing editor Keats Speed of the *New York Herald* began shopping redacted copies of the grand jury transcript to various newspapers for a $25,000 syndication fee.[28] Hoyne denied responsibility for the situation, later testifying that his copy of the grand jury record never left his personal safe.[29] A furious Ban Johnson publicly accused Arnold Rothstein of arranging the theft.[30] Rothstein denied it, threatening to sue Johnson for defamation (but never doing so).[31] When the finger of suspicion pointed his way, lead Attell lawyer William J. Fallon casually dismissed the fuss, stating that the grand jury record had been supplied to him by his Chicago associate counsel Henry Berger.[32] This produced an agitated response from Berger who disclaimed any formal affiliation with Fallon but did not actually deny his claims. "I only met him twice," Berger protested.[33] Trying to pinpoint culpability, newly installed Cook County SA Crowe hauled Hoyne, Kenney, Replogle, Berger, and Weaver defense counsel Thomas Nash before the grand jury, but all denied any knowledge of how the grand jury records had been purloined from the SAO and the matter officially remained a mystery.

Author Note: Most, but not all, Black Sox sleuths accuse Rothstein of engineering the thefts. Documents in the Black Sox file at the Giamatti Research Center postulate the theory that Rothstein paid Fallon $50,000 to procure the grand jury minutes. For that purpose, Fallon transmitted $15,000 to Berger, his associate counsel in Chicago. The bulk of this money then went to SAO secretary Kenney, the actual thief. The original source of this account is reputed to be Eugene F. McGee, Fallon's Fordham Law School classmate and erstwhile law partner. Sometime after McGee's disbarment in 1925, the story was apparently circulated by *New York Sun* sports editor Joe Vila. Another tale has Black Sox payoffs being laid out in affidavits by Abe Attell, Sport Sullivan, Fallon, and McGee seized in an FBI raid on Rothstein offices shortly after Rothstein's death in November 1928. The affidavits had supposedly been obtained by Rothstein from Boston lawyer William J. Kelly (Sullivan's counsel during the Black Sox affair) for $53,000, as reported a crime feature in the *Chicago Tribune*, published on April 28, 1940. That Rothstein considered Kelly a blackmailer is indisputable. Rothstein explicitly called Kelly a blackmailer while testifying in the notorious Fuller & McGee bucket shop case, as reported in the *Chicago Tribune* and *New York Times*, October 9, 1923. And Kelly was later disbarred on blackmail grounds arising from an unrelated matter. But otherwise, the story is dubious, at best. The notion that men as familiar with the criminal justice system as Attell, Sullivan, and particularly criminal defense attorneys Fallon and/or McGee would attest to their own misconduct in writing is farfetched. So too is the notion that Rothstein would have retained, rather than destroyed, such documents if he ever got them in the first place.

The stolen grand jury transcript was hardly the only Black Sox-related problem facing Crowe. Almost from the day that the new SAO administration took office in December 1920, it was on the defensive in the case. Public revelation that grand jury evidence had been stolen came only one day after Crowe took the oath of office as the new State's Attorney. Then within weeks, the viability of the Black Sox indictments was beclouded by the dismissal of the charges in the PCL case. Notwithstanding the press of other business in crime-ridden

Cook County, Crowe was pressured by baseball officials to give a high priority to the Black Sox case. After conferring with prosecutors, AL President Johnson announced that the league had retained recent SAO alumnus James C. O'Brien to assist the prosecution at the trial of the Black Sox defendants.[34] Sox owner Comiskey also offered to place team attorneys at SAO disposal.[35] Largely to placate worried MLB executives, Crowe assigned the Black Sox case to Second Assistant State's Attorney George E. Gorman, a former congressman and perhaps the most experienced litigator on the reorganized SAO staff.[36]

On January 21, 1921, Judge Landis was installed as baseball's new all-powerful chief executive. In his inaugural remarks, Landis sent a sobering signal to the indicted players and their partisans. Said the Commissioner, "If they [the Black Sox players] are found not guilty by a jury or judge, they will not necessarily be allowed to return to organized baseball."[37] The following day, Landis assembled major league team owners in his headquarters and instructed them to suppress gambling in their ballparks and to petition their state legislatures to criminalize betting on professional baseball.[38] Before the month was out, however, those looking to the prosecutorial process to cleanse baseball of gambling were jolted by a wire service story that began: "The vigorous prosecution, which all baseball lovers hoped to have meted out to the debauchers of the 1919 world's series, will never come to pass. Today it is a memory — yes, it is an odor — because the eighteen indictments found by the Cook County grand jury implicating eight former members of the White Sox team, two former ball players and three gamblers are declared by the State's Attorneys Office to be faulty. 'The indictments are a lemon,' declared one of the assistant prosecutors.... If the case is ever set for trial — and I don't think it will ever see the light of a criminal court calendar — the result is inevitable. It will be rejected."[39]

Apparently taking his cue from the Willis ruling in the PCL case, the anonymous ASA allowed that "he couldn't see where the alleged fixers had committed a crime," and, thus, the only forums available for redress were likely the new Commissioner's office or the civil courts.[40] As for the probable fate of the criminal case, the prosecutor continued, "The indictments are a joke, and, rather than spend a lot of the people's money in trying a case that is destined to result in acquittal, there is a strong probability that before many weeks the indictments will be stricken off the calendar."[41] The response of 2nd ASA Gorman provided little rebuttal. "Really, I have been too busy with other matters to give the baseball scandal much of my time," said the case prosecutor.[42] Nor was much confidence in the prosecution instilled by Gorman's recitation of the truism that convicting those accused of crime was a lot harder than indicting them. The prosecutor also indicated that he was not particularly conversant with the Willis ruling. Given all this, Gorman advised the press that he was not yet ready to ask the court to set a trial date in the Black Sox matter.[43]

The credence given to pronouncements of some anonymous member of his staff infuriated SA Crowe. Nor was he happy with the tepid response of his designated prosecutor. Crowe immediately ordered Gorman to concentrate on the Black Sox matter and relieved him of his other cases. Hoping to quiet naysayers, Crowe then publicly announced that the Black Sox case "will be brought to trial as quickly as it can be prepared."[44] Crowe next set about searching for the office traitor, but was unable to identify the culprit. So he turned on the press, targeting Leonard G. Edwardson, local correspondent for the *New York Herald* and *New York Sun*, who had written an article that reiterated the claim that the Black Sox case had been "pigeonholed" for dismissal.[45] In time, Crowe would obtain a measure of satisfaction, with Edwardson ultimately being convicted of criminal libel (and fined $1).[46] But by then the Edwardson prophecy had been fulfilled by the dismissal of the Black Sox indictments.

Notes

1. As reported in the *Boston Globe* and *Chicago Tribune,* October 19, 1920.

2. As earlier chronicled in the *Los Angeles Times,* August 5 to 18, 1920.

3. As reported in the *Los Angeles Times,* October 20 to 23, 1920. Eight years later, Raymond was a participant in the Manhattan card game that ended in the mortal gunshot wounding of Arnold Rothstein. See *New York Times,* November 7, 1928.

4. As reported in the *Los Angeles Times, New York Times* and *Washington Post,* December 11, 1920. The grand jury declined to charge Dale, no longer active in the PCL and refusing to set foot within California, reportedly based on jurisdictional misgivings.

5. As per the *Los Angeles Times,* December 11, 1920.

6. *Ibid.* The panel took no action on the slush fund allegation directed toward the Vernon team as a whole.

7. As reported in the *Los Angeles Times* and *New York Times,* December 25, 1920, and elsewhere.

8. As reported in the *Washington Post,* December 25, 1920.

9. Remedial legislation which made the throwing of a professional baseball game a felony was enacted in California in April 1921. Other states, including New York, Pennsylvania, Ohio, Oregon, North Carolina, and Illinois, adopted similar laws.

10. As quoted in the *Chicago Tribune*, December 25, 1920.

11. As reported in the *Atlanta Constitution* and *New York Times,* January 13, 1921. The action was officially taken by the National Association of Minor Leagues.

12. As briefly mentioned in the *Chicago Tribune,* November 2, 1920.

13. It is sometimes reported that Berger was a Black Sox grand jury prosecutor who later switched sides to represent the accused. This is incorrect. Berger resigned from the SAO in May 1919, months before the tainted World Series was even played. See *Chicago Tribune,* May 4, 1919, regarding Berger's departure from the SAO.

14. As quoted in the *Chicago Evening Post,* November 5, 1920. Weaver's bond was posted by Dr. Prettyman. Chicago tailor Joseph Kauffman posted surety for McMullin.

15. As reported by the *Los Angeles Times,* November 13, 1920.

16. As reported by the *Boston Globe* and *Los Angeles Times,* November 24, 1920.

17. As quoted in the *Boston Globe* and *Chicago Tribune,* November 24, 1920. As previously observed, public comment by a judge on matters pertaining to a pending court case was proscribed by the canons of judicial conduct, but no attention was paid to that restraint in the Black Sox affair.

18. See e.g., *Atlanta Constitution*, *Chicago Tribune* and *New York Times,* November 17, 1920.

19. As per the *Chicago Tribune,* November 18, 1920.

20. As reported in the *Chicago Tribune,* November 20, 1920.

21. As per the *New York Times,* November 17, 1920.

22. Published in the *Atlanta Constitution,* November 28, 1920, and syndicated nationwide via the United News wire service.

23. *Ibid.*

24. As reported in the *Chicago Tribune,* November 17, 1920. Replogle had resigned from the SAO only days earlier, as reported in the *Boston Globe,* November 17, 1920.

25. As reported in the *Boston Globe*, *Chicago Tribune* and *Washington Post,* December 8, 1920.

26. As quoted in the *Washington Post,* December 8, 1920.

27. As reported in the *Chicago Tribune,* December 8, 1920, and elsewhere.

28. As revealed in various documents preserved in the Black Sox file at the Giamatti Research Center.

29. As reported in the *Chicago Tribune,* February 2, 1921.

30. As reported in the *Boston Globe* and *Chicago Evening American,* July 26, 1921, and elsewhere. See also, David Pietrusza, *Rothstein: The Life, Times, and Murder of the Criminal Genius Who Fixed the 1919 World Series* (New York: Carroll & Graf, 2003), 189–190.

31. As reported in the *Boston Globe,* July 26, 1921.

32. As reported in the *Boston Globe,* July 27, 1921.

33. As per the *Chicago Evening American,* July 26, 1921, and *Chicago Herald Examiner,* July 27, 1921.

34. As reported in the *Chicago Daily News,* December 20, 1920, and *New York Times,* December 23, 1920.

35. As per the *Chicago Daily News,* December 20, 1920.

36. *Ibid.*

37. As reported in the *Chicago Tribune,* January 12, 1921.

38. As reported in the *Chicago Daily News,* January 13, 1921.

39. As published in the *Washington Post,* January 24, 1921, and elsewhere.

40. *Ibid.*

41. *Ibid.*

42. *Ibid.*

43. *Ibid.* Gorman's nonchalant attitude apparently disturbed Judge McDonald, as well. McDonald immediately removed the Black Sox case from the crowded criminal courts docket and specially assigned it to the first available county court judge, as per *The Sporting News*, February 10, 1921.

44. As quoted in the *Washington Post,* February 2, 1921.

45. Ironically, the basis of the Edwardson charge was unrelated to his reportage about the likely disposition of the Black Sox case. Rather, Edwardson was cited for criminal libel based upon published commentary maligning Judge McDonald's stewardship of the Black Sox grand jury, as reported in the *Chicago Tribune* and *New York Times,* March 2, 1921.

46. As per the *Los Angeles Times* and *New York Times,* April 27, 1921. The verdict was rendered and sentence imposed by Cook County Circuit Court Judge Thomas Taylor.

9

Grand Jury Redux

The events that led to the dismissal of the indictments began with the assignment of the Black Sox case to Judge William E. Dever on February 4, 1921.[1] The pace of proceedings immediately quickened. Within days, the court set a prospective March 14 trial date.[2] In the interim, the customary pre-trial motions would be entertained. One defense application sought a bill of particulars, a written statement that specifies factual events pertinent to the charges for the accused's benefit. Supporting the application were sworn assertions by Weaver, Jackson, and Williams which averred that (1) while acquainted with codefendants Burns and Chase, they had had "no business transactions or personal relations" with the two ex-players; (2) that they had never met the other gambler codefendants (although Williams had once been introduced to strangers named Sullivan and Brown); and (3) that they were "entirely innocent" of the charges made against them. As proof of honest play, the application proffered the World Series stats of Weaver and Jackson — but not Williams.[3] Of far more consequence was a motion to exclude the Cicotte, Jackson, and Williams grand jury statements from evidence. The grounds for the motion were deliberately vague. Said defense counsel Benedict J. Short, "we expect ... to take advantage of every legal process and technicality. Whether the alleged confessions will be repudiated, ignored or defended cannot be said now."[4] Notwithstanding this lawyerly obfuscation, the motion was widely viewed as one of repudiation, a denial by the defendants that they had made the statements attributed to them in the grand jury record.[5] Prosecutor Gorman professed indifference toward the motion but Judge McDonald was not so blasé. "If these witnesses repudiate the statements sworn before the grand jury, they will simply have to take the consequences" of a potential perjury prosecution,[6] said the judge, likening defense legal maneuvering to "jump[ing] from the frying pan to the fire."[7] For the time being, Judge Dever reserved judgment on the exclusion application, whatever its underlying thesis.

The court promptly denied, however, a motion for a separate trial filed by the Weaver defense.[8]

The showdown came just prior to the scheduled March 14 trial date when the prosecution formally requested an adjournment. The application had been anticipated for some time. On the eve of the proceedings, Commissioner Landis announced that the indicted players had been placed on baseball's ineligible list.[9] Although he regretted the anticipated delay in judicial reckoning, Landis declared that "baseball is not powerless to protect itself. All of these players ... must vindicate themselves before they can be readmitted to baseball."[10] Charles Comiskey concurred. "Those players are on my ineligible list," said the Sox owner. "It was not necessary for Judge Landis to put them on his, but I am glad he did. There is absolutely no chance for any of them to play on my team again unless they can clear themselves to my satisfaction of the charges."[11]

Accompanied by press predictions that the adjournment would be granted as a matter of routine, the parties gathered in court for a hearing on the motion. Among the excuses for the delay request offered by the prosecution was the entry of new counsel for the American League. James C. O'Brien, the previous AL attorney, had since been engaged to represent defendant Chick Gandil, and his replacement, recently retired Illinois Circuit Court judge George F. Barrett,[12] needed time to familiarize himself with the case.[13] The prosecution also wanted additional time to supplement its evidence, now that the defense had given notice that the confessing players (Cicotte, Jackson, and Williams) would not plead guilty.[14]

Author Note: This aspect of the adjournment request constituted tacit acknowledgment of the core weakness in the prosecution case against non-confessing defendants. Apart from Billy Maharg, at most a peripheral fix actor, the State had little independent proof of fix participation against those accused Sox players who maintained their innocence or against the gambler defendants. Barrett, therefore, was in earnest when he informed the court that the prosecution needed time to supplement its evidence. Desperately needed was the cooperation of a knowledgeable fix insider.

In addition, counsel asserted that the government required an adjournment so that it could expand the case to include currently unindicted wrongdoers.[15] Taking the lead at oral argument, Barrett declared that more time was needed because the prosecution was "fighting for baseball and for the public.... A trial improperly handled would kill baseball. We are not going to let that happen. A proper trial is much more important than an immediate trial. What we want to do is purge baseball of the unclean element and we don't care how long it takes."[16]

To the surprise of courthouse pundits, Judge Dever was unimpressed and indicated that he intended to start trial shortly. But as a courtesy to SA Crowe, then ill and unable to attend the proceedings personally, the judge deferred a definitive ruling, continuing the adjournment motion for a few days to permit Crowe to recover and further argue the motion himself.[17] But when Crowe appeared, he was no more persuasive than Barrett had been. The court set a deadline of May 2 for commencement of the Black Sox trial. Now Crowe was faced with a real predicament. The prosecution's case was not in trial shape, nor likely to be by May 2. Faced with the looming prospect of indictment dismissal if the government was unable to proceed on the scheduled trial date, Crowe opted for a strategic alternative. On March 17, 1921, he announced that the criminal charges against the seven White Sox players who had posted bond — Cicotte, Jackson, Williams, Felsch, Risberg, McMullin, and Weaver — had been *nolle prossed,* that is administratively dismissed by the SAO without prejudice to the initiation of new charges at a later date. The charges against the remaining defendants (Gandil and the gamblers) were stricken from the trial calendar, effectively placing their indictments on inactive status for the next six months.[18] Crowe coupled this stunning news with a vow to reinstitute prosecution of the accused. "These men will not escape punishment," promised Crowe. "We are going after the evidence that will convict these men and we know where to get it. And there will be no mistakes this time."[19] When new indictments were returned, moreover, "several other players not previously named will be included."[20] Among those declining to await further legal developments was Comiskey, who immediately voided all existing contracts signed by the accused players and granted them their unconditional releases.[21] But even with release in hand, there was little chance that any of the Black Sox would be back in uniform soon. Their status with the Commissioner's Office remained unchanged and no respectable baseball team was likely to employ the players. The fate of the Black Sox was forecasted by Kid Gleason following dismissal of the charges: "I am positive that they will never be allowed back in the ranks of organized ball. They are out of baseball."[22]

True to his word, SA Crowe reinitiated grand jury proceedings against the alleged World Series fixers almost immediately. On March 18, 1921, Crowe personally outlined the evidence that would be presented to the panel and then relinquished the floor to 2nd ASA Gorman. Thereafter, the case was presented in more conventional fashion with virtually no public disclosure of what was transpiring behind closed doors. The proceeding were abbreviated, with only five men later identified as grand jury witnesses: Sam Pass, Ban Johnson, Joe Gedeon, Harry Redmon, and Joe Pesch.[23] The majority of the evidence consisted of a reading of prior grand jury minutes by Gorman.[24] In all, the re-presentment of the Black Sox case took only a matter of days.

On March 26, 1921, the second grand jury returned superseding true bills that expanded both the scope of the charges and the roster of the defendants. To the originally accused, all of whom were re-indicted, were added St. Louis gamblers Carl Zork and Ben Franklin, and the Des Moines trio of Ben Levi, Lou Levi, and David Zelcer.[25] And as before, self-admitted fix conspirator Billy Maharg was not charged. Given the relaxation of evidence rules in grand jury proceedings, Maharg could have been indicted upon no more than a reading of his published *Philadelphia North American* interview to the panel. Prosecutors, however, appeared to have made a calculated decision to keep Maharg from being charged. As the only cooperative fix insider available, Maharg would be needed as a prosecution witness if the State was to have any chance of convicting the non-confessing defendants, a reality subsequently acknowledged by Ban Johnson in a private letter to Maharg interviewer James Isaminger.[26] The new indictments, couched in stilted legal verbiage, charged each defendant with a variety of statutory and common law forms of conspiracy to defraud via false pretenses and/or a confidence game.[27] In a backhanded swipe at the Willis ruling, certain charges expressly criminalized the Black Sox players' failure to honor a contractual duty to utilize "their best skill and ability" while performing in the 1919 World Series and thereby fulfill their duty to "play to win."[28] Those named as victims of defendants' conduct were Sox teammates John (Shano) Collins and Ray Schalk; the Chicago White Sox as a corporate entity; one Charles K. Nims, a losing World Series bettor representing a victim class, and the public generally.[29] With this, the stage, at long last, was set for a criminal trial of the Black Sox case.

Notes

1. As reported in the *Chicago Tribune* and *New York Times,* February 4, 1921. A respected jurist, "Decent Bill" Dever would be elected Chicago mayor in 1923 as a reform candidate.

2. As reported in the *New York Times,* February 10, 1921.

3. As per the *Chicago Tribune* and *New York Times,* February 13, 1921. A copy of the bill of particulars is available on the clerk of court website.

4. As quoted in the *Los Angeles Times,* February 13, 1921.

5. As reflected in the headlines "Black Sox to Repudiate Confessions" in the *Chicago Tribune,* February 13, 1921, and "Confessions of Players Denied" in the *Los Angeles Times,* February 13, 1921. In fact, the Black Sox defense would never allege that Eddie Cicotte, Joe Jackson or Lefty Williams had not uttered the statements memorialized in the grand jury record. Rather, the defense would maintain that the statements were inadmissible on legal grounds, induced by the reneged promise that the players would not be criminally prosecuted if they confessed.

6. As quoted in the *Chicago Tribune,* February 13, 1921.

7. As per the *Los Angeles Times,* February 13, 1921.

8. As reported in the *Chicago Tribune,* February 17, 1921.

9. As reported in the *Chicago Tribune,* March 12, 1921.

10. As quoted in the *Boston Globe* and *Hartford Courant,* March 13, 1921. In both word and deed, Landis was now setting upon the course charted by PCL President McCarthy.

11. As quoted in the *New York Times,* March 14, 1921.

12. As reported in the *Chicago Tribune,* March 5, 1921. At times, scandal reportage confused George F. Barrett with younger brother Charles V. Barrett, a Cook County Republican Party powerbroker and an attorney in Ban Johnson's employ. At the time of the Black Sox case, the Barrett brothers were close political allies of SA Robert Crowe.

13. As reported in the *Chicago Daily Journal,* March 14, 1921.

14. As per the *New York Times,* March 13, 1921, and *Chicago Tribune,* March 15, 1921.

15. As per the *Boston Globe* and *Hartford Courant,* March 13, 1921.

16. *Ibid.*

17. As per the *Chicago Daily Journal,* March 14, 1921, and *Boston Globe,* March 15, 1921.

18. As reported in the *Chicago Daily Journal* and *Chicago Tribune,* March 17, 1921, and elsewhere.

19. As quoted in the *Chicago Daily Journal,* March 17, 1921, and *Chicago Tribune* and *New York Times,* March 18, 1921.

20. As per the *Washington Post,* March 19, 1921, quoting 2nd ASA Gorman.

21. As reported in the *New York Times,* March 17, 1921, and elsewhere.

22. As quoted in the *Chicago Tribune,* March 18, 1921.

23. The names of the second grand jury witnesses were recorded on the cover of the true bills, a copy of which can be viewed at http://www.law.umkc.edu/faculty/projects/ftrials/blacksox/indictmentscan.jpg.

24. As reported in the *Washington Post,* March 22, 1921. See, Associated Press dispatch subsequently published in the *Olean (NY) Evening Herald,* June 27, 1921, and elsewhere. For reasons of strategy and convenience, prosecutors often resort to reuse of the prior record (as opposed to having witnesses re-testify) when charges have to be re-presented to the grand jury.

25. See *Chicago Tribune, Los Angeles Times* and *New York Times,* March 26, 1921. Investigative work by Cal Crim and other private detectives engaged by Ban Johnson had succeeded in identifying Zelcer as the fixer posing as *Bennett,* as per material in the Black Sox file at the Giamatti Research Center and Dellinger, 177–181, 311–317. The Levi brothers, who apparently considered the possibility of corrupting Reds players as well as the Black Sox, were well-known Midwest gamblers and related to Zelcer by marriage.

26. The Johnson letter, dated April 18, 1921, is now preserved in the Black Sox file at the Giamatti Research Center.

27. The superseding true bills were returned in the form of multiple indictments, eight in all against each defendant. Each indictment, in turn, contained three separate conspiracy/fraud-related offenses, making a total of 24 charges against the accused. A condensed version of the March 1921 charges in the Black Sox case is viewable on-line at *http://www.law.umkc.edu/faculty/projects/ftrials/blacksox/indictpartic.html.*

28. *Ibid.,* para. 6 and 8.

29. *Ibid.*

10

Extradition Follies

To those uninitiated in the legal process, the return of the superseding indictments seemed to signal the imminent resolution of the Black Sox case. But in reality, guerrilla warfare, criminal justice style, was about to commence. At regular turns, the prosecution would be confronted by procedural maneuvers — motions to dismiss, discovery demands, adjournment applications, and the like — designed to delay, if not prevent, trial of the accused. The first and foremost challenge to prosecutors, however, was an elementary one: getting the defendants into a Cook County courtroom.

In part, difficulty in gaining jurisdiction over the accused — a constitutional prerequisite to any trial[1] — stemmed from the atypical manner in which the charges had been developed. Unlike the case of a burglar caught in the act or a killer tracked down by the police, no one had been taken into law enforcement custody in the Black Sox matter. Indeed, no contemporaneous legal action had been taken, by police or anyone else, when the alleged offenses occurred in Fall 1919. Rather, the charges arose from a year-after-the-fact investigation conducted by a grand jury. The accused, meanwhile, were at liberty. This meant that jurisdiction over the corpus (the physical person) of the various defendants had to be acquired, a problem compounded by the fact that almost all of those charged were non–Illinois residents. Fortunately for the prosecution, the suspended White Sox players, looking to return to the diamond after hoped-for exoneration, were eager to go to trial. All, save Fred McMullin, would appear in court when needed. So would the gamblers from St. Louis (Carl Zork and Ben Franklin) and Des Moines (David Zelcer and the Levi brothers). For those who declined to come to Chicago voluntarily and thereby submit themselves to the court's control, the only alternative available to the prosecution was extradition, a relatively straightforward legal procedure but one that the prosecution would prove unable to master.

Besides McMullin, pleading poverty in Los Angeles and seeking travel expense reimbursement from the SAO, the defendants unaccounted for were Chick Gandil, Bill Burns, Hal Chase, Abe Attell, Sport Sullivan, and Rachael Brown, some of whom were believed to have fled the country. About a month after the new charges were returned and with these defendants still at large, the SAO announced that warrants would be prepared for their arrest, a precursor to extradition.[2] Among the fugitives, Sullivan had disappeared from the view of Chicago officials following his post-indictment outburst of the previous October. And while prosecutors had been in sporadic contact with defense counsel Kelly, Sullivan himself had never been served with process. Of more practical concern, Sullivan was reportedly in Montreal with no plans for appearing at trial.[3] In time, this situation precipitated a trip by AL President Johnson to Washington, D.C., where he hoped to persuade government officials to pressure their Canadian counterparts into expelling Sullivan as an undesirable.[4] All of this, however, came as news to Boston police, who reported seeing the well-known Sullivan, a resident of nearby Sharon, in their city on almost a daily basis.[5] This made perfect sense, as it was highly improbable that Sullivan, reputedly the biggest bookmaker in New England, would have left his operation untended for a lengthy stay out of the country. Perhaps more telling was the fact that Boston officials had received no request for assistance regarding Sullivan from Cook County prosecutors.[6] This lack of initiative betrayed a telltale weakness in the SAO case against Sullivan. For without the testimony of Lefty Williams or some other cooperating Black Sox defendant (which prosecutors did not have), the charges against Sullivan were unprovable. But whatever the reason, the SAO made no tangible effort to secure Sullivan's presence in Chicago. He would remain at large throughout the ensuing proceedings.

No such prosecutorial apathy was exhibited when it came to defendant Rachael Brown. On April 27, 1921, the SAO obtained a warrant for Brown's arrest.[7] But this, too, had charade overtones, as prosecutors had no firm idea who this "Brown" really was. Until midway through the original grand jury proceedings, ASA Replogle believed that "Brown, the gambler from New York," had merely been an alias used by Abe Attell.[8] Eastern newspapers covering the grand jury proceedings, however, presumed that "Brown" was Abraham Braunstein, a small-time hustler known in the New York demimonde as Rachel Brown. In time, this reportage took effect in Chicago, where the accused evolved from *Brown* to *Raphael Brown*[9] to *Rachael Brown,* the appellation ultimately adopted for the Black Sox indictments. Like Sullivan, this Brown had reportedly fled the country, headed for somewhere in Europe, according to an unidentified news item reprinted in *The Sporting News,* October 7, 1920. But, in fact, the whereabouts of Braunstein/Brown were no mystery. He had been swept up in a summer 1919 Saratoga, New York, gambling raid and had spent most of January 1920 in and out of a nearby Ballston Spa courthouse as defendant turned prosecution star witness, as reported in the local press.[10] But even assuming that Braunstein/Brown was their man, Chicago prosecutors faced a Sullivan-like dilemma with him. Without a cooperating codefendant to testify about the Warner Hotel meeting, the charges could not be proved against defendant Brown, whoever he was. The warrant for Brown's arrest, therefore, went unexecuted.

To this point, the initial SAO effort to obtain custody of uncooperative non-resident defendants had come up empty. And from there, things only got worse. There had been no problem locating Hal Chase, gadding about California in avoidance of a Cincinnati divorce court.[11] On April 25, 1921, San Jose police arrested Chase at the behest of the Cook County State's Attorneys Office. The event would quickly prove an embarrassment to prosecutors, exposing virtual malpractice by the government when it came to extradition proceedings. By way of explanation, extradition between states is the procedure through which the executive branch of government (invariably a law enforcement agency) of one state obtains custody of a fugitive criminal defendant located in another state.[12] The process is initiated by the delivery of a formal demand for the surrender of the accused signed by the governor of the demanding state. This document is commonly called a governor's warrant. Upon presentation of the governor's warrant, police in the receiving state arrest the accused. Those seeking to avoid extradition are entitled to a judicial hearing, but rarely to any avail, since no argument on the validity of the underlying charges or on the innocence of the accused will be entertained by the court during an extradition proceeding. The proceeding is essentially mechanical in nature, confined to demonstration that: (1) the person before the court is the same person named in the governor's warrant, and (2) the extradition documents are in proper form. Once these two pro forma requirements have been demonstrated, an order surrendering the wanted man into the custody of the demanding state is entered by the court. In most instances, the defendant is removed to that jurisdiction immediately thereafter.[13]

Simple as the process may seem, the SAO was unable to manage the task when it came to Chase. The problem lay with the papers dispatched to California. Rather than the requisite governor's warrant, the SAO had merely sent a copy of the superseding indictment and a letter requesting Chase's arrest to authorities in San Jose.[14] This procedural deficiency was immediately detected by James P. Sex, the San Francisco lawyer who had represented Chase in expulsion proceedings recently instituted by the Mission League. Upon being retained for extradition purposes, Sex immediately secured Chase's release on $3,000 bail pending disposition of a habeas corpus petition.[15] At the hearing subsequently held before Superior Court Judge J. R. Welch, the defective character of the extradition papers — which the SAO had done nothing to cure in the interim — proved fatal. The court granted the writ and discharged Chase from custody.[16] No further action was taken by the SAO, making Hal Chase the first defendant in the Black Sox case effectively in the clear — so long as he stayed outside of Illinois.

If the bumbling in the Chase extradition proceeding had been good for an occasional chuckle, it was nothing compared to the comedy about to be staged in the Bronx. The scene was set by the May 10, 1921, arrest of Abe Attell in Times Square, prearranged by his counsel William J. Fallon.[17] No sooner had Attell been arraigned as a fugitive from justice before Magistrate Robert C. Ten Eyck in the West Side Police Court, than Fallon had Attell sprung on bail pursuant to an order signed by New York State Supreme Court Justice John A. McAvoy.[18] Attell would remain at liberty pending the disposition of habeas corpus proceedings assigned to Justice John M. Tierney, sitting in the Bronx. Seeking to avoid the blunders of the Chase matter, Chicago prosecutors followed up news of Attell's arrest by transmitting model extradition papers to New York.[19] The New York (Manhattan) County District Attorney's Office then bolstered extradition prospects by handing the Attell file to a courtroom team led by Assistant DA John Caldwell Myers, an able and experienced prosecutor. But neither Myers nor Justice Tierney would be able to control Fallon, the irrepressible bad boy of the New York criminal defense bar. In short order, Fallon would make a shambles of the Attell hearing.

One-time featherweight boxing champ Abe Attell was indicted by the grand jury but successfully resisted efforts to extradite him to Chicago for trial.

At the outset, Fallon frustrated the proceedings by forcing adjournments, or by simply not showing up in court on scheduled hearing dates.[20] When finally trapped in the courtroom, Fallon demanded Attell's release on the ground that his client had not been in Chicago during the Series and thus could not be the man sought. This defense, however, was quickly gutted by the appearance of John O. Seys, Cubs team secretary and the stakeholder for Attell bets on the first two Series games.[21] Undaunted by Seys' testimony, Fallon then unveiled an audacious fallback position. Attell had been in attendance at the World Series, all right, but he was not the same Abe Attell cited by the Cook County grand jury. The person wanted in Chicago was not Fallon's client, but his double — some unidentified character who had impersonated Attell in meetings with co-conspirators and/or in swindling Chisox bettors.

To no surprise, the claim was met with howls of derision in the press. "Is Abe Attell Himself or Is He Somebody Else?" mocked the *New York Sun,*[22] while a headline in *The Sporting News* informed fans that the "Mystery of the Two Attells Should be Solved This Week."[23] But the shameless defense was Fallon's forte, and he proceeded to pull it off. First, Fallon placed Attell on the stand to protest his innocence, such testimony being permitted at habeas proceedings. Attell calmly maintained that he had not conspired with any White Sox players, did not know anyone named Rachael Brown, and had only recently made the acquaintance of Sport Sullivan. The World Series wrongdoing attributed to him must, therefore, be the work of some Abe Attell imposter. Fallon next produced White Sox sidekick Sam Pass, who flabbergasted prosecutors by testifying that he had never met the Abe Attell seated in the courtroom. Nor had Pass placed any World Series bets with him.[24] Left unmentioned during the Pass appearance was a small fact unknown to prosecutors and Justice Tierney — that Fallon had intercepted Pass the day before at Grand Central Station and reimbursed him for his Series betting losses via cash supplied by Arnold Rothstein.[25]

Fallon followed up the Pass coup by announcing that Joe Jackson, Eddie Cicotte, Lefty Williams, and Fred McMullin would appear in court on the next hearing date to testify that they did not know the Abe Attell present in court. Nor had they ever conspired with him prior to the 1919 World Series. Predictably, none of the players, only a fortnight away from standing trial on their own in Chicago, ever took the stand on Attell's behalf. But that did not trouble Fallon. In their place, he offered in evidence the transcript of Joe Jackson's grand jury testimony, among the confidential court documents notoriously stolen from authorities in Cook County. A sustained objection thwarted this stratagem, but Fallon's antics were taking their toll, with prosecutors unnerved by this unpredictable circus of events.[26] Misfortune then befell the prosecution from a different direction when Justice Tierney relinquished the gavel — either because of illness or to take an extended vacation, accounts differ.[27] The proceedings would therefore have to be restarted before a replacement judge entirely unfamiliar with the record. On June 21, 1921, the Attell extradition hearing resumed before Justice Thomas F. Donnelly. But at this point, ADA Myers proved unable to move forward.[28] Five days later, habeas corpus relief was granted by Donnelly[29] and Abe Attell became the second Black Sox defendant to beat the charges.

Back in Chicago, lead Black Sox trial prosecutor Gorman reacted mildly to the Attell extradition debacle. Said Gorman, "It simply means that Attell will not stand trial and consequently there will be one less man in the penitentiary when this case is finished."[30] The prosecutor's cockiness was not entirely unwarranted, for not all had ended badly in the fugitive roundup. For one thing, alleged fix ringleader Chick Gandil was back in Chicago, available for trial. Gandil had been arrested in Los Angeles on April 26, 1921.[31] Unlike Chase, Gandil was not averse to facing the charges, producing a prepaid train ticket to Chicago as proof of his intention to appear for trial. With the concurrence of the SAO, Gandil was released on nominal bail with instructions to report to Chicago authorities by May 1.[32] Days later, his arrival placed at least one fugitive Black Sox defendant safely in the dock. Of far greater import to prosecutors was the return of Bill Burns, retrieved from the Mexican border by his pal Billy Maharg.[33] On May 7, 1921, Burns was spotted strolling the streets of Chicago by a reporter for the *Chicago Tribune* who tailed Burns to the Barrett law office.[34] When contacted by the press, AL President Johnson would neither confirm nor deny that Burns was now cooperating with the prosecution, referring such inquiries to the SAO.[35] Such evasions aside, it was soon obvious that the State had a major Black Sox defendant in camp.

With a majority, if not all, of the defendants accounted for,[36] Judge McDonald assigned the Black Sox case to Circuit Court Judge Hugo M. Friend on June 21, 1921.[37] An unidentified prosecutor greeted the news with the boast, "Our case is absolutely complete. Our investigations during the past few months have uncovered every detail of the conspiracy and we have more witnesses than we need."[38] That confidence was about to be put to the test. Judge Friend had scheduled the Black Sox case to begin in six days.

Notes

1. The right of a criminally accused to be in attendance during court proceedings against him is of constitutional dimension, a guarantee of the Due Process Clause. See *Hopt v. Utah,* 110 *U.S.* 574 (1884). Apart from certain peculiar situations, American courts do not permit fugitive defendants to be tried *in absentia.*

2. As reported in the *New York Times,* April 5, 1921, and *Los Angeles Times,* April 27, 1921.

3. As reported in the *New York Times,* April 27, 1921.

4. *Ibid.*

5. As per the *Boston Globe,* April 27, 1921.

6. *Ibid.*

7. As per the *Los Angeles Times,* April 27, 1921.

8. As reported in the *Chicago Daily News,* September 29, 1920.

9. The discovery that the first name of defendant Brown was *Raphael* was announced by ASA Replogle, as reported in the *Boston Globe,* October 6, 1920.

10. As reported in the *Saratoga Sun,* December 31, 1920, *Albany Evening Journal,* January 4, 1921, and elsewhere. See also, *New York Times,* May 13, 1921, re witness testimony identifying "Rachie Brown, indicted in the World Series baseball scandal," as a Saratoga casino roulette wheel operator. In the meantime, Ban Johnson had detectives keep surveillance on his own candidate for the role of fix operative *Brown:* Nat Evans, confidant and casino business partner of Arnold Rothstein, as reflected in documents contained in the Black Sox file at the Giamatti Research Center. In April 1921, Evans and other Rothstein associates were arrested in St. Louis on a vagrancy-type charge but promptly released on bond, as reported in the *New York Times,* April 2, 1921. Decades later on October 8, 1957, *The Sporting News* would publish a far-fetched account of this event's supposed significance to the Black Sox case. But in April 1921, there was little to connect the suave Evans to the World Series fix. The notion that Nat Evans was the fixer posing as *Brown* at the Warner Hotel would not gain currency until the publication of *The Big Bankroll,* Leo Katcher's biography of Rothstein, in 1958.

11. Second wife Anna had sued Chase for divorce, alleging adultery and non-support. In proceedings before the Hamilton County Domestic Relations Court, Anna shoveled some Black Sox dirt on Hal, testifying that her husband had "admitted he knew all about the crooked deal put over by the members of the White Sox in the World Series of 1919, and he was helping it along," as reported in the *Chicago Tribune,* January 27, 1921. See also, *Cincinnati Commercial Tribune,* January 27, 1921, for a truncated, less incriminating version of the above testimony.

12. More particularly, United States Constitution, Art. 4, Sec. 2, provides that "a person charged in any state with treason, felony or other crime, who shall flee from justice, and be found in another state, shall on demand of the executive authority of the state from which he fled, be delivered up, to be removed to the state having jurisdiction of the crime."

13. The outcome of such proceedings is so foreordained that of the brigade of fugitives processed by the author during 33 years as a state/county prosecutor, only a handful requested a court hearing. The vast majority of apprehended fugitives simply waived the extradition process and submitted voluntarily to removal to the demanding state.

14. As per Dewey and Acocella, 342, who report that this action was taken by San Jose police against the advice of local DA Clarence Coolidge, who counseled waiting for proper extradition documents.

15. *Ibid. Habeas Corpus* is a constitutionally based legal proceeding through which the prisoner may obtain his release from unlawful custody. In the Black Sox case, it was used by several fugitive arrestees in lieu of requesting an extradition hearing.

16. As reported in the *Chicago Tribune,* May 28, 1921, and *New York Times,* May 29, 1921.

17. As reported in the *Boston Globe* and *New York Times,* May 11, 1921.

18. As per the *Los Angeles Times* and *New York Times,* May 11, 1921.

19. The governor's warrant for Attell was signed by Illinois Governor Len Small, as reported in the *New York Times,* May 14, 1921. Given this demonstration of professional competence, the failure of Cook County authorities to correct the deficiencies in the Chase

extradition papers takes on a curious cast. For some slightly overheated speculation on possible reasons, see Dewey and Acocella, 343–344.

20. Avoiding one judge on the representation that he was scheduled to appear at the same time and date before another was a Fallon standby. If that maneuver was not available, Fallon would oft-times simply fail to appear in court, relying on a roguish charm with judges to forestall disciplinary measures. And during his brief heyday at the bar — which included the time period of the Attell hearing — Fallon got away with it.

21. In her account of the 1919 Series from Edd Roush's perspective, Roush's granddaughter Susan Dellinger spots Attell in the background of a pre–Game One photo taken at Redland Field. See *Red Legs and Black Sox,* 210, for the photo.

22. *New York Sun,* June 2, 1921.

23. *The Sporting News,* June 7, 1921.

24. As reported in the *New York Times,* June 6, 1921, and *Chicago Tribune,* June 7, 1921.

25. In her life-with-Arnold memoir, Rothstein's widow reduced the amount to $1,000 — and reported that is was furnished by Rothstein as a loan to Pass, not a bribe. See Carolyn Rothstein, *Now I'll Tell* (New York: Vanguard Press, 1934), 184.

26. The courtroom travails of the prosecution are recounted in contemporaneous correspondence from James Price to Ban Johnson, preserved in the Black Sox file at the Giamatti Research Center.

27. Compare *The Sporting News,* June 23, 1921 (vacation) to the Price correspondence to AL President Johnson (illness). The latter seems more likely as Justice Tierney underwent surgery at Mount Sinai Hospital in late June, as reported in the *New York Times,* June 24, 1921.

28. As per the *New York Times,* June 21, 1921.

29. As reported in the *Boston Globe, Los Angeles Times* and *New York Times,* June 26, 1921.

30. As quoted in the *Boston Globe* and *New York Times,* June 26, 1921.

31. As per the *Chicago Tribune* and *Los Angeles Times,* April 27, 1921.

32. As per the *Chicago Tribune,* April 27, 1921.

33. Like virtually every other significant pretrial investigative measure, the Maharg mission had been financed by AL President Johnson. More than anyone else, Johnson was determined to have the Black Sox defendants tried, convicted, and punished. Among other places, Johnson's zeal is reflected in documents preserved in the Black Sox file at the Giamatti Research Center.

34. As reported in the *Chicago Tribune,* May 7, 1921.

35. *Ibid.*

36. In addition to the fugitive gamblers Sullivan and Brown and those defendants who had beaten extradition (Chase and Attell), Fred McMullin, scraping up travel funds in California, had not yet appeared in court.

37. As reported in the *Chicago Tribune* and *The Sporting News,* June 21, 1921, and elsewhere. According to Gene Carney, the Black Sox case had previously been headed for Judge John J. Sullivan, a veteran criminal court jurist. See *Burying the Black Sox,* 144.

38. As reported in the *Boston Globe* and *New York Times,* June 21, 1921.

11

Criminal Trial Preliminaries

In a nation saturated by coverage of courtroom proceedings — both real life and the Hollywood variety — most Americans have a rudimentary understanding of how a criminal trial works. Ultimately, the verdict turns on whether or not the charges against the accused have been proved to the jury beyond a reasonable doubt. What may not be fully appreciated is the extent to which a trial's outcome may be shaped by courtroom events that occur outside the jury's presence. These matters, typically involving the legal soundness of the charges, the admissibility of contested evidence, the specifics of the court's final instructions to the jury, and the like, present mixed questions of fact and law or purely legal ones and are decided by the judge alone. The trial of the Black Sox included pitched battles on many such issues. One especially crucial dispute focused on the elements of a conspiracy under Illinois law, circa 1919, the time of the alleged offenses. A better comprehension of the trial narrative may be fostered by a brief précis on that subject.

Although susceptible to varying definitions, the essence of conspiracy is an agreement between two or more persons to commit an unlawful act.[1] In most states, that agreement must be ratified by an overt act, i.e., action or conduct by one or more of the conspirators that moves the plot past the talking stage.[2] But that was not true in 1919 Illinois. Under both its common law and statutory definitions of the offense, a conspiracy in that state was complete upon the mere agreement to commit an unlawful act.[3] Illinois, moreover, permitted simultaneous prosecution of conspiracy charges on both common law and statutory grounds.[4] In addition, as elsewhere in this country, conspiracy was a crime separate and distinct from the offense that was the object of the conspiracy.[5] For a simple example, conspiracy (agreement) to rob a bank is one crime while the actual bank robbery is a second crime — although conviction on the two offenses might later be combined for sentencing purposes.

Black Sox defense counsel included some of Chicago's finest criminal trial lawyers. From left, James C. O'Brien, Benedict Short, Thomas D. Nash, Michael Ahern, Max Luster, and Henry Berger in their summer courthouse attire.

In the Black Sox case, these principles gave a huge advantage to the State, since prosecutors were not obliged to prove that the Sox players had actually dumped the 1919 World Series, or any particular game of it. The law only required proof positive that the accused players and the gambler defendants had reached an agreement to do so.[6] A trickier task for the State was establishing that the object of the conspiracy — the World Series fix — was itself an unlawful act. Here, the prosecution was hamstrung by the fact that Illinois did not have a statute that criminalized the corruption of sporting events on the books at the time that the Series was played. Like other states, Illinois adopted a specific sports corruption statute in the wake of the World Series scandal, but this new law could not be applied retroactively to the Black Sox accused.[7] This statutory deficit necessitated arguing that the World Series fix was a form of criminal fraud, like obtaining money by false pretenses and/or via a confidence game.[8] During the proceedings, considerable argument would be devoted to the legitimacy of this interpretation.

Doing battle on these issues would be a cast of legal heavyweights, the cream of the Midwest criminal bar. Appearing on behalf of defendants Buck Weaver, Swede Risberg, and Happy Felsch was Thomas D. Nash, a former Chicago alderman and veteran criminal defense counsel. Assisting Nash was his junior partner, the capable Michael J. Ahern, later attorney for Al Capone.[9] Joe Jackson and Lefty Williams had retained Benedict J. Short, an experienced former prosecutor and now perhaps Chicago's most respected criminal defense attorney. Short's second chair would be his law partner George Guenther, another veteran of high-profile criminal cases. In the run-up to the Black Sox trial, Short and Guenther had managed, against considerable odds, to save a particularly unsympathetic double-murderer named Carl Wanderer from the gallows.[10] Their opposition in the Wanderer case had been ASAs James C. O'Brien and John Prystalski, now joint defense counsel for Chick Gandil.[11]

During his tenure as a prosecutor, O'Brien's sway over juries in Chicago death penalty cases trials had been celebrated, earning him the fearsome nickname "Ropes," while the unsung Prystalski had performed the pair's trench work on cross-examination. Working in tandem, O'Brien and Prystalski had placed more than a dozen murderers on death row while employed in the Cook County State's Attorneys Office. Leaving the SAO in December 1920, O'Brien and Prystalski had formed a private law practice with former SAO colleague John Owen.[12] This would be their firm's first major case as defense attorneys. Eddie Cicotte was nominally represented by his personal attorney and long-time friend Daniel P. Cassidy, a Detroit civil lawyer who prudently left Cicotte's defense largely to Short.[13] The gamblers were also in good hands. David Zelcer and the Levi brothers were represented by the seasoned Max Luster and former Chicago jurist J.J. Cooke, while St. Louis defendants Carl Zork and Ben Franklin[14] entrusted their fate to hometown attorneys A. Morgan Frumberg and H. C. Lewinson, with Henry Berger, formerly of the Attell defense, retained as local counsel.

Though outnumbered, the prosecution was hardly outgunned.[15] Lead prosecutor George E. Gorman had been admitted to the bar in 1895 and had more trial experience than anyone else in the courtroom. At his side was Special Prosecutor Edward A. Prindiville, once First Assistant Cook County State's Attorney and now a member of the influential Chicago law firm of Barrett & Barrett.[16] ASA John Tyrell, formerly of Barrett & Barrett and an expert in matters of criminal law and procedure, was also on the prosecution trial team. Affiliated with the prosecution was retired judge George F. Barrett, counsel for the American League.[17] And quietly operating behind the scenes was a battery of able lawyers in the employ of Ban Johnson, headed by Charles V. Barrett, George's younger brother and a powerful force in local Republican Party circles.

Former congressman George E. Gorman assumed the role of lead prosecutor in the Black Sox case.

About the only untested figure in the courtroom was the judge. Although he would subsequently go on to a distinguished 46-year career on Illinois trial and appellate benches, Judge Hugo M. Friend was a judicial novice in June 1921. At the time of the Black Sox trial, Friend was better known for his athletic accomplishments. Friend had captained the

University of Chicago track team to a Big Ten Conference championship in 1905 and was the national AAU titlist in the long jump and high hurdles. Friend had gone on to win a long jump bronze medal in the 1906 Olympic Games in Athens. Since his admission to the bar, Friend had practiced mostly civil law and also had been active in Jewish philanthropies.[18] Finally, like his boss Judge McDonald, Friend was an avid Chicago baseball fan.

Given his judicial inexperience, the assignment of the highly charged Black Sox case to Friend's court was a puzzler. Later, during the trial of the Jackson civil suit, Judge McDonald would reveal that assignment of the Black Sox trial to Judge Friend was one of the few things that the opposing sides had agreed upon.[19] In any event, the choice would prove a sound one. Dealing with a battalion of fractious barristers would often test his mettle, but Judge Friend's intelligence and basic sense of fairness would see him through. The Black Sox case would be generally well tried, if not error-free.

Author note: As with the grand jury record, only fragments of the criminal trial transcript remain extant. The most extensive collection of trial-related documents is the one acquired by the Chicago History Museum in December 2007 and reviewed by the author in May 2010. Aspects of the criminal trial record are also embedded in the transcript of the Jackson v. White Sox civil trial, likewise inspected by the author in May 2010. The following chapters also incorporate material contained in the Black Sox file at the Giamatti Research Center, National Baseball Hall of Fame and Museum, Cooperstown, New York, and Black Sox trial reportage, particularly the verbatim accounts of testimony published in the newspapers that covered the proceedings first-hand. Using these sources, the following narrative of the Black Sox trial has been crafted with care. But no claim of inerrancy can be asserted.

The trial of the Black Sox case was the first significant matter handled by Judge Hugo M. Friend during his distinguished 46-year career as an Illinois jurist.

Judge Friend's management skills would be tested immediately.

As soon as the court set a trial date, two defendants, Ben Franklin and Carl Zork, asked to be excused on grounds of illness. According to the affidavit of Dr. Charles H. Vosburgh, Franklin was confined to his bed in a St. Louis sanitarium with articular rheumatism and would need a minimum of three weeks to recover. Thereafter, his condition and fitness to travel would have to be reevaluated.[20] Zork, meanwhile was said to be suffering from neurasthenia and melancholy.[21] "When I would question him," defense counsel Frumberg informed the court, "he would turn white and cry and tremble. It is impossible to carry on a conversation with him."[22] Counsel feared that standing trial might cause Zork to go insane.[23]

Judge Friend was unmoved, particularly after AL counsel Barrett testified that Zork had sounded fine to him during a telephone conversation a few weeks earlier.[24] The prosecution also presented an affidavit from Paul A. Rickert of *The Sporting News*, who maintained that he had seen Zork walking St. Louis streets only days ago.[25] Accordingly, the court ordered the Zork defense to be ready for trial as scheduled. But the Franklin illness evidence stood unrefuted. This forced Judge Friend to grant the adjournment request and sever the trial of Franklin from the immediate proceedings.[26] Thus another of the Black Sox defendants slipped out of the prosecution net.

While dealing with his malingering suspects, Judge Friend also had to contend with the avalanche of last-minute motions filed by defense counsel Berger, the legal beagle of the Black Sox lawyering corps. First and foremost, the Berger filings sought dismissal of the indictments as to all defendants. The centerpiece argument, premised largely on the Willis decision in the PCL case, was that the indictments failed to allege conduct condemned by Illinois criminal law.[27] Berger also sought dismissal on the grounds that: (1) the indicted players were not legally under contract to the White Sox during the playing of the 1919 World Series; (2) even if under contract, the Sox players had no legal duty to play well during the Series; they could perform poorly, if they so chose[28]; (3) bribery-type offenses could only be leveled at government officials; and (4) the combination of different classes of victims (Sox teammates/the White Sox corporation/defrauded White Sox bettors/the sporting public) in the indictments was improper.[29]

Moving on to specific charges, Berger sought dismissal of the indictment counts that were based on depriving Collins/Schalk or the White Sox corporation of the difference between the winning and losing shares of the Series purse. According to Berger, these purported victims could not be defrauded of property (the winner's share) that they never possessed in the first place. The defense also demanded a separate trial on each of the numerous counts of the indictments.[30] In the event that the motions were denied and the case proceeded to trial, the moving papers sought restriction on the evidence that could be used against the accused. Targeted for exclusion were: (1) all evidence of gambling on the 1919 World Series, as the indictments did not charge any gambling offenses or mention the word *gambling* in their text; (2) the grand jury statements of defendants Cicotte, Jackson, and Williams; and (3) testimony by any grand juror relating to such statements (on the almost laughable ground that grand jury secrecy in the Black Sox case needed to be preserved).[31] The defense also asked the court to order the arrest of Bill Burns, a defense turncoat who was at liberty without bond,[32] and to issue subpoenas for all members of the 1919 White Sox team.[33]

For the most part, the relief granted by Judge Friend was nominal. All defense complaints about the indictments were rejected and the charges would be adjudicated together in a unitary proceeding.[34] The trial, however, would not include the indictment counts alleging victimization of World Series bettor Charles K. Nims. Those counts were voluntarily dismissed by lead prosecutor Gorman, citing the need to avoid multiplicity of charges and resultant juror confusion.[35] (Left unmentioned by Gorman was an unsuccessful extortion attempt by Nims at the Berger law office earlier in the proceedings.)[36] The prosecution would also be precluded from mentioning the Cicotte, Jackson, and Williams statements in front of the jury until the court had ruled on their admissibility in evidence.[37] But mention of gambling, a topic of crucial importance to the Black Sox case, would not be prohibited by the court. With pretrial rulings now rendered, the lone obstacle forestalling the trial's start was a formidable one: empanelling a jury.

Given the notoriety of the Black Sox scandal and the 120 peremptory challenges[38] allotted both the prosecution and defense, Judge Friend requisitioned a jury pool of 600. Nevertheless, the selection process proceeded at a snail's pace, with both sides using the voir dire interrogations for indoctrination purposes or to evoke sympathy. Defense counsel Berger was the most gleeful practitioner of the art, weaving the accusation that Sox owner Comiskey had been too cheap to launder his players' uniforms without charging them and other damaging allegations into his questioning of prospective jurors.[39] Prosecutors, meanwhile, tried to gauge juror receptivity to accomplice testimony (but without mentioning Bill Burns by name).[40] After almost two weeks of this, Judge Friend had had enough, threatening to extend court sessions into the evenings and weekends, if required.[41] That seemingly did the trick. On July 16, 1921, the empanelling process concluded with twelve mostly working-class white men seated in the box, none of whom professed to being much of a baseball fan. The foreman was a hydraulic press operator named

William Barry.[42] Despite the duration of the jury selection process, it had gone by too quickly for cash-strapped Fred McMullin. Having arrived in Chicago too late to attend jury impaneling, McMullin was barred from being a trial defendant and a recipient of its verdict, good or bad. Instead, he would have to return home to Los Angeles and await the call of another trial at a later date.[43]

With the jury finally in place, the Black Sox trial appeared set to start. First, however, Judge Friend had to consider a flurry of new motions—requests to dismiss the charges, suppress evidence, etc.—submitted by defense counsel Berger. All were summarily denied by the court, except one: an application to compel listed prosecution witnesses Bill Burns and Joe Gedeon to submit to interviews by defense counsel. Such interview sessions were mandated by an Illinois pretrial discovery statute. That same statute, however, did not require a reluctant witness to answer any questions once the interview began. This quirk in the law resulted in one additional day of court time being devoted to a futile exercise—the production of Burns and Gedeon in court where, as expected, they politely declined to answer any of defense counsel's queries.[44] This was followed by another predictable event but one of significantly more consequence: the announcement by the SAO that the indictments against Bill Burns had been dismissed and that he had been granted immunity from prosecution on any Black Sox-related charges.[45]

Notes

1. See *Black's Law Dictionary,* 351.
2. *Ibid.*
3. As determined by the Illinois Supreme Court in *People v. Lloyd,* 304 *Ill.* 23, 136 *N.E.* 505 (Sup. Ct. 1922). See also, *United States v. Shatine,* 513 *U.S.* 10 (1994): A common law conspiracy is complete upon the formulation of the unlawful agreement. No act in furtherance of the conspiracy need be proved. The Illinois statutory version of conspiracy also omitted the overt act component. See *Chicago Daily Journal,* September 9, 1920, for the text of the Illinois conspiracy statute.
4. Generally speaking, the common law is non-statutory precedent derived from court decisions on a particular issue. The enactment of a statute on a specific subject ordinarily supersedes the common law. Thus, in most places legislative passage of a penal code preempts prior criminal law and precludes prosecution of an offense on common law grounds. But not in Illinois where the state's highest court had expressly held that "if an act is an offense against the common law and the statute, the prosecutor may proceed under either the statute, the common law or both." *People v. Curran,* 286 *Ill.* 302, 121 *N.E.* 637 (Sup. Ct. 1918).
5. See *Black's Law Dictionary,* 351, and *Callanan v. United States,* 364 *U.S.* 587 (1961).
6. In his 1956 account of the scandal, Chick Gandil maintained that the Black Sox players had gotten cold feet and never went through with their agreement to throw Game One or any other World Series games. See Chick Gandil, as told to Mel Durslag, "This Is My Story of the Black Sox Series," *Sports Illustrated,* September 17, 1956. Under Illinois

law, however, the purported abandonment of the fix would have provided no defense to the conspiracy charge. That offense was committed the moment that the agreement to dump the Series was reached.

7. The Illinois sports anti-corruption statute would not take effect until July 1, 1922.

8. Fraud arises from injury or loss to a person caused by deceit. Obtaining money by false pretenses or via a confidence game are specific types of fraud, and involve gaining the victim's trust in order to induce him to part with money or property voluntarily. See *Black's Law Dictionary,* 339, 448.

9. Nash and Ahern were also counsel for Fred McMullin, still not arrived in Chicago.

10. The first Wanderer trial was conducted while the original Black Sox grand jury proceedings were in progress. Without Short and Guenther as defense counsel at his trial for the second murder, Wanderer was tried, convicted, and then hanged in September 1921.

11. As previously noted, O'Brien had initially been retained by Ban Johnson to represent American League interests during the Black Sox proceedings. But by the time that the case came before Judge Dever in March 1921, O'Brien was at the defense table, representing Chick Gandil. Why this was countenanced is unknown since, absent the improbable consent of the AL, O'Brien was ethically prohibited from changing sides and representing a client whose interests were in conflict with the party who originally retained him, as per Canon 6, Illinois State Bar Association Canons of Professional Ethics, adopted June 24, 1910.

12. Gene Carney names John Owens as co-counsel for Gandil. See *Notes from the Shadows of Cooperstown,* No. 276, November 22, 2002. But John E. Owens, a prominent Chicago attorney/politician and former judge, was not involved in the Black Sox litigation. John Owen, partner in the newly formed law firm of O'Brien, Prystalski and Owen, appears with O'Brien and Gandil in a courthouse corridor photo published in the *Chicago Daily News.* The extent, if any, of Owen's participation in the Gandil defense is unknown.

13. It has long been speculated that Charles Comiskey financed the Black Sox players' defense. No evidence accompanies this speculation because there is none. It should also be noted that, while Joe Jackson, Lefty Williams, et al., may arguably have been underpaid in terms of their value as major league baseball stars, their 1920 salaries far exceeded the income of the typical Chicago criminal defendant in search of a good attorney. It also bears noting that, in an era when lawyers were prohibited from publicly advertising their services, appearance as counsel in the high-profile Black Sox case provided defense lawyers with a marketing windfall, not to mention a major ego boost.

14. Occasionally in trial reportage, and more often in ensuing Black Sox literature, Franklin is called Frankel, apparently the original family name.

15. At times, it has been asserted that the prosecution of the Black Sox defendants was hampered by defections from the SAO to the defense. This is erroneous. None of the four defense lawyers who had once served in the Cook County State's Attorneys Office (Short, Berger, O'Brien, and Prystalski) played any role whatsoever in the construction of the Black Sox case. Berger, who left the SAO in May 1919, and Short, a prominent SAO member a decade earlier, were not in government employ when the corruption of the 1919 Fall Classic was being investigated. And while O'Brien and Prystalski had been in the SAO in 1919, they had spent their time co-prosecuting the first Wanderer case and had had no connection to the Black Sox probe.

16. According to Bill Veeck, Jr., the engagement of former ASA Replogle as a special Black Sox trial prosecutor was nixed by White Sox corporation counsel Alfred Austrian, as per *The Hustler's Handbook,* 272. At the time of the Black Sox trial, Replogle served as legal counsel for the Tamms Silica Company of White Haven, Pennsylvania.

17. Although a rare occurrence nowadays, certain jurisdictions have permitted the attorney for a party claiming to be injured by the conduct of a criminal defendant to appear at trial to assist the prosecutor, or even to assume prosecution of the case entirely.

18. For a brief profile with a photo of Judge Friend, see the *Chicago Tribune,* February 22, 1921.

19. See JTT, p. 545.

20. Copies of the Vosburgh affidavit, dated June 18, 1921, as well as other documents related to Franklin's medical condition, are contained in the Black Sox file at the Giamatti Research Center.

21. As per the *Chicago Tribune,* June 28, 1921.

22. As quoted in the *New York Times* and *Washington Post,* June 28, 1921, and elsewhere.

23. As reported in the *Chicago Tribune,* June 28, 1921.

24. Note that ethical precepts forbade uncounseled contact on case-related matters between an attorney like George Barrett and an adverse party represented by counsel like Carl Zork. See Canon 9 of the Illinois code of legal ethics. Bur this, like other instances of seeming professional impropriety in the Black Sox case, was paid no mind.

25. As reported in the *Chicago Tribune* and *New York Times,* June 28, 1921.

26. As per the *New York Times,* June 30, 1921.

27. As reported by the *Los Angeles Times,* June 30, 1921, and other AP wire service outlets.

28. Clause 2 of the standard MLB contract explicitly obligated the player to perform with "his best skill and ability."

29. As per the *Los Angeles Times,* June 30, 1921.

30. As per the *Chicago Daily Journal,* July 18, 1921, and *Chicago Evening American,* July 19, 1921, reporting the denial of this particular application.

31. As per the *Boston Globe* and *Los Angeles Times,* July 6, 1921.

32. *Ibid.* The inclusion of Burns' name on a prospective prosecution witness list (as reported in the *Boston Globe* and *New York Times,* July 2, 1921) confirmed the suspicion that Burns had agreed to turn State's evidence.

33. As per the *Chicago Tribune,* July 9, 1921. Needless to say, the issuance of such subpoenas threatened serious disruption of the American League playing schedule. Berger and Sox club secretary Grabiner, however, subsequently worked out an accommodation that minimized the disturbance potential.

34. As reported in the *Boston Globe* and *Chicago Tribune,* July 6, 1921, and elsewhere.

35. As reported in the *Boston Globe* and *Washington Post,* July 19, 1921.

36. As per the bill of particulars supplied defense counsel, Nims had allegedly been victimized by Abe Attell. Months prior to the start of the Black Sox trial, Nims offered to "sell out" to the defense if reimbursed for his Series gambling losses. Attorney Berger, then Chicago associate counsel for Attell, refused the proposition and had Nims thrown out of the office. Berger then reported the incident to Judge Dever, as reported in the *Chicago Tribune,* March 15, 1921.

37. As reported in the *Chicago Daily Journal* and *New York Times,* July 19, 1921. The preferred practice is to resolve major evidential issues prior to trial, particularly when a testimonial hearing is required. Given the timing of the assignment of the Black Sox case to Judge Friend, the disruption attending the mid-trial proceedings held on the challenged player statements is not fairly ascribed to him.

38. A peremptory challenge enables a party to excuse a prospective juror without cause or explanation.

39. As reported in the *Chicago Tribune,* July 7, 1921.

40. As per the *Boston Globe,* July 6, 1921, and *Chicago Tribune* and *Los Angeles Times,* July 7, 1921.

41. Under the guise of seeking out partiality, lawyers frequently tried to indoctrinate potential jurors via loaded questions designed to stimulate juror indignation or evoke sympathy for the client. Lawyer abuse of the voir dire process and its often interminable length

eventually prompted many jurisdictions to assign the questioning of veniremen entirely to the trial judge.

42. The names, addresses, and occupations of the selected trial jurors were published in the *Chicago Tribune,* July 16, 1921. A photograph of the panel later appeared in *The Sporting News,* July 28, 1921.

43. As subsequently reported in the *Chicago Evening Post* and *Washington Post,* August 4, 1921.

44. As reported in the *Atlanta Constitution* and *Chicago Tribune,* July 18, 1921, and elsewhere.

45. As reported in the *Chicago Daily Journal* and *Chicago Herald Examiner,* July 18, 1921, and elsewhere.

12

The Prosecution Case Begins

As in all criminal trials, the prosecution commenced its case against the Black Sox defendants with an opening statement to the jury.[1] In his remarks, 2nd ASA Gorman offered a highly detailed account of the events attending the plot to throw the 1919 World Series. In the process, Gorman described the roles played by both the defendants seated in court and by other fix actors, including Arnold Rothstein and Abe Attell, who were not.[2] To legally sophisticated listeners, the indispensability of Bill Burns and, to a lesser extent, Billy Maharg to the prosecution case was quickly made evident. For without the testimony of a fix insider, the State would be unable to prove the existence of any conspiracy to rig the outcome of the 1919 World Series. Nor without Burns and Maharg would the State have the means of establishing the fix involvement of specific conspirators, save for those who had confessed before the grand jury (Cicotte, Jackson, and Williams) or to the press (Felsch).[3] Although the contours of the case were familiar to many in the gallery, particular revelations still elicited "ohs and ahs" from the otherwise silent throng.[4] The defendants, however, remained stoic during the lengthy Gorman address.

Although no opening statements were made on behalf of the accused, one aspect of defense strategy quickly became evident. The Black Sox defense would stipulate nothing, forcing the prosecution to prove every facet of its case, no matter how uncontroverted the point, apparently in hopes that prolonging the proceedings in a sweltering mid-summer courtroom would be held against the State. Thus, the prosecution was obliged to initiate its case by presenting elementary information, summoning witnesses from baseball's establishment for such purposes. To help substantiate the damage to his team, Charles A. Comiskey testified about his ownership of the White Sox, the value of the franchise, the seating capacity of the Chicago ballpark, and other prosaic matters. The tedium produced by this testimony was only disturbed by an angry exchange between the witness and defense counsel Short. Taking offense at Short's implication that he had been a contract jumper during the Players' League conflict of 1890, an enraged Comiskey bellowed, "Don't you dare to say that I ever jumped a contract. I never did in my life."[5] After things had calmed down, John E. Bruce, secretary of the late National Commission, concluded the opening day's testimony by providing minutiae about the 1919 Series, including its gate receipts of $722,414.[6]

The second day of trial began with more of the same. White Sox manager Kid Gleason related that he had read the official rules of the World Series to his charges prior to Game One.[7] The testimony of World Series official scorer J.G. Taylor Spink then placed the final score of each 1919 Series game into the trial record.[8] White Sox secretary Harry Grabiner was summoned to clarify a technical point about the players' World Series obligations. After identifying the signatures on the 1919 contracts of the Black Sox players, Grabiner testified that an exhibition game clause in those contracts covered World Series play and obligated the players to perform in the 1919 Series. For their efforts, the Black Sox would be paid per diem at their regular-season contract rate, in addition to receiving their individual World Series shares.[9] With these preliminaries out of the way, the stage was now set for the dramatic highlight of the Black Sox trial: the testimony of Bill Burns. Once on the witness stand, the raffishly dressed (bow tie, lavender shirt, dark green checked suit) Burns began perspiring noticeably, wiping his brow frequently with a large handkerchief. Burns also spoke in a low monotone, his voice often inaudible to spectators in the rear of the courtroom. But those who had associated Burns' "Sleepy Bill" nickname with his intellect were in for a shock. Quick-witted and unflappable, Burns would prove more than a match for antagonistic defense lawyers — to the astonishment and then delight of a jaded Black Sox press corps.[10]

The performance of star prosecution witness Bill Burns garnered rave reviews from the Black Sox press corps.

For reasons grounded in strategy

and law, Burns spent parts of three days on the witness stand. During his initial appearance, Burns confirmed the existence of a plot to fix the 1919 World Series. The scheme was devised and/or financed by a group that included Burns, Arnold Rothstein, Abe Attell, Billy Maharg, and a man named Bennett — whom Burns identified in court as defendant Zelcer.[11] In the beginning, Burns and Maharg approached Rothstein at New York's Aqueduct Racetrack and later in the grill room of the Astor Hotel. At first, Rothstein was not interested in the fix proposition, so Hal Chase put Burns in touch with Abe Attell and Bennett (Zelcer). Burns discussed the fix and its financing with them and then met with Eddie Cicotte and Chick Gandil at the Ansonia Hotel. Two days before the start of the Series, Burns sat down with Chisox players at the Sinton Hotel in Cincinnati and offered $100,000 for their agreement to lose the Series to the Reds. Present during the fix negotiations were Cicotte, Gandil, Swede Risberg, Lefty Williams, Happy Felsch, Buck Weaver, and Fred McMullin, with Cicotte, Gandil, and Risberg doing most of the talking for the players. The players wanted the $100,000 paid up front in a lump sum but eventually agreed to accept payment in $20,000 per loss installments, with Burns to get his fix cut from the players' money. Cicotte, the ace of the Sox pitching staff and the presumed opening game starter, agreed to lose Game One, saying he would do so "even if he had to throw the baseball clear out of the Cincinnati park."[12] Cicotte, however, also wanted to win a Series game for 1920 contract purposes. Williams, the anticipated starter for Game Two, agreed to lose that contest. Burns testified that problems subsequently arose when the players were not paid after the Sox loss in Game One and Gandil began to suspect a double cross. Shortly thereafter, the witness was excused for the day.

Before resumption of the Burns testimony the following morning, the prosecution returned Harry Grabiner to the stand to inform the jury that the White Sox World Series player pool had amounted to $73,104.[13] Former National Commission chairman (and Reds President) Garry Herrmann then testified about the official rules of the World Series.[14] Burns then returned to the stand and his narrative of fix events was resumed.[15] After the White Sox lost Game Two, Burns and Maharg went to the Sinton Hotel to collect the players' money. Inside a room there, the pair observed Attell, Zelcer, and a horde of other gamblers, with money everywhere. Zelcer wanted to stiff the players again but Attell was persuaded to pay them something. With the Black Sox owed $40,000 at this point, Attell pulled $10,000 in cash from beneath a bed mattress and offered it to Burns, take it or leave it. Burns took the money and proceeded to another Sinton room, where he met Gandil, Cicotte, Risberg, McMullin, and two other players whose identity Burns could no longer recall. When Burns tossed the $10,000 on the bed, Gandil renewed his complaints about being double crossed. Nevertheless, Gandil later told Burns that the Sox would play to lose Game Three, information that Burns, in turn, relayed to Attell and Zelcer. Acting on Gandil's assurances, Burns and Maharg wagered their entire stake on the Reds in Game Three and were wiped out when the Sox won, 3–0, behind the pitching of Dickie Kerr. In the aftermath of this misadventure, Attell offered to pony up $40,000 of his own money if Burns could persuade the corrupted Sox players to return to the fix. Later, Burns conveyed this offer to Gandil at the Warner Hotel in Chicago but Gandil turned him down flat. On a street outside the hotel, however, Burns ran into Risberg, who pledged his commitment to continuing with the fix. Burns then went to Attell's room at the Sherman Hotel and notified Attell that the fix was off.

Prior to Burns' third and final appearance on the stand, Judge Friend ruled that sufficient evidence of the conspiracy had been presented to establish its existence. This judicial determination was crucial to the prosecution, as it sanctioned the introduction of more expansive testimony by the witness, including mention of conversations that Burns had with fix conspirators prior to the time frame specified in the indictments.[16] Granted this leeway, Burns testified that Cicotte had approached him late in the 1919 season, holding out the promise of "something good" if the White Sox won the pennant.[17] At a subsequent September 18 meeting with Cicotte and Gandil at the Ansonia Hotel, the two Sox leaders offered to throw the upcoming Series in return for $100,000. To this, Burns replied that he would "see what he could do." Shortly after being rebuffed by Rothstein, Burns met with Hal Chase, Abe Attell, and Bennett (Zelcer) who informed him that Rothstein had changed his mind and was now agreeable to financing the fix. Burns was thereupon dispatched to Cincinnati to meet with the Sox players.

Eagerly anticipated, the cross-examination of Burns was largely a dud. Apart from producing some waffling on meeting dates, the defense made little headway, extracting nothing strikingly inconsistent or damaging to the credibility of the witness. Burns took everything that sneering defense lawyers could muster in stride. He effectively parried hostile questions, bantered at times with his interrogators, and even managed a joke at attorney Short's expense.

> SHORT: You don't like me much, do you Bill?
>
> BURNS: Sure I do, Ben. You're a smart fellow, and I wish we had someone like you at the head of this deal. We'd all be rich now.[18]

Spectators laughed. Short fumed. Through it all, Burns remained seated serenely on the witness stand, waiting for the next ineffectual defense attack upon him. By the time that Burns stepped down, prosecutors were jubilant.[19] The *Los Angeles Times* gave an assessment that was typical of glowing, if sometimes trite, press reviews thereafter accorded Burns' performance: "The State's chief witness ... hurled excellent ball, permitting the defense few hits in the grilling cross-examination."[20]

The first testimony implicating Midwestern gamblers was given on July 22. Cubs team secretary John O. Seys informed the jury that he had served as stakeholder for certain bets placed on Game One and Game Two by Abe Attell.[21] Attell was frequently in the company of defendant Lou Levi, for whom Seys also held a few World Series bets. Both Attell and Levi were wagering heavily on the Reds. As a loyal National League man, Seys was also backing Cincinnati — until Attell warned him against betting on the Reds in Game Three. By the time that the Series had switched to Chicago, Seys had accumulated approximately $2,250 in winnings for Attell but was unable to find him in the Windy City. This led Seys to deposit the Attell winnings with Paul Gores, the assistant manager of the Congress Hotel.

At the conclusion of the Seys testimony, the two sides entered a rare mutually agreeable stipulation of fact. It was agreed that if called as a witness, the aforementioned Gores would testify that he had accepted $2,200 from Seys and had later turned that sum over to Attell.[22] Once the jury was so advised, East St. Louis theater owner and habitual sports bettor Harry Redmon was placed on the witness stand to incriminate Carl Zork and Ben Franklin, the severed defendant. According to Redmon, he first learned of the World Series fix from Franklin, who told him that eight White Sox players had agreed to lose the Series to the Reds.[23] But after Game Two, there had been a falling out between the corrupted players and the fix backers. Franklin and some others were trying to reinstate the fix for Game Four and Game Five, and Franklin wanted to know if Redmon and traveling companion Joe Pesch would contribute $5,000 each to a fund being collected to achieve that purpose. The two declined. Sometime later, Redmon and Pesch encountered Zork and an unidentified man at Chicago's Morrison Hotel. There, Zork boasted of masterminding the Series fix. "I'm the little red-headed fellow from St. Louis that was responsible for it all," crowed Zork. Redmon further testified about subsequently running into Abe Attell at the Sherman Hotel. Attell was carrying a "treasure box" packed with cash and had a message for Redmon to deliver: "Tell Zork that little Abie is not hooked this time." Redmon understood this to mean that Attell had continued to profit on the Series despite the breakup with the Sox players.

Sparks flew during the cross-examination of defense counsel Berger, who pressed Redmon about his gambling activities and accused him of being a bookmaker. Redmon heatedly denied it. An even sorer subject for the witness was his post–World Series meeting with White Sox brass in Chicago. Redmon denied that club attorney Austrian had called him a "blackmailer" during the meeting and then challenged Berger to repeat the accusation to Redmon's face outside the courthouse.[24] Several more insults were traded before Judge Friend regained control of the proceedings. Shortly thereafter, Redmon was excused. So was the jury, clearing the courtroom for the pivotal evidentiary hearing of the Black Sox trial: proceedings to determine whether or not the Cicotte, Jackson, and Williams grand jury testimony would be admitted in evidence.

Notes

1. In most jurisdictions, an opening statement by the prosecutor is mandated by court rules. This address must be confined to the facts that the prosecutor, in good faith, believes will be adduced during the government's case and may not be argumentative in nature. The timing of opening defense statements varies, sometimes being given immediately after the prosecutor's opening statement, sometimes immediately prior to the commencement of the defense case. And, if it so chooses, the defense need not make an opening statement at all. In the Black Sox case, no reference to an opening statement by any of the defense counsel was uncovered by the author. Nor was an opening statement delivered by AL counsel George Barrett, a near invisible presence during the trial.

2. For a detailed recapitulation of the Gorman opening, see *Chicago Daily Journal,* July 18, 1921.

3. Rules of evidence would prohibit the jury from utilizing the admission of fix participation made by one defendant against any of the other accused. In other words, the Cicotte grand jury confession could only be used as evidence of Cicotte's guilt, and not as evidence of fix involvement by Jackson, Williams, or the other defendants. This is a mandate of the Confrontation Clause of the Sixth Amendment and a by-product of the fact that an inanimate object like the Cicotte grand jury transcript could not be subjected to cross-examination by the others named in it. The testimony of a live witness like Bill Burns, however, was different, as Burns could obviously be made to answer questions by counsel for defendants other than Cicotte. Thus, the Burns testimony could be used against any co-conspirator incriminated by Burns. The same was true of any testimony provided by unindicted co-conspirator Billy Maharg.

4. As reported by the *New York Times,* July 19, 1921.

5. As reported in the *Chicago Herald Examiner* and *Chicago Tribune,* July 19, 1921, and elsewhere. Comiskey's outrage apparently amused his former players, observed laughing at the witness, according to the *Washington Post,* July 19, 1921.

6. As per the *Chicago Tribune,* July 20, 1921.

7. As per the *Chicago Herald Examiner,* July 20, 1921, and *Chicago Tribune* and *New York Times,* July 21, 1921.

8. As per the *Chicago Tribune,* July 21, 1921.

9. As per the *Chicago Herald Examiner* and *New York Times,* July 21, 1921.

10. For examples of reportage extolling Burns' performance on the witness stand, see *Chicago Daily Journal,* July 20, 1921; *Chicago Tribune,* July 21, 1921; *Los Angeles Times,* July 22, 1921; *New York Times,* July 23, 1921.

11. Nothing related to the Burns testimony is contained in the Chicago History

Museum documents. This account is drawn from verbatim passages from the Burns testimony published in the *Chicago Herald Examiner,* July 20, 1921. Extensive verbatim excerpts of the Burns testimony were also published in the *Chicago Daily Journal* and *New York Times,* July 20, 1921.

12. According to the *New York Times,* July 20, 1921: "A wave of laughter ran through the courtroom at the answer. Even the defendant players laughed. Cicotte appeared at first puzzled, then broke into a grin."

13. As reported in the *Chicago Herald Examiner* and *New York Times,* July 20, 1921.

14. As per the *Chicago Herald Examiner,* July 20, 1921.

15. This account of Burns' second day on the witness stand is derived from verbatim testimonial excerpts published in the *New York Times,* July 21, 1921.

16. The order of proof protocol in a 1921 criminal conspiracy case is not a matter easily encapsulated. In short, however, the minuet that the prosecution had to dance derived from the principle of vicarious liability. In lay terms, each and every participant in a conspiracy is personally responsible for any act committed in furtherance of achieving the conspiracy's object or goal by any of his co-conspirators. But before wide-ranging testimony about co-conspirator statements or conduct can be admitted at trial, the judge first has to be persuaded that some independent evidence of the conspiracy exists. In the Black Sox case, this principle extended Bill Burns' stay on the witness stand. Judge Friend first had to be persuaded that there was, in fact, some evidence of a plot to fix the outcome of the 1919 World Series — apart from the alleged statements of the conspirators themselves — *before* he would permit the Burns testimony to proceed into matters about events precedent to that plot or into conversations that Burns had with his alleged cohorts.

17. The account of Burns' third day of testimony is drawn largely from verbatim excerpts published in the *Chicago Tribune,* July 22, 1921.

18. As recounted in the *Los Angeles Times,* July 22, 1921.

19. According to the *New York Times,* July 23, 1921.

20. *Los Angeles Times,* July 22, 1921.

21. The account of the Seys testimony is taken from testimonial excerpts published in the *Chicago Daily Journal* and *Chicago Herald Examiner,* July 23, 1921.

22. As reported in the *Chicago Daily Journal,* July 23, 1921.

23. The account of the Redmon testimony is drawn largely from testimonial excerpts published in the *Chicago Herald Examiner,* July 23, 1921. See also, *Chicago Daily Journal* and *New York Times,* July 23, 1921, for reportage of the Redmon testimony.

24. As reported in the *Atlanta Constitution* and *New York Times,* July 23, 1921, and elsewhere.

13

The Missing Confessions

Because the issue had not been determined prior to trial, proceedings before the jury had to be suspended so that Judge Friend could conduct an evidentiary hearing to determine whether, and to what extent, the grand jury testimony of Cicotte, Jackson, and Williams could be utilized by the prosecution.[1] In seeking to suppress this testimony, which amounted to confessions by the three players, the Black Sox defense made no claim that the accused had not spoken the words attributed to them in the grand jury record. Rather, relief was sought on a couple of legal grounds. The first was a half-hearted claim of duress. But this was quickly supplanted by the argument that the players' grand jury testimony had been induced by broken off-the-record promises of immunity from prosecution. If that were true, such promises would render the testimony involuntary in the legal sense and, hence, inadmissible in evidence before the jury.

Accompanying the break in the trial was public revelation that the original transcriptions of the Cicotte, Jackson, and Williams grand jury testimony, as well as the waiver of rights signed by each player, were among the items of evidence missing from the SAO. Although sensationalized in the press, this development had little, if any, effect on the outcome of the proceedings. The prosecution merely had to resort to alternative means for establishing the content of the testimony and the validity of the defendants' relinquishment of their rights. The hearing itself would be restricted in scope, with inquiry into the playing of the 1919 World Series and player-gambler interaction prohibited. The evidence would be confined to the events attending the players' appearance before the grand jury on September 28–29, 1920. As a result, the hearing would come down to a test of credibility, with Cicotte, Jackson, and Williams maintaining that they had been promised immunity in return for their testimony and former ASA Replogle and Judge McDonald denying it.[2]

Author Note: A number of Black Sox commentators give the impression that something irreplaceable was lost when the Cicotte, Jackson, and Williams grand jury transcripts went missing. But this was hardly the case. In the 1920s (before the advent of modern recording devices), grand jury testimony was taken down in shorthand by a grand jury stenographer. The stenographer then created a typed transcript of the testimony from his or her notes. These transcripts were customarily transferred to the prosecutor's office for safekeeping. When the original transcripts of the Cicotte, Jackson, and Williams grand jury testimonies were discovered missing, the SAO simply had grand jury stenographers Walter J. Smith and Elbert M. Allen create new copies of the testimony transcripts from their shorthand notes. That solved the problem. Indeed, the accuracy of these second-generation transcripts was not even contested by the Black Sox defense. The loss of the signed waivers, being the best evidence of the defendants' voluntary relinquishment of their legal rights, did pose a problem for the prosecution, but only a minor one. The absence of the signed waivers could be overcome by testimony from former ASA Replogle, grand jury foreman Brigham, or the other 22 grand jurors, all of whom had witnessed the waiver process. All in all, the missing documents were a non-issue during the Black Sox proceedings.

Because it bore the burden of persuasion, the prosecution went first at the hearing, presenting Hartley Replogle, the grand jury prosecutor who had dealt directly with the defendants. Replogle testified that he initially met with Cicotte at the office of White Sox attorney Alfred Austrian on the morning of September 28.[3] Later that day, he met Jackson in Judge McDonald's chambers. That was also the location of the first meeting between Replogle and Williams on the following morning. On the central issue, Replogle was resolute: no promise of immunity from prosecution had been made to any of the three players. In addition, their rights had been fully explained by Replogle and voluntarily waived by Cicotte, Jackson, and Williams prior to their respective grand jury appearances. Replogle added that he had personally witnessed each player sign the original waiver of rights document now missing from SAO files.[4]

A dramatically different version of events was offered by the Black Sox defense. Shielded from interrogation about the alleged crimes,[5] Eddie Cicotte testified at length about his grand jury experience. According to Cicotte, he was already aware of the Maharg newspaper exposé when directed to the Austrian office by club secretary Grabiner.[6] Minutes after Cicotte's arrival, ASA Replogle appeared. In short order, Austrian informed Cicotte that they had "the goods" on him and wanted his cooperation. In return, Cicotte would not be punished, a promise ratified by Replogle. The two then escorted Cicotte to the courthouse, where he met with Judge McDonald. Cicotte revealed what he knew about the Series fix but Judge McDonald was unsatisfied, accusing Cicotte of withholding information about the gamblers behind the plot. When Cicotte protested, the judge turned to Replogle and said, "Indict him." With that, Cicotte raised the assurances that he had received from Austrian and Replogle. McDonald, Austrian, and Replogle then went into private conference, after which Replogle told Cicotte that the promise that he would not be punished was still good. Upon hearing that, Cicotte agreed to testify and entered the grand jury room.

A more elaborate account of the day's events was drawn from Joe Jackson. On the morning of September 28, he was ordered to the Austrian office by Kid Gleason.[7] Upon arrival, Jackson was told that he had been implicated in the 1919 World Series fix by Cicotte and was going to be indicted in the next 15 to 20 minutes. Jackson was also handed a letter notifying him of his immediate suspension from the White Sox. Jackson wanted to contact an attorney but was dissuaded from doing so by Austrian, who promised Jackson that he would not be punished if he confessed. Shortly afterward, Jackson telephoned Judge McDonald and asked for the same consideration afforded Cicotte. But when Jackson later spoke to McDonald personally in chambers, the judge did not like Jackson's story and told him to expect no sympathy from the court. McDonald then sent for ASA Replogle, who led Jackson to the grand jury room. Prior to entering, however, Jackson was met in the corridor by Austrian, who advised him that the grand jury did not intend to indict the ballplayers. It was the gamblers behind the fix that "they wanted to trample under their feet."[8]

Before testifying, Jackson had signed some type of waiver but he did not really know what the document was. At that point, Jackson "would have signed my own death warrant if they wanted me to."[9] But Jackson did not believe himself in legal peril. He had been promised his freedom after testifying and was told that he could go anywhere that he wanted — Judge McDonald had suggested "the Portuguese Islands" — as soon as he was finished. Jackson would only have to come back to the courthouse if he was needed as a witness. He would not be jailed, fined, or required to post bond. His only punishment would be banishment from organized baseball.[10] Jackson had been drunk the night before his grand jury appearance but was not intoxicated when testifying before the panel. He asked for and received police protection after completing his testimony, but not because of any supposed threat from Swede Risberg. The recent slashing of Buck Herzog by a scandal-incensed fan was what had concerned Jackson.[11] After he departed the courthouse, Jackson telephoned Lefty Williams and informed him of the guarantees that he had received from authorities. Jackson and his bailiff-protectors then proceeded to get drunk together.[12]

The testimony of Lefty Williams presented a similar scenario, but not without significant discrepancies.[13] According to Williams, he learned of courthouse developments from his wife Lyria. She, not Williams himself, had spoken on the telephone to Jackson. Williams then placed a call to the office of lawyer Jerome Crowley, but before getting a return call, Williams was ordered to the Austrian office. In front of the building that housed the Austrian firm, Williams met with Jackson and Kid Gleason, who accompanied him inside to meet the Sox counsel. Once inside the office, Austrian assured Williams that he did not need an attorney and promised him the same guarantee of no punishment extended to Cicotte and Jackson. When Williams then denied knowledge of the Series fix, Austrian reiterated the "no sentence of any kind and no fines" guarantee provided his two teammates. Austrian even asked Jackson to confirm the terms of that deal to Williams. Williams was subsequently transported to the courthouse but denied that he had received any promises of leniency from Judge McDonald. "I never talked to him," maintained Williams. Instead, Williams had relied on further assurances provided to him in the courthouse hallway by ASA Replogle. The prosecutor repeated the no sentence, no fine pledge made by Austrian, if Williams "would come in and make a clean confession."[14] On that basis, Williams entered the grand jury room, where he signed a document that was read to him. Williams then provided the grand jury testimony that the Black Sox defense now wanted suppressed.

After the defendants had testified, the prosecution called Judge McDonald in rebuttal. In no uncertain terms, McDonald denied that anything resembling immunity from prosecution had been offered to Cicotte, Jackson, or Williams.[15] McDonald had harbored some sympathy for Williams, believing him to have been underpaid by the White Sox and essentially a follower in the fix, so he had told him that his cooperation would probably be viewed favorably by prosecutors and the sentencing court. But McDonald had had no sympathy for Cicotte or Jackson. "They would have to take their chances with the trial court," McDonald had informed each of them. "I could make [them] no promises."[16] The McDonald testimony also disclosed aspects of what Cicotte, Jackson, and Williams had told the judge during brief pre-grand jury conversations in chambers. Cicotte, for example, confirmed Bill Burns' placement of the first player-gambler meeting in the Ansonia Hotel and stated that his price for participation in the fix was $10,000. At a second meeting held at the Warner Hotel several days before the Series opener, Cicotte demanded his payment in cash. Later that evening, Cicotte found his payoff under the pillow in his hotel room. In Game One, Cicotte was supposed to confirm his commitment to the fix by walking the Reds leadoff batter, but had hit him with a pitch unintentionally. Immediately after that, Cicotte's conscience began to bother him, but not to the point where Cicotte returned the $10,000.[17]

As for Jackson, McDonald had been curt with him when Jackson denied involvement in the Series fix during an initial September 28 telephone call to the courthouse. Fifteen minutes later, Jackson called back, saying he now wanted to tell all to the grand jury. Following his arrival in chambers, Jackson informed McDonald that he had first been approached about participating in the World Series fix outside the Ansonia Hotel. Chick Gandil offered him $5,000, a sum rejected by Jackson as "that wasn't enough to influence a laborer to do a dirty deed."[18] Later, Jackson agreed to join the fix for $20,000, payable in $5,000 installments. Jackson also told the judge that when his wife Katie subsequently found out about Joe's involvement, she cried. As for Jackson's post-testimony protection, that was occasioned by Jackson's fear of Swede Risberg's reaction to news that Jackson had appeared before the grand jury. Accordingly, McDonald assigned bailiffs to accompany Jackson home from the courthouse.[19] Williams arrived the following day and informed McDonald that he had split the $10,000 that he had received with Jackson. For the most part, however, McDonald's conversation with Williams had focused on the player's plight, with McDonald walking a fine line between offering Williams hope that his cooperation would be rewarded and avoiding any promises to that effect.[20]

During the suppression hearing, numerous excerpts from the grand jury testimony of Cicotte, Jackson, and Williams were read aloud by one side or the other.[21] At the conclusion of the testimony, Judge Friend ruled that the Cicotte, Jackson, and Williams testimony had been voluntarily rendered and would thus be admissible in evidence.[22] Of necessity, this meant that the court had determined the Replogle and McDonald version of disputed events to be the believable one, a decision doubtless made easier by the improbable testimony of Lefty Williams. But before defendants' grand jury testimony could be used by the prosecution, the transcript of each player's testimony would have to be edited to remove references in that testimony to any other defendant apart from the speaker. In other words, the names Gandil, Jackson, Felsch, etc., would have to be deleted from Lefty Williams' testimony before that testimony was heard by the jury.[23] This tedious process would have to be completed by ASA Tyrrell and the grand jury stenographers back in the office. In the meantime, the prosecution would resume the presentation of its case to the jury.

Notes

1. The admissibility of evidence is a legal issue, decided by the court outside the presence of the jury. In the Black Sox case, the prosecution bore the burden of proving that the Cicotte, Jackson, and Williams grand jury testimony had been provided voluntarily. The testimony was also subject to redaction, i.e., the excision of specific parts, in this case the names of the other defendants mentioned by Cicotte, Jackson, and Williams during their grand jury appearances.

2. Outside the courtroom, SAO officials announced that yet another grand jury investigation into the disappearance of Black Sox evidence — telegrams, correspondence, and other documents had just been discovered missing, as well — would be instituted shortly, as reported in the *Chicago Tribune* and *New York Times,* July 26, 1921, and elsewhere. Meanwhile, the public battle of words between Ban Johnson and Arnold Rothstein about the stolen grand jury transcripts raged on. See, e.g., *Atlanta Constitution* and *New York Times,* July 26, 1921.

3. Among the Black Sox documents obtained by the Chicago History Museum were abridged transcripts of the testimony given at the suppression hearing. See CHM, Black Sox file, Box 1, Folder 4. Testimonial excerpts of the proceedings were also published in the *Chicago Herald Examiner* and *Chicago Tribune,* July 26, 1921, and elsewhere.

4. CHM transcripts and as reported in the *Atlanta Constitution* and *Chicago Daily Journal,* July 23, 1921.

5. An attempt by Prosecutor Gorman to question Cicotte about the fix itself was quickly squelched by the court as being outside the scope of the suppression hearing. Testimony would be restricted to what was said and done at the time of defendants' grand jury appearances in late September 1920.

6. This account of the Cicotte hearing testimony is derived from the CHM transcripts.

7. The account of the Jackson hearing testimony is based on the CHM transcripts and reportage in the *Chicago Tribune* and *Savannah Morning News,* July 26, 1921, and elsewhere.

8. *Ibid.*

9. *Ibid.*

10. *Ibid.* Jackson's "quaint phraseology and dialect" were noted in the *New York Herald,* July 26, 1921. Left unmentioned in such reportage was the breadth of Jackson's vocabulary and his ability, when he so chose, to speak with both grammatical precision and clarity, neither of which fit his amusing public image as an illiterate bumpkin.

11. CHM transcripts. Left unnoted was the fact that Jackson had justified his need for bailiff protection on the basis of an event that had not yet happened. Buck Herzog was not slashed until September 30, 1920, two days after the Jackson grand jury appearance.

12. CHM transcripts.

13. The account of Williams' hearing testimony is drawn entirely from CHM transcripts.

14. *Ibid.* Williams' assertion that he had never spoken to Judge McDonald was in direct contradiction of the grand jury record at WGJ23–11 to 21 and was perhaps the most glaring of the various credibility problems presented to the defense by the Williams testimony.

15. CHM transcripts and the reportage of McDonald testimony in the *Boston Globe, Chicago Herald Examiner* and *Chicago Tribune,* July 26, 1921.

16. *Ibid.*

17. CHM transcripts and *Chicago Tribune,* July 26, 1921.

18. CHM transcripts and *Boston Globe, Chicago Herald Examiner* and *Chicago Tribune,* July 26, 1921.

19. CHM transcripts.

20. CHM transcripts and *Chicago Herald Examiner,* July 21, 1921.

21. As reported in the *Chicago Tribune,* July 26, 1921, and elsewhere.

22. As reported in the *Boston Globe* and *Chicago Herald Examiner,* July 26, 1921, and elsewhere.

23. As reported in the *Chicago Daily Journal,* July 26, 1921, and *New York Times,* July 27, 1921. As previously noted, this editing process (called redaction) was mandated by the Confrontation Clause of the Sixth Amendment. In the Black Sox case, this meant that any reading of the Jackson grand jury testimony could not include mention of, say, Chick Gandil or Lefty Williams by name. As part of the redaction process, the anonym *Mr. Blank* would be substituted whenever the name of Gandil or Williams appeared in the Jackson transcript.

14

The Prosecution Rests

While the grand jury transcripts were being redacted, the jury was recalled to the courtroom to hear testimony from Judge McDonald.[1] Taking care not to divulge the names of third parties mentioned to him, McDonald repeated what Eddie Cicotte, Joe Jackson, and Lefty Williams had told him about the Series fix prior to their grand jury appearances. McDonald added that Jackson had told him that "he played hard but could have played harder" during the Series.[2] On cross-examination, Black Sox defense lawyers treated Judge McDonald deferentially, avoiding challenges to his credibility and contenting themselves with testimony about the remorse exhibited by the players while speaking to McDonald. When the witness had concluded his testimony, Judge Friend imparted a limiting instruction, advising the jury that the McDonald testimony was not admissible as to any of the defendants except the individual defendant who allegedly made the statement to McDonald.[3] The court day then concluded with a brief appearance by White Sox counsel Alfred Austrian to describe his role in persuading Cicotte, Jackson, and Williams to confess.[4] When asked about Harry Redmon, Austrian testified that he had only met Redmon once — with White Sox officials in the Austrian law office on December 30, 1919. Redmon wanted club management to reimburse him for $5,500 that he had lost betting on the Sox, and in exchange Redmon would provide information about the fix of the Series. Austrian described the encounter as a cordial one and denied that he had called Redmon a blackmailer during the meeting. Nor had he ever used that term subsequently to describe Redmon.[5]

The morning proceedings of July 27 were recessed to permit defense counsel to review the redacted versions of the Cicotte, Jackson, and Williams grand jury testimonies. No objections to the accuracy of the of the product resulted.[6] Special Prosecutor Prindiville and grand jury stenographer Walter J. Smith assumed speaking roles in a reading of the edited versions of that testimony.[7] The boredom pervading the courtroom during these lengthy recitals was palpable and it was exacerbated by the fact that segments of the grand jury record had been redacted to the point of near unintelligibility. The grand jury, for example, had heard Cicotte testify that "a few weeks before the World Series, I had a conversation with seven other ballplayers at the Ansonia Hotel, their names being Claude Williams, Joe Jackson, Arnold Gandil, George Weaver, Oscar Felsch, Charles Risberg and Fred McMullin." After the redaction process, the passage was transformed into "...with seven other ballplayers at the Ansonia Hotel, their names being *Mr. Blank, Mr. Blank, Mr. Blank, Mr. Blank, Mr. Blank, Mr. Blank,* and *Mr. Blank.*"[8] Fearful of losing momentum and sensitive to the mood of jurors confined to a stifling courtroom, prosecutors then made the calculated strategic decision to close their case quickly and on a high note. To that end, the remainder of the scheduled government witnesses — Joe Gedeon, Ban Johnson, Joe Pesch, et al.,— would be jettisoned. Prosecution hopes for conviction would be anchored on one final witness: Billy Maharg.[9]

After outlining his current circumstances — he was a low-paid shop repairman in a Philadelphia Ford plant — Maharg recounted his involvement in the plot to prearrange the outcome of the 1919 World Series.[10] In the process, Maharg provided substantial corroboration of the testimony of Bill Burns. Like Burns, Maharg positively identified defendant Zelcer in court as the fixer posing as "Bennett" at the Sinton Hotel. Before beginning his narrative of events, Maharg addressed the issue of his identity. Prosecutor Gorman: "It has been intimated by the attorneys for the defense that you are Peaches Graham. Is that correct?" Maharg: "No. I have never been known by anything but Billy Maharg. I know Peaches Graham, but I am not he."[11] Maharg then testified that he was initiated into the fix by his friend Burns, whom he accompanied to the Ansonia Hotel in September 1919 for a meeting with Eddie Cicotte and Chick Gandil. There, the two players offered to throw the upcoming World Series for a $100,000 payoff. Burns and Maharg got the brush-off, however, when they approached Arnold Rothstein about underwriting the fix. Maharg then returned home to Philadelphia thinking that the scheme was dead. But just before the Series started, Maharg got a telegram from Burns summoning him to Cincinnati. After being reunited, Burns and Maharg proceeded to the Sinton Hotel for a conference with Abe Attell and Bennett (Zelcer). Those two claimed to be acting as agents for Rothstein, now agreeable to financing the Series fix.

Ensuing Maharg testimony essentially reiterated Burns' account of how the Sox players were short-changed on fix payoffs by Attell and Bennett/Zelcer and then retaliated by posting an unscripted win in Game Three, wiping out the heavily invested Burns and Maharg in the process. Prior to Game Four, he and Burns saw Attell at the Sherman Hotel in Chicago. Attell was holding a "tin box" full of cash and was waiting on "some bankers to make arrangements for the game."[12] Shortly afterward, a man unknown to Maharg appeared. According to Maharg, "Attell gave him a lot of money," and then explained that "the fellow had been working percentages for him."[13] Maharg then departed for home, his participation in the fix over. A year later, "Ban Johnson came to Philadelphia to see me [and] I told him the whole story straight through, just as it happened."[14] With the AL president covering all expenses, Maharg subsequently undertook a mission to southwest Texas to retrieve Burns. After locating Burns near the border of Mexico, Maharg delivered him to Chicago, where Burns was interviewed by Johnson and ASA Tyrrell. Maharg added that he first told his account of the fix publicly to sportswriter James Isaminger of the *Philadelphia North American.*[15] But Maharg denied having sought the $10,000 Comiskey reward for Series fix information. He claimed that a telegram demanding the money in Maharg's name had actually been sent by Isaminger, who was trying to call Comiskey's bluff on making payment.[16]

As with Burns, defense cross-examination of Maharg was intense but ineffectual. When it was over, the affable and seemingly guileless Maharg stepped off the stand and was adjudged a credible and effective government witness by most observers.[17] The prosecution then rested its case, knowing full well that it would now have to accept the consequences of truncating its presentation. By shortening the case, the State accentuated, unavoidably, the inherent unevenness of its evidence, which was strong against some defendants, but paper-thin or non-existent versus others. In particular, the prosecution had presented a compelling prima facie case against the confessing defendants, Cicotte, Jackson, and Williams. In many respects, the sworn admissions of fix participation made by these three were also corroborated by the testimony of Bill Burns, Billy Maharg, and Judge McDonald. If Burns and Maharg were to be believed, there was likewise ample proof of complicity in the Series fix lodged against Chick Gandil, David (Bennett) Zelcer, and, to a lesser extent, Swede Risberg.

But the State's case against the other accused was problematic, at best. Unlike the grand jury, the trial jurors had not heard Buck Weaver or Happy Felsch specifically identified by name as a fix participant in the confessions of Cicotte, Jackson, and Williams. All the trial jurors heard in the redacted versions of the grand jury testimonies read to them was that the other Sox players involved in the fix were the unnamed *Mr. Blank,* etc. And if they were to abide by the instruction of Judge Friend, the jurors were not to speculate about whether Weaver and/or Felsch were one of the *Blanks.* This reduced the evidence against Weaver and Felsch largely to Bill Burns' placement of the two at the pre–Game One fix meeting at the Sinton Hotel, and the inferences reasonably drawn from it — a slender reed (and one which renders inexplicable the prosecution's failure to put the Felsch newspaper confession before the jury via testimony by *Chicago Evening American* reporter Harry Reutlinger).[18] The case against gambler Carl Zork was similarly slim, resting almost entirely on the testimony of the volatile and embittered Harry Redmon. But that was more than the incriminating evidence presented by the State against the Levi brothers. That amounted to virtually nothing at all, leaving courthouse observers to wonder what those two defendants were doing in the case.

As is common in a criminal trial, the close of the prosecution case against the Black Sox precipitated a flurry of defense applications.[19] Most of these motions — to strike the testimony of Harry Redmon; to dismiss the charges on the ground that the prosecution had utilized the minutes of the original grand jury proceedings in obtaining the superseding indictments; to quash the indictments because Judge McDonald had acted as a prosecutor in facilitating the grand jury appearances of Cicotte, Jackson, and Williams; to vacate the charges because McDonald may have been present in the grand jury room when the indictments were voted — were frivolous on their face and were summarily denied by the court.[20] Taken more seriously were motions to dismiss for lack of proof in the government's case the charges against defendants Ben Levi, Lou Levi, Carl Zork, Buck Weaver, and Happy Felsch.[21] Having presented little evidence against Lou Levi and none at all against his brother, the prosecution voiced no objection to the dismissal of the charges against the Levis.[22] The State, however, refused to dismiss the charges against Zork, Weaver, and Felsch. Following argument, the prosecution's desire to proceed prevailed, but not without drawing a warning from the court. Said Judge Friend: "There is so little evidence against these men that I doubt I would allow a guilty verdict to stand if it were brought in. But as some evidence has been brought against them, I will not dismiss them unless the State is willing to *nolle prosse* (i.e., dismiss the charges unilaterally)."[23] The trial would therefore continue with nine defendants, including Zork, Weaver, and Felsch.

No judicial relief had been sought by the attorneys representing Gandil. Lead counsel O'Brien proclaimed, "I am going to put him on the stand and he will make a categorical denial of everything they charge against him. We want our vindication from the jury."[24] Other defense lawyers announced that Weaver, Risberg, and Felsch were also definitely taking the stand.[25] Player partisans packing the courtroom would have to wait, however, for their favorites to testify. The gamblers were going first.

Notes

1. A transcript containing excerpts of Judge McDonald's trial testimony is another artifact contained in the Chicago History Museum collection. See CHM, Black Sox file, Box 1, Folder 4.

2. As quoted in the *New York Times,* July 26, 1921.

3. As per the CHM transcripts. This reinforced the court's earlier instruction that, if the jury accepted as true what Cicotte was alleged to have said to Judge McDonald about the fix, such statements could be used by the jury only in determining the innocence or guilt of Cicotte. The Cicotte statements could play no part in juror assessment of the culpability of any other defendant standing trial.

4. See the *Chicago Tribune,* July 26, 1921.

5. As reflected in the CHM transcript of the Austrian testimony. See, also, *Savannah Morning News,* July 27, 1921, and *The Sporting News,* July 28, 1921.

6. As noted in the *Chicago Daily Journal* and *Chicago Herald Examiner,* July 26, 1921.

7. As reported in the *Chicago Daily Journal* and *Chicago Herald Examiner* and *New York Times,* July 27, 1921.

8. According to the *Chicago Herald Examiner,* July 27, 1921, taking note of the oppressive conditions in the mid-summer courtroom and the boredom induced by the repetitious reading of grand jury statements redacted to the point of near gibberish.

9. As reported in the *Chicago Daily Journal,* July 26, 1921.

10. The account of the Maharg testimony is taken from testimonial excerpts published in the *Chicago Daily Journal,* July 27, 1921, and *Chicago Herald Examiner* and *New York Times,* July 28, 1921.

11. As excerpted in the *New York Times,* July 28, 1921. Philadelphia resident William J. Maharg appears in every U.S. census through 1940, the last currently available. Although still sometimes published as fact, the notion (spread by Black Sox lawyers prior to trial) that William Joseph Maharg (1881–1953) and one-time Phillies catcher George Frederick "Peaches" Graham (1877–1939) were the same person is inane.

12. As per the *New York Times,* July 28, 1921.

13. *Ibid.*

14. *Ibid.*

15. In coverage of the Maharg testimony, the name *Isaminger* was frequently transposed into *Izzy Meyer.* See, e.g., *Chicago Daily Journal,* July 27, 1921, and *New York Times,* July 28, 1921.

16. As earlier reported in the *Washington Post,* September 30, 1920.

17. Maharg, "an articulate witness, ... added a strong layer of testimony to the State's already strong case," according to Asinof, *Eight Men Out,* 202.

18. The Black Sox file at the Giamatti Research Center contains a letter from *Chicago Evening American* correspondent Harry Neily to Ban Johnson urging him to bring the Reutlinger-Felsch interview to the attention of prosecutors. But it is difficult to conceive that prosecutors would not already have known about the widely reported interview.

19. These motions were argued before the court outside the jury's presence.

20. As reported in the *Chicago Daily Journal,* July 27 and 28, 1921, *Chicago Daily News,* July 28, 1921, and *Washington Post,* July 29, 1921.

21. As reported in the *Boston Globe,* July 28, 1921. The *Globe* account included Joe Jackson among the defendants seeking dismissal on failure of proof grounds, but this seems unlikely. The establishment of a prima facie case against Jackson — at least for mid-trial acquittal motion purposes — was not a matter that could be seriously disputed.

22. As reported in the *Chicago Daily Journal* and *Chicago Herald Examiner,* July 28, 1921, and *Chicago Evening American,* July 29, 1921. The Levi brothers had been particular

targets of Ban Johnson. In pretrial correspondence with private detective Cal Crim, Johnson declared, "We want to convict the Levi brothers" and counseled rough treatment of Fred Mowbray, a well-to-do Cincinnati lumberman and longtime friend of the Levis, if Mowbray declined to assist the conviction effort, as reflected in an April 22, 1921, Johnson letter contained in the Black Sox file at the Giamatti Research Center. The steps, if any, taken by Crim in response to the Johnson directive are unknown. The name Fred Mowbray, however, never appeared on any prosecution witness list and the evidence ultimately presented at trial against the Levi brothers was embarrassingly meager.

23. As reported in the *Los Angeles Times* and *New York Times,* July 28, 1921. An endnote is not the place for a lengthy discussion of the differences between the mid-trial dismissal of charges on evidential ground and the post-verdict entry of a judgment of acquittal by the court notwithstanding the jury's guilty verdict. Suffice it to say that the distinctions between the two are significant. Most important, mid-trial dismissal rulings are completely dispositive of the charges, such rulings not being appealable by the State. Thereafter, the Double Jeopardy Clause of the Fifth Amendment permanently prohibits any retrial of the charges. Court rulings that overturn a jury's guilty verdict afford no such protection to the accused. Such rulings are subject to appeal by the State and the reinstatement of the conviction or the ordering of a new trial by an appellate court.

24. As quoted in the *Los Angeles Times* and *New York Times,* July 28, 1921.

25. As reported in the *Chicago Herald Examiner*, *Los Angeles Times* and *Washington Post,* July 27, 1921, and elsewhere. Lawyers for Cicotte, Jackson, and Williams were noncommittal, keeping their options open about having their clients testify.

15

THE BLACK SOX DEFENSE

Denial was the watchword of the Zelcer defense. Taking the stand in his own behalf, David Zelcer unequivocally denied any involvement in the plot to rig the 1919 World Series.[1] Most particularly, Zelcer denied that he had posed as someone named Bennett during the Fall Classic. Burns and Maharg, whom the accused claimed never to have laid eyes on before they appeared in court, "have made a big mistake in saying I am the man they knew as Bennett."[2] Zelcer also denied any connection to codefendant Zork, a stranger to him until the two men had been charged and met at the courthouse.[3] Nor did Zelcer know Arnold Rothstein.[4] And Zelcer had never even heard of New York's Ansonia Hotel prior to being indicted.[5] Zelcer did acknowledge being acquainted with Abe Attell, but was evasive about contact with him during the 1919 World Series until confronted with the register of the Sinton Hotel by Special Prosecutor Prindiville. Zelcer then admitted that he had shared a room at the Sinton with Attell, the Levi brothers, Jack Davis, and Sam Lauswick while the first two Series games were played in Cincinnati.[6]

To counteract prosecution testimony that placed him in conference with other Series fixers on September 28, 1919, Zelcer provided a narrative of his whereabouts on that date. That afternoon, Zelcer, Ben Levi, and Davis had attended the White Sox-Tigers game at Comiskey Park. The trio then took the train to Cincinnati, registering at the Sinton Hotel under their own names upon arrival.[7] While there, Zelcer never encountered Burns or Maharg, much less engaged in fix-related activity with them, though he had now conceded his presence at the Sinton on the dates that Burns and Maharg placed him there.[8] Returning to Chicago for Game Three, Zelcer had become ill and was confined to his bed at the Sherman Hotel for the remainder of the Series.[9] To bolster Zelcer's version of events, his lawyers then introduced hotel records, medical bills, and other documentary evidence.[10] The Zelcer defense also presented Sherman Hotel desk clerk Harold Schwind, who produced ledger accounts that seemed to indicate that Zelcer had paid his bill at the hotel in Chicago on the same date that Burns testified about meeting fix conspirators including Bennett (Zelcer) in New York.[11] With that, the defense of David Zelcer rested, yielding the floor to the Zork forces.

Electing to keep their client off the witness stand, Zork lawyers pursued a twofold strategy: (1) attack the credibility of principal accuser Harry Redmon, while (2) portraying Zork, ostensibly a manufacturer of women's apparel, as a pillar of the community. Summoned for the former task were two respectable newspapermen who had been in Zork's company on the evening of his alleged encounter with Redmon at the Morrison Hotel. E.P. Melrose, financial secretary of *The Morning Press* of Logansport, Indiana, testified that he and Zork had dined with Joe Pesch and Redmon on the evening in question. While the four were in the hotel grill room, there had been "a general discussion of baseball with some reference to the poor playing of the White Sox," recalled Melrose. But Zork had "said nothing at all about a plot to throw [Series] games nor did anyone else." Nor did Zork "brag about having fixed the games."[12] After dinner, Melrose and Zork left the grill room and met *St. Louis Times* sports editor Sid Keener in the lobby.[13] Later that evening, Melrose accompanied Zork to the station, where the two men caught the train to St. Louis — all of this occurring at about the same time that Redmon had Zork boasting about fixing the Series.[14] In addition to substantive testimony directly contradicting that of Redmon, the Melrose appearance also started a procession of character witness, all of whom attested to Zork's civic virtue. When given their chance, prosecutors were unable to undermine Melrose's credibility, doing scant more than badgering the witness about knowledge of Zork's association with Henry "Kid" Becker, a notorious Midwestern gambler, recently murdered.[15] Melrose knew little about that and specifically denied that Zork had ever spoken to him about any Becker/Zork joint effort to corrupt ballplayers.[16]

The appearance of Sid Keener continued the defense assault upon the Redmon testimony. Like Melrose, Keener had spent time with Zork at the Morrison Hotel and had not heard the braggadocio about fixing the World Series attributed to the accused. At about the time that Redmon claimed Zork was making his dinner table boast, Keener testified that he and Zork were playing billiards in an auxiliary hall of the hotel.[17] Thereafter, Zork took the train to St. Louis.[18] Not content with the testimony of two fact witness who had "scored heavily,"[19] the Zork defense then pressed the attack on Redmon's credability via some secondhand defamation. Chicago newsman Gregory T. Dillon and Zork senior defense counsel A. Morgan Frumberg both took the stand to relate that White Sox attorney Alfred Austrian had, indeed, called Redmon a blackmailer who had tried to shake down club management.[20]

This last bit of testimony evidently provoked 2nd ASA Gorman beyond endurance. Gorman's cross-examination of Frumberg grew so testy that the two men, both experienced litigators pushing 50, almost came to blows.[21] Meanwhile, real violence was breaking out down the corridor, where Judge McDonald was filling in for another jurist in an acrimonious property dispute case. Upset about being found in contempt, defendant Harry Kellogg, an off-duty suburban patrolman, withdrew his service revolver and began firing. Kellogg's first shot whizzed over McDonald's head. His second fatally wounded plaintiff's attorney Lemuel Ashley and set off a courtroom stampede that resulted in numerous injured spectators. Kellogg then turned the revolver on himself.[22] When the gunsmoke cleared and courthouse proceedings were permitted to resume, the Zork defense restarted its parade of character witnesses, upward of twenty in all, including insurance broker J.C. Punch, jeweler J.H. Lowenblatt, former judge and current St. Louis mayoral candidate John K. Talty, and furniture dealer Fred Roosenfeld. All testified that Zork was an honest and law-abiding citizen.[23]

The torch was then passed to the defense of the Black Sox players, with the Gandil defense going first. As a prelude to the much-anticipated testimony by the accused players, defense counsel O'Brien called Gandil's former teammates Nemo Leibold and Shano Collins, as well as the Reds Dutch Ruether, all presumably in order to prove the publicly declared defense contention that the Series had been honestly contested.[24] But efforts to elicit the witnesses' expert opinion regarding the caliber of the performance of the Black Sox were stymied when Judge Friend sustained a prosecution objection to this line of inquiry.[25] Given that a trial lawyer of O'Brien's ability and experience would never have sought opinions on this subject unless utterly confident that it would be beneficial to his client, prosecution concerns were doubtless well-founded.[26] But in retrospect, the court's ruling appears legally dubious, as the prerequisites for expert opinion on the integrity of defendants' World Series play were seemingly met. More particularly, (1) all three witnesses manifestly possessed the necessary expertise; (2) the subject was beyond the understanding of the casual, at most, baseball fans seated on the jury; and (3) expert opinion on the integrity of Black Sox play indisputably addressed an important issue in the case. Nevertheless, the court refused to allow it. The defense had better luck when White Sox club secretary Harry Grabiner was recalled to the stand. Grabiner's portrait of team finances — gross revenues had risen from $521,175.76 in 1919 to $910,306.59 for the 1920 season with a corresponding jump in profits[27] — was both revelatory and powerful, effectively eviscerating the claim that Comiskey and the corporate franchise had suffered injury from the outcome of the 1919 World Series.[28]

The defense then hurled bricks at the testimony of Bill Burns, focusing primarily on his assertion that he had met with the corrupted players at the Sinton Hotel on the morning before Game One. Manager Gleason and Clean Sox Eddie Collins, Ray Schalk, Roy Wilkinson, and Dickie Kerr were trooped in to help portray Burns as a liar on this point.[29] With varying degrees of certainty, each witness placed the Black Sox contingent at practice in Redland Field on the morning in question.[30] In mitigation of the dismal Series play of Swede Risberg (an .080 batting average and shaky play in the field), the defense then presented White Sox team trainer Harry "Doc" Stephenson, who revealed that Risberg had complained of a chest cold prior to Game One and been given some unspecified medicine.[31] Defense counsel O'Brien then retrained his fire on Burns, producing apartment superintendent Albert Kafka, who testified that at the time the 1919 World Series was played, Chick Gandil and his wife were tenants at 4295 Grand Boulevard.[32] The government's assertion that Gandil had lodged at the Warner Hotel during the Series (as per the testimony of Bill Burns and other prosecution evidence) was also contradicted through the introduction of hotel records showing that Gandil had not been registered at the Warner.[33]

With the stage now finally set for the promised testimony of the accused players, the Gandil defense abruptly rested. No further evidence was offered by the other Black Sox either, all of whom simultaneously rested their cases as well. Little public explanation was provided for this unanticipated change in defense strategy. All that could be gotten from counsel was the comment that it was not necessary to put the players on the witness stand because the "state has made no case."[34]

Caught off guard by the quick close of the defense case, prosecutors scrambled to collect their rebuttal witnesses. But the absence of a defense by most of the accused made presentation of rebuttal legally tenuous, since there was no defense evidence to rebut regarding those defendants. Generally speaking, rebuttal is restricted to evidence that tends to disprove or contradict proof presented by the opposing side. In a criminal case, the prosecution may offer rebuttal after all defendants have rested. Rebuttal, however, does not afford the prosecution a second chance to present evidence that should have been presented in its initial case-in-chief. For this reason, the belated presentation of Joe Gedeon as a prosecution witness was prohibited by the court.[35] Nor was Judge Friend impressed by prosecution excuses for failure to call *Chicago Evening American* reporter Harry Reutlinger during its direct case. Prosecutors claimed, implausibly, that they had only just learned of the published out-of-court confession given by Felsch to the reporter some eleven months earlier. In barring testimony by Reutlinger, the court scolded prosecutors, declaring that "negligence in the State's Attorneys Office should not jeopardize a defendant's liberty. You should have brought in this testimony during your case-in-chief. It is not rebuttal evidence."[36]

The court was also ill-disposed to a prosecution application to recall defendant Zelcer to the stand for further cross-examination.[37] The State, however, would be permitted to impeach the Zelcer testimony via the introduction of additional evidence regarding the Sherman Hotel. This precipitated the return of hotel clerk Schwind, who testified that one N.E. Zelcer had also been registered at the Sherman in September 1919. Schwind disclosed that the accounts of both Zelcers had been settled on September 28, 1919, but he was now unsure if David had actually been at the hotel on that date, as he had testified previously.[38] The proof phase of the Black Sox case then closed with the State's recall of Alfred Austrian for elicitation of an evidential trifle: formal denial that he had ever referred to Harry Redmon as a blackmailer in the presence of reporter Dillon or defense counsel Frumberg.[39]

Notes

1. As reported in the *Boston Globe, Chicago Daily Journal* and *Chicago Herald Examiner,* July 28, 1921, and elsewhere.
2. As quoted in the *Des Moines Register* and *Washington Post,* July 28, 1921.
3. As per the *Chicago Daily Journal* and *Chicago Herald Examiner,* July 28, 1921.
4. As per the *New York Times,* July 28, 1921.
5. *Ibid.*
6. As reported in the *New York Times* and *Washington Post,* July 28, 1921.
7. As per the *Chicago Daily Journal* and *Chicago Herald Examiner,* July 28, 1921. See also, *Washington Post,* July 28, 1921.
8. As noted in the *New York Times,* July 28, 1921.
9. As reported in the *Washington Post,* July 28, 1921. The impressions made by Zelcer while on the witness stand differed markedly. To one press observer, Zelcer "was nervous while testifying and continually rubbed perspiration from his face," as reported in the *New York Times,* July 28, 1921. To another, "Zelcer's statements were made without hesitation and he answered questions on cross-examination promptly," as per the *Washington Post,* July 28, 1921.
10. As reported in the *Des Moines Register, New York Times* and *Washington Post,* July 28, 1921.
11. As per the *Chicago Daily Journal* and *Chicago Herald Examiner,* July 28, 1921, and *Washington Post,* July 29, 1921.
12. As reported in the *Chicago Daily News,* July 28, 1921. See also, *Chicago Daily Journal,* July 28, 1921, for a variant of this testimony.
13. As per the *Chicago Daily News,* July 28, 1921.
14. As per the *Chicago Evening American* and *Des Moines Register,* July 28, 1921.
15. As reported in the *Des Moines Evening Tribune,* July 28, 1921. Various Black Sox authors relate that the fix of the 1919 World Series had been conceived the year before by Becker who wanted to rig the 1918 Red Sox–Cubs match, but could not raise the cash in time to do it. See e.g., Pietrusza, *Rothstein,* 159–160; Dellinger, 178. After Becker was shot to death in April 1919, his ambitions were supposedly carried forward by acolytes Zork and Franklin.

16. As reported in the *Chicago Herald Examiner* and *Des Moines Evening Tribune,* July 29, 1921.

17. As per the *Chicago Daily Journal,* July 28, 1921.

18. As reported in the *Chicago Herald Examiner* and *Des Moines Daily Capital,* July 28, 1921, and *Chicago Evening American,* July 29, 1921. From available press accounts, it appears that the Keener testimony was confined to the impeachment of Harry Redmon. The jury did not learn of the investigation of fix rumors conducted personally by the young St. Louis sports editor. Well prior to trial, Keener offered his findings — based largely on admissions by the Browns' Joe Gedeon that wholly exonerated Zork — to both sides in the criminal case. But only the Zork defense took up the offer. Defense counsel A. Morgan Frumberg subsequently provided detailed affidavits by Keener and Zork to White Sox attorney Alfred Austrian. These documents ultimately found their way to Cook County prosecutors via Johnson lawyer Charles V. Barrett, and are now preserved in CHM, Black Sox file, Box 1, Folder 2. A July 26, 1921, letter by Keener to AL President Johnson tartly defending his appearance at trial for the Zork defense is contained in the Black Sox file at the Giamatti Research Center.

19. In the estimation of the *Chicago Daily News,* July 29, 1921.

20. As reported in the *Chicago Daily Journal* and *Chicago Evening Post,* July 29, 1921.

21. Hours later, Gorman asked that his cross-examination be stricken from the record and apologized to Frumberg, as per the *Chicago Herald Examiner,* July 29, 1921.

22. As reported in the *Chicago Evening Post,* July 29, 1921, *Chicago Tribune,* July 30, 1921, and elsewhere. Kellogg survived his self-inflicted gunshot wound, only to commit suicide in his jail cell some months later, as reported in the *Chicago Tribune,* February 21, 1922.

23. As reported in the *Chicago Daily Journal,* July 29, 1921.

24. At the outset of the trial, defense counsel Berger had informed the press, "We expect to prove by the teammates of those accused players that there was no crooked playing. We will ask the umpires if they detected anything off-color and the same question will be asked of the Cincinnati players," as quoted in the *Chicago Tribune,* July 9, 1921.

25. As reported in the *Chicago Daily Journal,* July 28, 1921, *Chicago Tribune,* July 29, 1921, and elsewhere.

26. Prosecution unease about the testimony was doubtless heightened by the cordial hallway greetings exchanged with the Black Sox when Manager Gleason and certain Clean Sox were summoned to the courthouse earlier in the proceedings.

27. As reported in the *Chicago Daily Journal* and *Chicago Daily News,* July 29, 1921, and newspapers nationwide.

28. During a visit to chambers sometime after the trial, jury foreman Barry told Judge Friend that the Grabiner testimony about the robust health of post-fix White Sox finances had been the most influential proof received by the jury in the entire case. See Eliot Asinof Papers, circa 1963 Asinof-Friend interview, in the white penny notebook, Chicago History Museum.

29. When pressed, Burns had equivocated on the date/time of the meeting but drawing attention to such ambiguity in the Burns testimony served no defense purpose.

30. As reported in the *Chicago Tribune* and *New York Times,* July 29, 1921, and elsewhere. While on the stand, Ray Schalk was briefly converted into a prosecution witness, placing the Black Sox players together in a Sinton Hotel room after the playing of Game Two, as per the *New York Times,* July 29, 1921.

31. As reported in the *New York Times,* July 29, 1921. See, also, *Des Moines Evening Tribune,* July 29, 1921.

32. As reported in the *Chicago Daily Journal,* July 29, 1921.

33. As per the *Boston Globe* and *Washington Post,* July 29, 1921.

34. As per an unidentified defense lawyer quoted in the *Chicago Evening Post,* July 29, 1921.

35. As reported in the *Atlanta Constitution* and *New York Times,* July 30, 1921.

36. As quoted in the *Des Moines Evening Tribune,* July 29, 1921, and *Atlanta Constitution.* July 30, 1921. See, also, *Chicago Evening Post,* July 29, 1921. As defendant Felsch had presented no defense, the court's ruling was legally sound.

37. As reported in the *Chicago Evening Post,* July 29, 1921.

38. N.E. was probably Nathan, the youngest of the four gambling Zelcer brothers. For an informative sketch of the Zelcer clan, see Ralph Christian, "Beyond Eight Men Out: The Des Moines Connection to the Black Sox Scandal," SABR annual conference presentation, 2003. Christian also relates that Zelcer's claim about attending a White Sox game on the date of the Ansonia Hotel fix meeting "was confirmed by a witness" at trial. The witness is not named by Christian but would seemingly have to have been Jack Davis. No mention of testimony by Davis, however, was found in the trial reportage reviewed by the author.

39. As per the *Chicago Daily Journal,* July 29, 1921. See also, *Atlanta Constitution,* July 29, 1921.

16

Closing Words, Verdict and the Landis Edict

As lengthy summations by counsel were a courthouse staple in the Black Sox era, ten hours were allotted to each side for closing arguments to the jury.[1] The order of presentation would be: prosecution, defense, prosecution rebuttal (with no separate closing address on behalf of the American League as an independent party to the proceedings). Special Prosecutor Prindiville delivered the State's primary address, taking the jury back through the events attending the conspiracy to fix the Series. In the process, Prindiville concentrated his arguments on defendants Gandil, Cicotte, Williams, Jackson, and Zelcer.[2] Prindiville took only a passing swipe at Risberg, deriding his purported World Series cold as "an overdose of conspiracy in his hide,"[3] with no individual denunciations of Weaver, Felsch, or Zork mentioned in newspaper coverage of the Prindiville summation. Anticipating defense attacks on star prosecution witness Bill Burns, the prosecutor emphasized the congruity between the fix as described in the Burns testimony and the fix details provided by the confessing players, especially Cicotte.[4] Prindiville identified Gandil as the ringleader of the corrupted players,[5] but reserved his scorn for Cicotte who, after demanding his fix payoff at the Warner Hotel, "Judas-like went down the stairs to hob-nob with his innocent teammates ... to allay the suspicions of the men he had just betrayed."[6]

As "Williams and Jackson have admitted their guilt," Prindiville continued, the jury had no choice but to "go the limit in punishing them."[7] The same was true for Zelcer, the fix representative and "self-styled lieutenant of Arnold Rothstein," the financier of the affair.[8] Prindiville tore into Zelcer's alibi defense, stressing the evidence that connected the Des Moines gambler to absent fix villain Abe Attell.[9] The prosecutor then closed his remarks with words calculated to strike a chord with jurors in the violence-weary Cook County of 1921:

> These men are killers. They conspired to kill baseball, to murder our greatest sport, to defraud the public and their comrades — even to defraud the children of this country — your children and my children who pay their bleacher admission fee to watch their heroes play a game they believe to be honest.
>
> A murderer deserves the utmost in punishment. Eddie Cicotte, Joe Jackson, Happy Felsch, Buck Weaver, Charles Risberg, Claude Williams, Chick Gandil and these gamblers conspired to murder baseball and I demand that you twelve gentlemen inflict the maximum punishment of a $2,000 fine and five years in the penitentiary on each of them.[10]

The next day and a half was consumed by speeches from defense counsel, beginning with Zork co-counsel Henry Berger. At first, Berger took a legalistic approach, pointing out that Illinois had only recently enacted a sports corruption statute and that no such law had been in force when the 1919 World Series was played.[11] Thus, conviction of the accused would be unfair. From there, Berger launched the initial defense strike against Burns and Maharg, the prosecution's "two aces in the hole: Burns, the club who knocks, and Maharg, the spade who dug up Burns."[12] The Zork summation was then taken up by senior counsel A. Morgan Frumberg, who resumed the task of identifying wrongdoers other than the accused. To Frumberg, the malefactor-in-chief was AL President Ban Johnson, accused of having protected fix financier Arnold Rothstein. Also denounced by counsel was the escape of reputed Rothstein henchmen Attell, Sullivan, and Brown. Decrying the prosecution of the beleaguered defendants in the courtroom, Frumberg asked the jury: "Why were these underpaid ballplayers, these penny-ante gamblers from Des Moines and St. Louis who bet a few nickels perhaps on the World Series, brought here to be the goats in this case?" Taking no chance on his audience's reply, Frumberg immediately rejoined, "Ask the powers of baseball. Ask Ban Johnson."[13]

Little newsprint was devoted to the closing of Zelcer attorney Max Luster, who focused upon the alibi defense of his client. According to counsel, that evidence disproved the Burns/Maharg claim that Zelcer was the Series fixer known as Bennett.[14] Considerably more newspaper coverage was afforded the summation of James C. O'Brien, lead attorney of the Gandil defense. Picking up on the Frumberg theme, O'Brien lambasted Ban Johnson, portraying him as anxious to conceal the endemic scope of gambling in baseball by having the Series fix depicted as an aberrant event.[15] As for the accused players, O'Brien maintained that their status in the eyes of the public stood undiminished, for "these boys are not fallen idols or broken idols. Send them back to Comiskey Park and listen to the applause that will come from the grandstand."[16]

Michael Ahern, associate counsel for Weaver, Felsch, and Risberg, unleashed an all-out attack on Johnson, the sinister hand behind the proceedings against the players. Said Ahern: "The State's attorneys have no more control over the prosecution than a bat boy has over the direction of play at a World Series game."[17] Nor was Ahern a fan of Billy Maharg: "He lied. He makes me think of a drink of moonshine. It looks good but when you drink it, it gives you a stomach ache."[18] Partner Thomas Nash continued the vilification of Johnson, accused of orchestrating the prosecution of White Sox stars in order to ruin a personal enemy, team owner Comiskey.[19] Johnson also was accountable, Nash charged, for the prosecution's failure to put Joe Gedeon and Joe Pesch on the witness stand. The AL President was fearful that the two might turn on the State and "tell the truth."[20]

Ben Short, the veteran trial lawyer retained by Joe Jackson and Lefty Williams, completed the defense summations.[21] Like Berger, Short offered a technical defense to the charges — the absence of proof that the defendants intended to injure or defraud anyone. Short maintained that neither the White Sox franchise nor the game itself would have suffered injury had the conspiracy remained a secret as the fixers had intended.[22] Shifting gears, Short then asserted that even if there had been a plot to throw the 1919 World Series, the statistics posted by his clients, as well as those of Weaver and Cicotte, belied their participation in it.[23] The Short summation also included the obligatory denunciation of the AL president. Over vehement objection, Short told the jurors that they, Judge Friend, and defense counsel were the only persons in the courtroom "not under Ban Johnson's thumb."[24]

The rebuttal remarks of 2nd ASA George Gorman were mercifully brief. The State, he declared, had presented "such a conclusive case that a long address was unnecessary."[25]Accordingly, Gorman confined his comments mostly to a defense of Comiskey's conduct in the affair and a reminder to the jury that Cicotte, Jackson, and Williams had confessed to the charges.[26] The highlight of the Gorman closing came when he invoked the plight of fans who had so eagerly come to see Cicotte pitch Game One. Observed Gorman, "They came to see a ball game. But all they saw was a con game."[27] And with that, the oratory in the Black Sox case came to a close.

Delivery of the court's final instructions to the jury was delayed by legal haggling over the more than 300 separate requests to charge submitted by counsel.[28] It was, therefore, midway through the afternoon of August 2, 1921 before Judge Friend was able to render the court's charge. For the most part, its précis text has not survived. Certain aspects of its content, however, were obligatory and hence can readily be reconstructed. The jury, for instance, would have been advised of bedrock criminal trial principles such as the presumption of innocence accorded the accused and the burden of proof placed on the prosecution. Regarding the latter, conviction would demand unanimous juror satisfaction that a particular charge against a particular defendant had been proved beyond a reasonable doubt.[29] In the Black Sox case, essentially eight criminal charges were ultimately submitted to the jury. All were variations of a single offense: conspiracy to defraud.[30] Because neither the common law nor the Illinois statute version of the crime required establishment of an overt act, the offenses would have been committed by a particular defendant the instant that he agreed to join the plot to throw the Series.[31] Thereafter, commission of the offense could not be undone by a defendant's failure to perform his part in the plot. This is because: (1) conspiracy is a criminal offense separate and distinct from the crime that is the conspiracy's objective, and (2) the offense of conspiracy is virtually irrevocable; once the agreement that is the essence of the crime is reached, it can almost never be rescinded.[32]

Theoretically at least, the law worked greatly to prosecution advantage. From a strictly legal standpoint, whether or not Jackson had played the Series to win and whether or not Cicotte had abandoned the fix after hitting the Reds leadoff batter in Game One were questions entirely irrelevant to the determination of their guilt or innocence. If either Jackson or Cicotte, or any other defendant, had agreed to participate in the plot to rig the Series outcome, their guilt was legally established — with one caveat. In what some commentators viewed as a major victory for the defense, Judge Friend had agreed with the contention that conviction required more than proof of simply an agreement to throw the 1919 World Series. To sustain a guilty verdict, prosecution evidence would also have to establish that in agreeing to fix the Series outcome, the accused had done so with the conscious intent of defrauding the public and/or the other victims specified in the indictments. More particularly, the court informed the jury, "The State must prove that it was the intent of the ballplayers and the gamblers charged with conspiracy through the throwing of the World Series to defraud the public and others, and not merely to throw games."[33] Shortly afterward, the jury was excused to consider its verdict.

Following deliberations of two hours and forty-seven minutes and the casting of a single ballot, the jurors informed bailiffs that a verdict had been reached. Another forty-two minutes, however, were required to round up the lawyers, defendants, and Judge Friend.[34] At approximately 11:22 P.M., the first verdict was announced by the court clerk: "We, the jury, find the defendant Claude Williams — Not Guilty."[35] The several hundred defense supporters packing the courtroom erupted in joy. After order was restored, the verdict poll continued to the drumbeat of Not Guilty — as to all defendants on all

Eddie Cicotte (1), Chick Gandil (2), David Zelcer (3), Michael Ahern (4), Max Luster (5), James C. O'Brien (6), Swede Risberg (7), Lefty Williams (8), Joe Jackson (9), Henry Berger (10), Carl Zork (11), J.J. Cooke (12), Daniel Cassidy (13), Benedict Short (14), and Thomas D. Nash (15) gather on the courthouse steps with shirtsleeved jurors and other well-wishers to celebrate the not guily verdicts.

charges. After the final acquittal was recorded, Judge Friend congratulated the jury, terming their verdict a just one.[36] With that, all restraint in the courtroom dissolved. Eddie Cicotte ran over to shake the hand of jury foreman Barry, while the other defendants warmly congratulated one another.[37] Hats and papers soared through the air, with courtroom attendants abandoning efforts to restore decorum after noticing the smile on Judge Friend's face. They, too, then joined the celebration.[38] For the next five minutes, "the courtroom was a love feast, as the jurors, lawyers and the defendants clapped each other on the back and exchanged congratulations."[39] Jurors then hoisted Jackson, Williams, and several other defendants on their shoulders and paraded them around the courtroom[40] before the celebrants finally gathered on the courthouse steps for a smiling group photo.[41]

When later asked by reporters for his reaction to the verdict, Cicotte declined, playfully invoking the unhappy consequences of the last time that he had spoken at the courthouse.[42] Others were not so reticent. Before slipping from the courthouse, Chick Gandil offered AL President Johnson "a sailor's farewell. Goodbye. Good luck. And to hell with you."[43] Buck Weaver was more effusive: "I knew I'd be cleared and I'm glad the public stood by me until the trial was over."[44] He then added, "Everybody knew I had nothing to do with the conspiracy. I believe that I should get my old position back. I'm going to fight for it."[45] No such intention was voiced by Joe Jackson ,who declared that he was "through with organized ball" and was weighing other employment opportunities, including a return to the vaudeville stage.[46] The comments of Happy Felsch and Lefty Williams were also muted. Felsch said little more than that he was "tickled to death" about the trial's outcome,[47] while Williams deemed the verdict a "true" one, adding that he was proud to have "come through clean."[48] The gamblers were mostly closed-mouthed, David Zelcer only repeating his courtroom denial of acquaintance with Arnold Rothstein and opining that acquittal was "the only kind of verdict that the jury could have returned."[49]

Crushed by the totality of their defeat, prosecutors had little to say. "We did our best," said a glum George Gorman. "But I did my talking to the jury."[50] This surrendered press attention to defense counsel Henry Berger, who theatrically described the verdict as nothing less than "a complete vindication of the most mistreated ballplayers in history."[51] Once outside the courthouse, jurors declined to comment on their verdict.[52] Instead, they repaired to a nearby Italian restaurant to wind down privately. There, by some coincidence, a number of the men on whom the jurors had just passed judgment had also gathered for a party. Upon discovering each other, the two groups promptly merged. Juror resolve to remain silent apparently evaporated soon afterward. Opening up regarding the trial, one unidentified juror related that, "We thought the State presented a weak case. It was dependent on Bill Burns and Burns did not make a favorable impression on us."[53] The panel was also displeased that the trial had been allowed to take so long. "We felt from the time that the State finished that we could not return any verdict other than not guilty," the anonymous juror added.[54] But disdain of Burns, and presumably Maharg as well, does not satisfactorily explain the jury's verdict — at least as it pertains to the acquittals of Cicotte, Jackson, and Williams. Each of these defendants had confessed the essential element of the conspiracy charges lodged against him: agreement to commit an unlawful act.[55] In addition, Cicotte, Jackson, and Williams had each admitted accepting a substantial cash payment in return for that agreement. The fact, moreover, that Cicotte, Jackson, and Williams had named teammates *Blank* as fix co-conspirators had an ineradicable spillover effect on them and the other accused, the instructions of Judge Friend about confining the confession evidence to the individual confessor notwithstanding.

Author note: These circumstances tend to posit that the Cicotte, Jackson, and Williams verdicts in that courtroom phenomenon that all prosecutors dread: jury nullification. Jury nullification is a jury's "knowing and deliberate rejection of evidence or refusal to apply the law either because the jury wants to send a message about some social issue that is larger than the case itself or because the result dictated by law is contrary to the jury's sense of justice, morality or fairness."[56] The potential for jury nullification is increased where, as in the Black Sox case, the prosecution is significantly grounded in accomplice testimony, a form of evidence that jurors, unlike news reporters, tend not to esteem or credit.[57] Or in matters in which the jurors identify with the accused, not the alleged victim. From the outset of the trial, Black Sox lawyers assiduously cultivated the working-class men on the jury, portraying the defendants as the underpaid laborers of a rich and unfeeling employer, whose business had not been injured by the reputed fix of the 1919 World Series. Indeed, while the defendants had lost their livelihood, Charles Comiskey and the White Sox corporation were flourishing, as established by club secretary Harry Grabiner's testimony about burgeoning team revenues in the aftermath of the 1919 Series outcome.[58] This strategy evidently had its intended effect. Juror bonding with the accused was reflected in the post-verdict sentiments of another unnamed panel member, who was quoted as telling Eddie Cicotte that "I know that every man on this jury hopes that the next time he sees you that you will be at the center of the diamond putting over strikes."[59] "And we'll be there in a box cheering for you and the rest of these boys, Eddie," added another juror.[60] Continued into early morning hours, the juror/defendant celebration reportedly ended with a chorus of "Hail, Hail, The Gang's All Here."[61]

Within 24 hours of the verdict, MLB Commissioner Kenesaw Mountain Landis banished the acquitted players from Organized Baseball.

Unfortunately for the acquitted men, the judgment of the Black Sox jurors was shared by few others. As observed by sports columnist H.G. Salsinger, "There has never been a jury verdict that has aroused such wide discussion and so much unfavorable comment."[62] A particularly frosty reception was accorded the trial's outcome by baseball's establishment. "They can't play for me," declared Comiskey.[63] Nor could Kid Gleason see any future in organized ball for the acquitted players.[64] Ban Johnson's attitude was revealed by the comment that "the fact that the outfit was freed by a Cook County jury does not alter the conditions one iota or minimize the magnitude of the offense."[65] To Johnson, "the players are as odious to a clean and right-thinking public as the thieves and crooks they dealt with."[66] More than a hint of the game's official response to the verdict was embodied in the remarks of PCL President William H. McCarthy, who dismissed the players' acquittal as "a technical verdict only ... [as] there was a question of whether throwing a baseball game constituted a crime in Illinois."[67] Notwithstanding the courtroom outcome, "The moral guilt of the players remains the same," asserted McCarthy. "The jury can throw buckets of whitewash on the players, but that will not affect their standing in organized baseball."[68]

But not all the news was bad for the Black Sox. The State's Attorneys Office was throwing in the towel, all lingering charges would be dismissed. "As far as I am concerned, the case is a closed book," declared State's Attorney Crowe.[69] Only the forlorn investigation into the disappearance of the grand jury material would continue.[70]

Then, the hammer fell on the Black Sox players. Quietly but keenly, major league baseball's new, all-powerful czar had been following the proceedings in Judge Friend's courtroom, reportedly receiving a transcript of the trial on a daily basis.[71] And before the jury's verdict had even been fully digested, Commissioner Landis acted. In his famous edict, Landis decreed,

> Regardless of the verdicts of juries, no player that throws a ball game; no player that undertakes or promises to throw a ball game; no player that sits in conference with a bunch of crooked ballplayers and gamblers where the ways and means of throwing games are planned and discussed and does not promptly tell his club about it, will ever play professional baseball.
>
> Of course, I don't know that any of these men will apply for reinstatement, but if they do, these are at least a few of the rules that will be enforced. Just keep in mind, regardless of the verdict of juries, baseball is entirely competent to protect itself against crooks, both inside and outside the game.[72]

With that, Joe Jackson, Eddie Cicotte, Buck Weaver and the others were consigned to the game's wilderness, playing out their careers in outlaw baseball.[73] Only Weaver, doggedly maintaining his innocence, would even seek reinstatement. But to no avail.[74] For certain of the Black Sox players, however, their acquittal was not a completely hollow victory. Rather, it would serve as the springboard for years of civil litigation against their erstwhile employer, Charles A. Comiskey.

Notes

1. As per the *Chicago Evening Post,* August 1, 1921. But see, *Chicago Tribune,* July 31, 1921, indicating that prosecutors were given only five hours for their closing arguments. Selected excerpts of prosecution and defense summations are posted at *http://www.law.umkc.edu/faculty/projects/ftrials/blacksox.trial summations.html.*
2. As noted by the *Boston Globe, Los Angeles Times* and *Washington Post,* July 30, 1921.
3. As per the *Chicago Herald Examiner* and *New York Times,* July 30, 1921.
4. As observed by the *Los Angeles Times,* July 30, 1921.
5. As per the *Atlanta Constitution* and *Los Angeles Times,* July 30, 1921.
6. As reported in the *Atlanta Constitution* and *Washington Post,* July 30, 1921, and elsewhere.
7. As per the *Atlanta Constitution* and *Boston Globe,* July 30, 1921.
8. As per the *Chicago Herald Examiner,* July 31, 1921.
9. As noted in the *Des Moines Daily News,* July 30, 1921, and *Atlanta Constitution* and *Boston Globe,* July 31, 1921.
10. As per the *Boston Globe* and *Washington Post,* July 31, 1921. The punishments sought by the prosecution were the legal maximums.
11. Again, the newly enacted Illinois sports anti-corruption statute would not take effect until July 1, 1922.
12. As quoted in the *Chicago Evening Post,* August 1, 1921. The Berger closing also alluded to the dismissal of the charges in the PCL scandal, employing the argument that "not every wrong constitutes a crime."
13. As quoted in the *Chicago Herald Examiner* and *Washington Post,* August 2, 1921, and elsewhere.
14. As summarized in the *Boston Globe* and *Washington Post,* August 2, 1921.
15. As per the *Chicago Evening Post* and *Chicago Herald Examiner,* August 2, 1921.
16. As quoted in the *Chicago Herald Examiner,* August 2, 1921.
17. As per the Black Sox summations website, 2.
18. *Ibid.* The Ahern summation also "delved into conspiracy law," according to the *Boston Globe* and *Washington Post,* August 2, 1921.
19. As per the *Washington Post,* August 2, 1921.
20. As reported in the *Boston Globe* and *Washington Post,* August 2, 1921.
21. The author was unable to locate any report of a summation by Cicotte counsel Daniel Cassidy. Presumably, the closing arguments of the Cicotte defense were covered by Short.
22. As per the *Chicago Evening Post,* August 2, 1921.
23. *Ibid.*
24. As reported in the *Boston Globe,* August 2, 1921.
25. As per the *New York Times,* August 3, 1921.
26. As per the Black Sox summations website, 2.
27. *Ibid.*
28. As reported in the *Chicago Herald Examiner,* August 2, 1921. A request to charge is a written submission that contains the precise language that a party wants the court to use in instructing the jury on a point of law. Not infrequently, such requests are a source

of contention that must be resolved by the court outside the jury's presence prior to the charge being given.

29. Proof beyond a reasonable doubt is the highest standard of proof in American jurisprudence and is reserved for criminal cases. In shorthand form, reasonable doubt is the state of mind that exists in the mind of a juror when, after a full consideration of the evidence, there is not an abiding certainty about the truth of the charges. See *Black's Law Dictionary,* 1380.

30. A capsule summary of the individual charges submitted to the jury was published in the *Los Angeles Times* and *New York Times,* August 3, 1921, and elsewhere.

31. In a pretrial ruling, Judge Friend had determined that the fixing of the 1919 World Series was a legally adequate predicate for the conspiracy charges, necessarily rejecting, in the process, the rationale of the Willis decision in the PCL case. By virtue of this determination, player failure to perform a contractual duty to play to the best of that player's skill and ability was more than just a breach of contract. In the context of the allegations made in the Black Sox proceedings, it was also a crime, provided, of course, that the other elements of the conspiracy charges were proved to the jury's satisfaction.

32. In most jurisdictions, conspiracy law recognizes a concept called renunciation. Renunciation is the complete and voluntary abandonment of criminal purpose before the crime is committed, usually coupled with announcement of that withdrawal to the other conspirators and/or an affirmative duty by the actor to thwart the success of the conspiracy. The concept of renunciation has no application in the Black Sox case, as the object of the conspiracy was achieved the moment co-conspirator Abe Attell or Sport Sullivan placed a bet with some unsuspecting White Sox backer prior to the start of Game One. And, once in motion, the conspiracy could not be undone or renounced, legally speaking, whatever the second thoughts of any of its participants.

33. As reported in the *Chicago Tribune* and *Los Angeles Times,* August 3, 1921, and elsewhere. In the view of some commentators, this aspect of the court's instructions virtually assured acquittal. See, e.g., James Kirby, "The Year They Fixed the World Series," *American Bar Association Journal,* February 1, 1988, 68: "If intent to throw games plus taking money, plus agreeing to lose and actually losing were not enough, the prosecution never had a chance. The law was simply inadequate for the Black Sox' offenses, even if the worst about them is believed."

34. As reported in the *Chicago Tribune* and *New York Times,* August 3, 1921, and elsewhere.

35. As per the *Chicago Tribune,* August 3, 1921.

36. As reported in the *Atlanta Constitution, Chicago Tribune* and *New York Times,* August 3, 1921, and elsewhere.

37. As per the *Atlanta Constitution* and *Chicago Tribune,* August 3, 1921.

38. As reported by the *Chicago Tribune* and *Los Angeles Times,* August 3, 1921.

39. As described by the *Chicago Tribune,* August 3, 1921.

40. As reported in the *Atlanta Constitution* and *New York Times,* August 3, 1921.

41. The photo was published in the *Chicago Tribune,* August 3, 1921.

42. As per the *Chicago Tribune,* August 3, 1921, referring to his self-incriminating grand jury appearance.

43. As quoted in the *Boston Globe* and *New York Times,* August 3, 1921, and elsewhere.

44. As per the *Atlanta Constitution* and *New York Times,* August 3, 1921.

45. As per the *Chicago Tribune,* August 3, 1921.

46. *Ibid.*

47. *Ibid.*

48. As reported in the *Los Angeles Times* and *New York Times,* August 3, 1921.

49. As per the *Chicago Tribune,* August 3, 1921.

50. *Ibid.*

51. As quoted in the *Boston Globe* and *New York Times,* August 3, 1921.

52. As reported in the *Chicago Tribune,* August 3, 1921.

53. As reported in the *Los Angeles Times,* August 3, 1921.

54. *Ibid.*

55. The argument that the jury's verdict turned on Judge Friend's instructions requiring that intent to "defraud the public and others" be demonstrated is unpersuasive to the author. Among other things, intent to defraud the public was self-evident, as surely no Sox backer would have bet his money with co-conspirators Attell and Sullivan if he knew the Series was rigged. Nor were the court's instructions cited as grounds for the not guilty verdict by anyone on the jury. Finally, the argument presupposes that highly charged criminal cases, such as the Black Sox case, are decided by juries on an intellectual basis, a proposition that many trial lawyers, as opposed to academics, would find contrary to their experience.

56. See *Black's Law Dictionary,* 936.

57. As a state court prosecutor, the author went 24 years (from 1982 until 2006) between using the testimony of a cooperating codefendant at a criminal trial.

58. See again, Note 28, Chapter 15, above, regarding the impact of the Grabiner testimony on the jury.

59. As quoted in the *Los Angeles Herald Examiner,* August 3, 1921.

60. As per the *Des Moines Evening Tribune,* August 3, 1921.

61. As reported in the *Des Moines Evening Tribune* and *Los Angeles Herald Examiner,* August 3, 1921.

62. As per *The Sporting News,* August 11, 1921. If in this regard only, there is a striking parallel between public rejection of the verdict in the Black Sox case and societal condemnation of the acquittal of O. J. Simpson in October 1995.

63. As reported in the *Chicago Evening Post,* August 3, 1921, and *Atlanta Constitution,* August 4, 1921.

64. As per the *Chicago Evening Post,* August 3, 1921.

65. As quoted in the *Chicago Evening Post,* August 3, 1921, and *Boston Globe* and *Los Angeles Times,* August 4, 1921.

66. As per the *Chicago Evening Post,* August 3, 1921, and *Atlanta Constitution,* August 4, 1921.

67. As reported in the *Los Angeles Times,* August 4, 1921.

68. *Ibid.* The same article reported Judge McDonald's disappointment with the verdict. The judge was consoled, however, by the belief that "those in control of baseball and club owners have decided for all times to keep the shady players from the game."

69. As reported in the *Boston Globe, Los Angeles Times* and *Washington Post,* August 4, 1921. But only days after being put in the clear in the Black Sox case, the incorrigible Abe Attell was back in police custody, arrested in Manhattan for unlawfully trying to resell a ticket after being evicted from the Polo Grounds, as per the *New York Times,* August 8, 1921, and *Los Angeles Times,* August 9, 1921.

70. As per the *Boston Globe, Los Angeles Times* and *Washington Post,* August 4, 1921. The investigation into the missing grand jury materials would come to naught.

71. As reported in the *Chicago Evening Post,* August 3, 1921.

72. As reported in newspapers nationwide.

73. In November, Joe Gedeon would join the Black Sox, permanently banished from organized baseball by Commissioner Landis, as reported in the *Chicago Tribune* and *New York Times,* November 4, 1921, and elsewhere.

74. Weaver's efforts to gain reinstatement are chronicled in Irving M. Stein, *The Ginger Kid: The Buck Weaver Story* (Dubuque: Brown & Benchmark, 1992), 274–279. But even a late-in-life Weaver petition supported by Judge Friend was fruitless.

17

Black Sox Lawsuits

Biding their time during the prosecution of the Black Sox case were counterstrokes contemplated by some of those charged. At various junctures in the proceedings, particularly when events seemed to favor the accused, player lawsuits were threatened against Charles Comiskey, the White Sox club, and major league baseball itself. The final impetus to such legal action was supplied by the post-acquittal blacklisting of the players by Commissioner Landis. In time, first Buck Weaver, and then Happy Felsch, Swede Risberg, and Joe Jackson, would file suit against the White Sox corporation. This, in turn, would compel Eddie Cicotte, Lefty Williams, Bill Burns, Billy Maharg, and other significant scandal figures to retell their stories. Ultimately, these lawsuits, like most civil litigation, would end in out-of-court settlements. But not before a perceptive, if somewhat misunderstood, judgment had been rendered by a civil jury sitting in Milwaukee and a treasure trove of scandal-related information had been generated for future Black Sox researchers.

Author Note: The cornerstone of this work's civil litigation narrative is the transcript of the 1924 Jackson v. White Sox breach-of-contract trial, reviewed at Chicago Baseball Museum offices. Regrettably, the author was not able to gain access to case-related pleadings possessed by the Cannon law firm of Milwaukee, but was the beneficiary of notes taken on these documents that were generously provided by Black Sox researcher Tim Newman of Austin, Texas. In addition, excerpts from the late Gene Carney's notes on civil case pleadings were supplied by Arlene Marcley, executive director of the Shoeless Joe Jackson Museum and Library in Greenville, South Carolina. Civil litigation material on file at the Chicago History Museum and the National Archives in Chicago, as well as pretrial pleadings embedded in the Jackson/White Sox trial transcript, were also utilized in reconstructing the civil litigation record. Contemporaneous newspaper reportage, particularly that published in Milwaukee, also proved highly useful.

The most assertive of the Black Sox defendants was always Buck Weaver, who maintained his innocence from the moment that his name surfaced in the scandal. Alone among the accused players, Weaver also sought reinstatement by baseball officialdom and a return to the big leagues, either with the White Sox or elsewhere. In the wake of the dismissal of the original indictments in March 1921, Weaver attorney Thomas D. Nash had announced that legal action would be taken if Weaver was not immediately restored to the Sox roster. If not reinstated, Weaver would initiate suit for the $7,250 salary due him for the 1921 season, the last of the handsome three-year deal that Weaver had inked in March 1919.[1] Nash would also utilize such litigation as a "test case to see if players are to be blacklisted by baseball which is no different than any other corporation."[2] Within days, however, plans for such action had to be shelved when Weaver and the other Sox players were recharged in superseding indictments.

A challenge to the "constitutionality of organized baseball" was promised by Nash in response to the banishment of the Black Sox following their acquittal that August. Nash planned to ground such litigation in the argument that baseball was "a trust ruled by an oligarchy."[3] Incorporated into the proposed suit, moreover, might be claims of defamation for injury to the banned players' reputations.[4] But when litigation was actually commenced by Weaver, it bore little resemblance to the suit advertised by Nash. All Weaver requested was $20,000. Filed in Chicago Municipal Court by new Weaver attorneys Charles A. Williams and Julian C. Ryer on October 18, 1921, the Weaver suit sought only monetary damages attributed to the White Sox' failure to pay Weaver his salary for the 1921 season.[5] The suit also laid claim to a $685.80 share of 1920 second-place team money withheld from Weaver.[6] Upon being served with the complaint, Sox lawyers[7] immediately petitioned for removal of the action to federal court on diversity of citizenship grounds, the White Sox then being incorporated in Wisconsin. The application was unopposed and an order of transfer was promptly entered by Municipal Court Judge George B. Holmes on October 22, 1921. All further proceedings in the suit would be conducted in the United States District Court for the Northern District of Illinois.[8]

With the consent of the Weaver attorneys, the deadline for the White Sox to file an answer to the complaint was extended. When submitted on February 9, 1922, the club's response denied indebtedness to plaintiff Weaver, maintaining that he was properly discharged from White Sox employ pursuant to the termination clause in his contract.[9] More particularly, the Sox answer asserted that Weaver had been contractually obligated to provide "his best services" as a ballplayer and was subject to fine, suspension, or termination of his contract if he failed to render his services "in the manner provided."[10]

Weaver had violated this requirement of his contract by conspiring with others to throw the 1919 World Series. Termination of the Weaver contract, furthermore, was not only a remedy afforded by the plaintiff's contract. The team maintained that it was also an action compelled by the American League Constitution of February 16, 1910, which mandated the expulsion of any franchise that failed to terminate a player who had conspired to lose a league game.[11] As for Weaver's continued play in a White Sox uniform during the 1920 season, this was excused by the club's lack of knowledge of the plaintiff's treachery until late–September 1920.[12] Following the submission of the White Sox' answer, visible proceedings in the Weaver suit abated, overtaken by events emanating from Milwaukee.

Firebrand Milwaukee attorney Raymond J. Cannon instituted civil suits on behalf of Happy Felsch, Swede Risberg, and Joe Jackson against the White Sox in Spring 1922.

The Spring of 1922 saw the initiation of civil suits by Black Sox who had been accorded far less public sympathy than Buck Weaver.[13] The first of these was an action instituted on behalf of Happy Felsch by firebrand plaintiff's attorney Raymond J. Cannon. Filed in the Circuit Court of Wisconsin, Milwaukee County, on April 26, 1922, the suit sought back pay and bonuses withheld by the White Sox.[14] As later amended, the Felsch complaint asserted four discrete damage claims. Sought were: (1) a $1,300 balance allegedly due Felsch on his 1920 contract; (2) a withheld $1,500 bonus for being a member of the 1917 World Series-winning White Sox team (the amount being the difference between the official $3,500 winners' share and the $5,000 purportedly promised Sox players by Comiskey if they won the Series); (3) injury to Felsch's professional reputation arising from the unfounded assertion that he was a participant in the fixing of the 1919 World Series; and (4) restraint upon Felsch's livelihood caused by a conspiracy to blacklist him and thereby prevent Felsch from playing organized baseball anywhere in the United States. The aggregate damages for the latter two causes of action were placed at $100,000.[15]

On or about May 12, 1922, civil actions in the Milwaukee circuit court were filed by Cannon on behalf of Swede Risberg and Joe Jackson.[16] The Risberg complaint was essentially a reprise of the Felsch pleading. But the Jackson suit was different, grounded in breach of contract. Jackson had signed a three-year, $8,000-per-season pact with the White Sox in February 1920 and had not been paid since the contract was voided by Comiskey in March 1921. The Gravamen of the Jackson complaint was fraud and overreaching by club secretary Harry Grabiner, who was accused of having taken advantage of the plaintiff's illiteracy to retain a termination clause in the contract that Jackson had been led to believe had been deleted. In addition to $16,000 in unpaid wages for the 1921 and 1922 seasons, the suit sought the disputed $1,500 World Series bonus for playing on the 1917 Series winner and the $100,000 defamation and restraint on livelihood damages claimed by Felsch and Risberg.[17]

Once the suits were filed, it was not long before brickbats began to fly, with lead plaintiff Felsch becoming the primary target of lawsuit critics. AL President Johnson denounced the litigation. Said Ban, "Felsch and the other indicted Sox ... are seizing this straw to get money out of organized baseball but they won't get a cent."[18] Grabiner also went after Felsch, informing the press, "There is no truth to the charges made by Felsch ... a discredited player kicked out of the game because he betrayed his employer."[19] Shortly afterward, White Sox supporters set their sights on Buck Weaver, who had publicly vouched for a Felsch claim that the White Sox had bribed Detroit players late in the 1917 season.[20] Tigers secretary Charles F. Navin angrily denied the charge, branding Weaver "a discredited man known to be dishonest [and] actuated by base motives."[21] Former Detroit catcher Oscar Stanage, a friend of Weaver and the recipient of money delivered by Buck, also weighed in on the matter. Stanage acknowledged that the Tigers had gotten cash from the Sox but denied that the money constituted a bribe. Rather, the money had been a sort of thank you present from Chicago players, who were appreciative of late-season Detroit wins over pennant rival Boston.[22] Plaintiffs' counsel Cannon, meanwhile, cast blame for the current unpleasantness on Comiskey, accusing him, among other things, of scuttling negotiations to settle his clients' claims without litigation.[23] Cannon further maintained that Felsch had wanted to testify during the original Cook County grand jury probe but had been prevented from appearing by Sox lawyers, who were fearful that Felsch's testimony would incriminate the Sox owner.[24]

As with the Weaver suit, defense of White Sox interests in the Felsch/Risberg/Jackson litigation was entrusted to Alfred Austrian. Retained as local counsel in Milwaukee was the firm of Bottum, Hudnall, Lecher and McNamara, Esqs. On July 27, 1922, answers formally denying the three plaintiffs' contentions and seeking dismissal of the actions were submitted by local counsel on White Sox behalf.[25] From there, the parties proceeded to the discovery phase of litigation wherein new scandal revelations, both large and small, would be generated.

Notes

1. As reported by syndicated sports columnist James L. Kilgallen in the *Atlanta Constitution,* March 4, 1921.

2. *Ibid*

3. Again as reported by Kilgallen, this time in the *Atlanta Constitution,* August 4, 1921.

4. *Ibid.*

5. As briefly noted in the *Chicago Tribune,* October 19, 1921.

6. The suit was captioned *George D. Weaver v. American League Baseball Club of Chicago,* Chicago Municipal Court Docket No. 855871, filed October 18, 1921.

7. Lead counsel for the White Sox in the Weaver suit were Alfred S. Austrian and Frederick Burnham of the Chicago firm of Mayer, Meyer, Austrian and Platt, Esqs.

8. As per documents and docket book entries preserved at the National Archives and Records Administration building in Chicago. The case was docketed on November 26, 1921, and assigned Civil Action Case No. 33870.

9. On various grounds, Clause 10 of the standard MLB player contract permitted a club to terminate the agreement upon ten days' notice to the player.

10. As per the answer of defendant, filed February 27, 1922, tracking the boilerplate of Clause 2 of the standard player contract.

11. Answer of defendant.

12. *Ibid.*

13. During the criminal trial, Weaver was the only defendant whose guilt was not publicly presumed, as reflected in a mid-trial Kilgallen column entitled "Weaver May Be Innocent," published in the *Atlanta Constitution,* July 25, 1921. Little sympathy was expressed in print for the other accused.

14. As reported in the *Chicago Tribune,* April 27, 1922.

15. As per the amended complaint filed in *Oscar Felsch v. American League Baseball Club of Chicago,* Wisconsin Circuit Court/Milwaukee County, Docket No. 64442, filed July 5, 1922, preserved in CHM, Black Sox file, Box 1, Folder 6.

16. As reported in the *Chicago Tribune* and *New York Times,* May 13, 1922.

17. See Jackson civil case pleadings, CHM, Black Sox file, Box 1, Folder 10, and as reported in the *Chicago Tribune,* April 10, 1922.

18. As quoted in the *New York Times,* May 13, 1922. Johnson, however, would provide little assistance to the White Sox, declining to appear voluntarily on behalf of the defense at the trial of the Jackson suit, as established by documents in the Black Sox file at the Giamatti Research Center.

19. As quoted in the *Chicago Tribune,* May 13, 1922.

20. As reported by Kilgallen in a syndicated column published in the *Lincoln* (*Neb.*) *Star,* May 12, 1922, and elsewhere.

21. As quoted in the *New York Times,* May 13, 1922.

22. As reported in the *New York Times,* May 14, 1922. In January 1927, the arrangement between the 1917 White Sox and Tigers would be explored by Commissioner Landis at awkward public hearings. Swede Risberg and Chick Gandil would appear in support

of the charges against their old team. But ultimately, Landis concluded that the funds passed to the Tigers were a reward for beating Boston in an important late-season series, not a bribe for rolling over in games against Chicago. For a more thorough discussion of the matter, see Pietrusza, *Judge and Jury,* 296–307.

23. As reported in the *New York Times,* May 13, 1922.

24. As per the *New York Times,* May 14, 1922. Just how Felsch would have incriminated Comiskey was not divulged.

25. A partial copy of the White Sox answer to the Felsch suit can be found in CHM, Black Sox file, Box 1, Folder 6.

18

Deposition Revelations

One of the hallmarks of civil litigation is the extensive use of pretrial depositions. A deposition is a sworn out-of-court statement given by a witness under questioning by attorneys for the litigants. For reasons of convenience or necessity, a litigant may subsequently choose to have the deposition read in court in lieu of live testimony by the witness.[1] Although many of the principal figures in the Black Sox scandal had testified previously, either before the grand jury or at the criminal trial, depositions furnished counsel for the civil litigants the chance to question them under oath anew. By agreement of counsel, depositions taken in the Weaver suit would be admissible in the Felsch/Risberg/Jackson actions, and vice versa. Consequently, lawyers for all parties would customarily be in attendance at deposition sessions. On occasion, depositions proved eventful, producing significant modification of a prior rendition of fix-related events by the witness. And in one instance — Joe Jackson — deposition testimony would be so at variance with a previous sworn account that it would serve as the precursor for a perjury citation.

White Sox forces began pretrial preparations by courting an unlikely ally: Eddie Cicotte. Perhaps surprisingly, Cicotte seemed receptive to defense overtures, telling White Sox private investigator John R. Hunter that "I am not suing Comiskey myself. He paid every nickel I was entitled to ... and I have no ill feelings against him."[2] While minimizing his own fix culpability — Cicotte told Hunter that the plot to throw the Series was already fully conceived before he was approached — Cicotte expressed willingness to provide a deposition on behalf of the Sox and "tell all the facts surrounding the conspiracy and the final result." He just needed to consult his friend and attorney Daniel P. Cassidy beforehand.[3] But it was not to be. Six weeks later, Cassidy informed Sox lawyers that Cicotte had had second thoughts and would not voluntarily submit to deposition, as he wanted to avoid all further public attention.[4] As a result, it would be another sixteen months before a recalcitrant Eddie Cicotte would appear at a fruitful deposition session.

The first notable non-party to be deposed was a far more cooperative one. Summoned to Chicago by the defense on October 5, 1922, Bill Burns gave a deposition that closely mirrored the testimony that he had provided at the criminal trial — except in one regard. The Burns deposition would feature an expanded account of events attending the post–Game Two payoff, one that was highly damaging to the Weaver and Felsch causes.[5] That aspect of the deposition, however, was preceded by Burns' familiar account of the first fix meeting at the Sinton Hotel in Cincinnati, also harmful to the plaintiffs because it: (1) explicitly placed Weaver, Felsch, and Risberg in the room when the Series fix proposition was broached by Burns; (2) had Weaver getting up once or twice during the meeting to check the hallway for signs of manager Gleason; (3) had Williams informing players' ringleader Gandil that he "was kind of representing Jackson" for fix purposes; (4) had Abe Attell and "Bennett" being subsequently admitted into the conference for direct negotiations about fix payment terms; and (5) had the players agreeing to deferment of the first installment on the $100,000 fix bribe until after the Sox had lost Game One.[6]

But the real kicker was Burns' new payoff account. As Burns now recalled, there were seven corrupted players in Room 708 when Burns delivered the $10,000 coaxed from Attell after the Sox had lost Game Two. Included by name as attendees of the payoff gathering were plaintiffs Weaver, Felsch and Risberg, as well as all the other Black Sox, save Joe Jackson.[7] The money, tied in packets wrapped into a single bundle, was removed to the bathroom for counting by Risberg and McMullin, and then recounted on the bed by Gandil before all present — including Weaver and Felsch.[8] When the payoff was less than the $40,000 due and expected, Gandil and Risberg angrily accused Burns of a double cross. Regarding subsequent fix events, Burns testified that Attell had joined a group of St. Louis gamblers after the unanticipated Sox win in Game Three. Burns then had conveyed a new fix proposal to Gandil but was turned down flat. A chance encounter with Risberg and McMullin on the street, however, afforded Risberg the opportunity to reassure Burns of his commitment to throwing the Series.[9]

As he had during the criminal trial, Billy Maharg corroborated Burns regarding those details of the fix that Maharg had witnessed. Deposed in Philadelphia on December 16, 1922, Maharg supplied more testimony damaging to plaintiffs, particularly in relation to the post–Game Two payoff. Although Maharg had not accompanied Burns to the Sinton, the two had spoken about the meeting upon Burns' return from the hotel. He also reported that Burns had mentioned Weaver, Felsch, and Risberg by name in recounting what had happened when the $10,000 payoff was delivered.[10] Joe Jackson, however, had not been present for the payoff. In fact, Maharg had had no personal contact with Jackson at any time during the Series fix.

On February 23, 1923, the lawyers gathered in Detroit for the deposition of Eddie Cicotte. Attempts to gain substantive information about the Series fix, however, were frustrated by Cicotte's invocation of the right against self-incrimination. The assertion was spurious. By virtue of the Double Jeopardy Clause of the Fifth Amendment, there was no prospect that Cicotte's deposition answers would incriminate him. His acquittal at the criminal trial effectively insulated Cicotte from further prosecution for any offense connected to the fix of the 1919 World Series. At the time, however, invocation of the constitutional right to remain silent — pioneered by William J. Fallon, no less[11] — was relatively novel and the deposition lawyers, none of whom specialized in criminal law, seemed befuddled by Cicotte's rights assertion and did not press the issue. Thus, nothing of value was learned during the session.

No more happy about being questioned but considerably more voluble was Charles Comiskey, deposed in Chicago on March 24, 1923. Comiskey testified that he first became concerned about the Series' integrity upon receiving a telephone call from Mont Tennes on the morning of Game Two. Tennes warned him that there was a "problem" with some of the White Sox players.[12] After the Series was over, fix rumors continued, prompting Comiskey to hire private detectives to investigate. But the detectives could uncover nothing to confirm the rumors. Acting on the advice of Sox attorney Alfred Austrian, Comiskey felt forced to offer 1920 contracts to suspected players, with the Cicotte, Jackson, and Felsch pacts containing hefty salary increases. Comiskey had remained without credible substantiation of Series fix rumors until the Cicotte admissions of late–September 1920. On this point, Comiskey denied that team captain Eddie Collins had complained to him about Black Sox players during the 1920 season. Collins had not raised the subject of their play with Comiskey until a week after the Cicotte grand jury testimony had been published in the press.

Also deposed on March 23 was White Sox secretary Harry Grabiner. To the extent that questioning focused on fix knowledge, Grabiner toed the party line, testifying that club management had lacked concrete evidence of the 1919 Series fix until the 1920 season was almost over.[13] For the most part though, the Grabiner deposition concentrated on the focal point of the Jackson lawsuit: the circumstances surrounding Jackson's signing of his contact with the White Sox for the 1920-1921-1922 seasons.

A few weeks later, the attorneys traveled to Savannah for the pivotal event of the pretrial period — the deposition of plaintiff Joe Jackson. Jackson was deposed before court commissioner Girard M. Cohen on April 23, 1923. The proceedings were closed to the press and public at defense insistence and only ill-informed snippets of the Jackson testimony found their way into immediate newsprint.[14] In time, however, verbatim excerpts of the deposition were published in a column written by syndicated sportswriter Frank G. Menke.[15] Those excerpts revealed a Jackson account of the World Series scandal strikingly different from Jackson's testimony before the Cook County grand jury in September 1920.

According to the Menke column, the deposition commenced with Jackson maintaining, "I knew absolutely nothing about the throwing of the 1919 World Series until two or three days after it was over."[16] Jackson further testified that "I played my very best during the series, threw everything I had into the effort to bring victory to my team. I think the facts and figures [of my performance] will bear me out."[17] Regarding his acceptance of fix-connected cash, Jackson explained,

> Two or three days after the series was over, Lefty Williams ... came to my room with two envelopes in his hand. Williams was in an intoxicated condition. He told me each envelope contained $5,000 cash. He threw one of the envelopes at my feet and told me that certain players had used my name in negotiating with the gamblers and that the players had informed the gamblers that I was to help throw the games against my own team.[18]

Jackson maintained that he was "dumbfounded" by Williams' remarks and immediately informed him that "they had a lot of nerve to use my name under the circumstances." Williams then departed the room.[19] "The very next day," Jackson continued, "I went to Charles Comiskey's office with the envelope to interview the club president concerning the transaction with Williams." He, however, was denied admission by Grabiner, who "slammed the door in my face" and told Jackson "to beat it."[20] Shortly after he got home to Savannah, Jackson received a wire from Comiskey soliciting "whatever information I had concerning the 1919 series." Jackson communicated his willingness to assist but never heard back from Comiskey.[21] When Grabiner arrived in Savannah the following February to negotiate new contract terms, he advised Jackson that the club had "the absolute goods on Cicotte, Williams and Gandil concerning their dishonest and crooked play during the 1919 series." Jackson then "admitted to Grabiner that I had received $5,000 in an envelope from Lefty Williams and gave Grabiner all the information concerning the manner under which it was paid."[22] The Jackson deposition then proceeded to an account of the signing of Jackson's contract for the 1920-1921-1922 seasons that depicted him as a victim of Grabiner's duplicity.[23]

The Savannah proceedings of April 23 also included the deposition of Katie Jackson, primarily for the purpose of establishing her absence when Grabiner came south to negotiate Joe's new contract. Katie Jackson customarily reviewed proffered contracts for her illiterate husband and counseled him before signing. But this had not occurred in February 1920, when Katie only learned of Joe's contract signing after the fact.[24] While Katie's testimony bolstered the Jackson lawsuit on its contract claim, her deposition was not without benefit to the White Sox, since Katie admitted to having been an eyewitness to Joe's acceptance of money from Lefty Williams. As she recalled, Lefty handed Joe an envelope and said, "Here's the money. There is $5,000 in it." Joe then put the envelope in his pocket.[25] Katie did not know why Williams had given Joe the money and neither of them explained.[26] Sometime after their return home to Savannah, Joe gave the $5,000 to Katie for safekeeping. Eventually, almost all of that money went to cover medical bills for Joe's ailing sister.[27]

Educated by their encounter with Eddie Cicotte, Sox lawyers were ready for the Fifth Amendment claim asserted by Lefty Williams when he was deposed in Chicago on May 23, 1923. The claim was swiftly dispatched as legally unavailable. But the attorneys had not anticipated the amnesia that now afflicted Williams. He could remember nothing about the plot to throw the 1919 World Series, including his receipt of $10,000 from Chick Gandil and his disbursement of half of that cash to plaintiff Jackson.[28] Nor did Williams' memory improve after he was shown the sworn statement that he had given on September 29, 1920. Said Williams, "I gave a statement at Austrian's office but I don't remember what the statement was."[29] Williams was also unable to recall his ensuing grand jury testimony, even when confronted with verbatim passages from the transcript. In particular, Williams could not recall his testimony about meeting fix arrangers Sullivan and Brown at the Warner Hotel; walking the streets afterward discussing ways to throw Series games with Weaver and Felsch, or any other specific event recounted during his grand jury appearance.[30] As for his testimony before the Cook County grand jury, Williams could only say that "I told the truth as far as I know."[31]

According to Black Sox expert Gene Carney, Joe Jackson was deposed a second time in Savannah on September 4, 1923.[32] The specifics of that deposition session are unknown to the author. Subsequent events, however, suggest (1) White Sox lawyers did not confront Jackson with the sworn testimony that he had given to the Cook County grand jury in late–September

1920, and (2) Sox lawyers either implied or specifically stated that they were not in possession of the Jackson grand jury transcript. Thereafter, the pace of pretrial discovery slackened. The only noteworthy event was the November 16, 1923, deposition of John J. Cornell, a cashier at the Chatham Bank & Trust Company in Savannah. With the help of a deposit slip completed by Katie Jackson, Cornell testified that $5,400 in large bills had been deposited into the Jackson account on December 1, 1919. Within the next eleven months, that entire sum had been withdrawn from the account.[33] The White Sox defense also secured depositions from Eddie Collins, Ray Schalk, and Red Faber, all of which contradicted the plaintiffs' 1917 World Series bonus claim.[34]

Notes

1. *Black's Law Dictionary,* 272.

2. Per letter of Hunter to Alfred S. Austrian, dated July 5, 1922, in CHM, Black Sox file, Box 1, Folder 6.

3. *Ibid.*

4. Letter of Daniel P. Cassidy to Alfred S. Austrian, dated August 22, 1922, CHM, Black Sox file, Box 1, Folder 6.

5. This summary is derived from aspects of the Burns deposition embedded in the transcript of the Jackson civil case trial (JTT). The Burns deposition is also summarized in Gene Carney, "New Light on an Old Scandal," *Baseball Research Journal,* Vol. 35, 2007, 76–78.

6. JTT, p. 591; 686.

7. JTT, pp. 686–695. At the criminal trial some fifteen months earlier, Burns had testified that these present for the payoff were Gandil, Cicotte, Risberg, McMullin, and two other Sox players whom Burns did not then recall. See again, the Burns testimony excerpted in the *New York Times,* July 21, 1921.

8. JTT, pp. 695–698.

9. JTT, pp. 707–707. The credibility of deposition testimony is difficult to assess but it is perhaps noteworthy that at trial, the Jackson side would decline to offer even a single passage of its cross-examination of Burns. Only the direct testimony given in response to questions by Sox lawyers would be admitted in evidence at the civil trial.

10. JTT, pp. 730–734.

11. Fallon's assertion of the right of gambler client Nicky Arnstein to decline to answer questions that might be self-incriminating was upheld by the United States Supreme Court in the ground-breaking decision of *Arnstein v. McCarthy,* 254 *U.S.* 71 (1920).

12. This account is drawn from portions of the Comiskey deposition extant in the civil record and from contemporaneous reportage in the *Boston Globe* and *Hartford Courant,* March 25, 1923.

13. As per Gene Carney's notes on the Grabiner deposition and *Notes from the Shadows of Cooperstown,* No. 388, February 7, 2007.

14. See, e.g., *Boston Globe* and *Chicago Tribune,* April 10, 1923.

15. The Jackson deposition was likely leaked to Menke by plaintiffs' attorney Cannon, the subject of an admiring profile penned by Menke two years earlier which bore the title "From Baseball to $100,000 a Year," published in the *Atlanta Constitution,* July 17, 1921, and elsewhere.

16. As quoted in a Menke column published in the *Lincoln Star,* April 23, 1923, and elsewhere.

17. *Ibid.*
18. *Ibid.* If faithfully reproduced by Menke, the vocabulary and grammatical command exhibited by Jackson in his deposition testimony are impressive, again not at all in keeping with his public persona.
19. *Ibid.*
20. *Ibid.*
21. *Ibid.* The Jackson-Comiskey post–Series communications, which began with an October 27, 1919 letter from Jackson seeking his World Series check, are reproduced in Donald Gropman, *Say It Ain't So, Joe! The True Story of Shoeless Joe Jackson*, revised 2nd ed. (New York: Citadel Press, 1992), Appendix B, 277–284.
22. *Lincoln Star,* April 24, 1923.
23. *Ibid.*
24. JTT, pp. 1145–1148.
25. JTT, pp. 1162–1163.
26. JTT, p. 1156.
27. JTT, p. 1156; 1163. See also, *Chicago Tribune,* April 10, 1923, for a variant on Katie Jackson's deposition testimony.
28. JTT pp. 746–751; 797–798.
29. JTT, p. 769.
30. JTT, pp. 795–799.
31. JTT, p. 768.
32. As per Carney, *Notes from the Shadows of Cooperstown,* No. 359, September 6, 2005.
33. JTT, pp. 1169–1178.
34. As per Carney, *Burying the Black Sox,* 331, n. 95.

19

Eve of Trial Maneuvers

As is customary in civil litigation, the setting of a trial date for the cases was preceded by the filing of motions and settlement discussions. Of the former, the most significant were demurrer/dismissal applications[1] submitted on behalf of the White Sox in the Felsch/Risberg/Jackson cases. On May 13, 1923, the scope of the litigation pending in Milwaukee was reduced by Circuit Court Judge John J. Gregory. Dismissed by the court were the 1917 World Series bonus and the restraint on livelihood counts of the Felsch and Risberg complaints. The Jackson lawsuit, however, was left untouched by the court and could proceed intact.[2] Plaintiffs' attorney Cannon then began making tactical decisions in order to expedite getting his cases to trial. To that end, Cannon decided to pare down his suits unilaterally. On October 1, 1923, Cannon voluntarily dismissed the defamation and restraint on livelihood claims of the Jackson complaint. The defamation counts in the Felsch and Risberg complaints then were jettisoned on October 29.[3] If nothing else, the dismissals got Cannon a trial date. The Jackson case would commence trial in late January 1924.

As the trial date approached, White Sox lawyers, sensing insecurity in the opposition, took a hard line on settlement. At a federal court pretrial hearing back in Chicago, defense counsel Frederick Burnham spurned a $5,000 settlement offer tendered by Weaver lawyer Williams. The Weaver case was then placed on the District Court trial calendar for February 29, 1924.[4] Meanwhile in Milwaukee, local Sox lawyers took pleasure in economic distress rumored at the Cannon firm. Representation of the Black Sox had apparently proved unpopular with other firm clients. In addition, being counsel to the banished men had had a particularly deleterious effect on Cannon's attempt to organize a new major league baseball players union. In correspondence with Alfred Austrian, local defense counsel smugly predicted that Cannon would propose a brink-of-trial settlement of the Milwaukee litigation.[5]

Time would prove counsel right but Sox lawyers would overplay their hand. At first, Cannon proposed settlement of all three suits — Felsch, Risberg, and Jackson — for $8,000 total. In reply, Sox lawyers low-balled, offering only $2,000. When Cannon countered at $6,000, the defense would only come up to $2,500. Unable to bridge the chasm, the attorneys on both sides began their final preparations for trial of the Jackson suit.[6]

In the run-up to the Jackson trial, attorneys for the White Sox took a second shot at deposing Lefty Williams and Eddie Cicotte. This time, however, the two would be interrogated by lead defense counsel George B. Hudnall, an experienced and hard-nosed trial lawyer accustomed to dealing with difficult witnesses.[7] When re-deposed on January 12, 1924, Williams reverted to memory loss on all things Black Sox-related. But Hudnall was having none of it. He quickly led Williams into acknowledging that his grand jury testimony — whatever it had been — was the truth. From there, Hudnall shoved the transcript of that testimony under Williams' nose and steered him through adoption of everything in it that was of use to the White Sox defense. As documented in correspondence now preserved in the Chicago History Museum file, Hudnall's firm had obtained the grand jury transcripts from the Austrian firm, which, in turn, had obtained them from Cook County prosecutors, only too happy to assist in the defeat of lawsuits brought by those whom the SAO had unsuccessfully prosecuted.[8] The grand jury testimony of Williams and Cicotte had been available during the original deposition sessions but Sox lawyers from Chicago evidently lacked the expertise needed to use the transcripts coercively when the witnesses turned uncooperative. But George Hudnall was a litigator far superior to the second-stringers generally attending depositions and before he was through, Williams had been maneuvered into effectively re-testifying that Weaver and Felsch had attended the fix meeting at the Warner Hotel when the players were introduced to fix front men Sullivan and Brown,[9] that Weaver, Felsch and he had discussed ways to throw Series games while walking Chicago streets after that meeting,[10] and that Weaver, Felsch, and Risberg had been present when a second Series fix proposal was presented by Bill Burns at the Sinton Hotel.[11] Williams was also obliged to adopt his grand jury testimony about the post–Game Four payoff to plaintiff Jackson[12] as well as his declaration, for the grand jury record, that the players involved in the plot to throw the 1919 World Series were "Cicotte, Gandil, Weaver, Felsch, Risberg, McMullin, Jackson and myself."[13]

Two days later, this exercise was repeated when Cicotte was re-deposed in Detroit. Those aspects of the grand jury record helpful to the White Sox cause were herded into the deposition transcript the moment that an uncooperative Cicotte stated that "what I told the grand jury was the truth."[14] He, too, would now be obliged, under pain of a potential perjury or contempt citation, to ratify his grand jury testimony. This was particularly harmful to Joe Jackson because Cicotte's grand jury account of scandal developments, whether accurately or not, had placed Jackson at the initial fix meeting of White Sox players at the Ansonia Hotel in New York.[15] As for the other plaintiffs, Cicotte, like Williams, had put Weaver and Felsch at the meeting subsequently held with gamblers at the Warner Hotel[16] and placed Felsch and Risberg at the Bill Burns conclave later conducted at the Sinton Hotel in Cincinnati.[17] When the second Cicotte deposition was over, so was the discovery phase of the Jackson suit. The time for trial had finally arrived.

Notes

1. A demurrer challenges the legal sufficiency of a civil complaint on its face.
2. As reported in the *Boston Globe* and *New York Times,* May 13, 1923.
3. The procedural history of the litigation is memorialized in correspondence between White Sox lawyers in Milwaukee and Chicago, preserved in CHM, Black Sox file, Box 1, Folder 7.
4. As noted in a letter to Charles Comiskey from the Austrian firm, contained in CHM, Black Sox file, Box 1, Folder 10.
5. As per correspondence from White Sox defense lawyers in Milwaukee to their counterparts in Chicago, dated January 8, 1924, in CHM, Black Sox file, Box 1, Folder 8.
6. The defense approach to settlement was decidedly odd, as the amounts sought by Cannon were modest, probably less than it would cost the White Sox in counsel fees for its battalion of lawyers to try the cases. But defense willingness to litigate in open court tends to refute the notion that Comiskey or other club officials feared exposure of their own conduct in the scandal.
7. At the original Williams and Cicotte depositions, the White Sox had been represented by attorneys from the Austrian firm in Chicago.
8. As documented by CHM correspondence.
9. JTT, p. 810; 829.
10. JTT, pp. 811–814; 826.
11. JTT, p. 816.
12. JTT, pp. 816–818; 833–836.
13. JTT, p. 831.
14. JTT, p. 1213.
15. JTT, pp. 1213–1214.
16. JTT, p. 1227.
17. JTT, pp. 1252–1261.

20

The Case of Plaintiff Jackson

The primary claim of the lawsuit that Joe Jackson brought to trial against his former employer sought payment of his salary for the 1921 and 1922 seasons.[1] At the height of the Black Sox scandal in March 1921, club management had terminated Jackson's contract for those seasons and released him unpaid. According to Jackson, this action was unjustified and constituted an unlawful breach of contract. But the legal argument behind the suit was something of a curiosity. In essence, Jackson wanted his contract with the White Sox enforced, but not as written. As plaintiff saw it, the bone of contention was Clause 10, the boilerplate MLB contract proviso that allowed a club to terminate a player's contract on ten days' notice. The Jackson suit alleged that the ballplayer had insisted on the deletion of Clause 10 during contract negotiations and that its existence in the pact that he signed was entirely the product of duplicity and misrepresentation by White Sox secretary Harry Grabiner.[2] To the White Sox, the Clause 10 brouhaha was a red herring because the team had not relied upon that clause in releasing Jackson. As trenchantly put by its lead trial counsel, "the club discharged Jackson because he was a crook. It did not give him ten days notice. It fired him outright."[3] Given the nature of the White Sox defense, one thing looked sure. Nothing less than a retrial in miniature of the Black Sox criminal case was in the offing. But there would be significant differences from that trial in the upcoming proceeding.

Civil litigation provides a forum for the redress of private grievances. It essentially asks the judicial system to resolve a dispute between parties and to award damages, usually in the form of money, to the injured side. As already noted, one of its characteristics is the extensive use of depositions, sworn out-of-court testimony that may be admitted in evidence at trial in lieu of live courtroom testimony by the witness. This serves to distinguish civil proceedings from a criminal trial, where the use of depositions is rarely, if ever, permitted.[4] Once at trial, the plaintiff— the party initiating suit — has the burden of proving his entitlement to damages. But that burden is not an onerous one. In most civil cases, the outcome favors the party who, on the whole, has the stronger evidence, however slight that edge might be.[5] And unlike a criminal trial, the verdict of the jury in a civil matter need not be unanimous. In the Jackson case, only ten of the twelve jurors would have to agree in order to return judgment, one way or the other.[6] If the plaintiff prevailed, or the amount of money damages to be awarded to him would also be determined by the jury.

Like the Black Sox criminal trial, the Jackson suit would be tried by star quality lawyers. The two principal figures were also polar opposites. Lead plaintiff's counsel Raymond J. Cannon was Horatio Alger material. Young (only 29), handsome, and dynamic, Cannon had been raised in a Green Bay orphanage until rescued at age 14 by a schoolteacher aunt.[7] Cannon took advantage to combine the pursuit of education with baseball talent, pitching for various Midwest semi-pro teams during summer recesses. At one time, he had even been a teammate of Happy Felsch.[8] Admitted to the Wisconsin bar in 1914, Cannon quickly established a thriving civil practice. He had recently been feted by admirers for having won 100 consecutive jury verdicts. He had earned some national attention as well, serving as counsel for heavyweight boxing champ Jack Dempsey[9] and attempting to organize a new union for major league baseball players.[10] Cannon was also active in Milwaukee Democratic Party politics. By the time of the Jackson civil trial, Cannon was a local celebrity, described by admirers as the "best trial lawyer in Wisconsin."[11] He was also heartily despised in certain quarters of the Milwaukee bar, where Cannon's brash nature and aggressive self-promotion were deemed not in keeping with the traditions of the profession.

Cannon's principal adversary could not have been more different. A generation older, lead White Sox trial counsel George B. Hudnall personified the Wisconsin political and legal establishment.[12] A senior member of the dominant LaFollette wing of the Republican Party, Hudnall had been a Wisconsin state senator, counsel to the governor, and president of the state bar association. His law firm, Bottum, Hudnall, Lecher and McNamara, Esqs., primarily represented large corporations, numbering International Harvester, Western Union, and various railroads among its clients. Hudnall himself was a keen and able debater as well as an experienced civil practitioner. He also held Raymond J. Cannon in particular disdain.

There was a personal history between the two lawyers. In February 1923 — while the Felsch, Risberg, and Jackson lawsuits were still pending disposition — Cannon had been indicted by a Milwaukee County grand jury on charges presented by specially appointed prosecutor George B. Hudnall. The indictment alleged that Cannon had supplied Democrat District Attorney Winfred C. Zabel with a case of bootleg champagne "with intent to bribe."[13] Cannon was also charged with misleading clients for financial gain.[14] In due course, and after Hudnall had been relieved of his duties as special prosecutor, the charges were dismissed on grounds of insufficient evidence.[15] But the resolution of the matter had done little to warm relations between the Jackson case's primary litigators and their dislike of each other was unmistakable during the proceedings.

Lead White Sox trial counsel George B. Hudnall was a pillar of the Wisconsin political and legal establishment (courtesy Milwaukee Historical Society).

The man in the middle was Wisconsin Circuit Court Judge John J. Gregory, an able and respected judicial veteran. Like Cannon, Gregory had endured youthful hardships.[16] A childhood fall precipitated a tubercular hip that would cripple Gregory for life. The premature death of his father thrust the crutches-dependent Gregory, the oldest of eight children, into the work force at age 14. He had gained an education at night while working in the post office and was admitted to the Wisconsin bar in 1895. First elected to the judiciary in 1910, Gregory, a Democrat, breezed to reelection for the remainder of his life. On the bench, Gregory was known for his intelligence, sunny disposition, and liberal views (except on the subject of Wisconsin divorce laws). He was given to treating lawyers kindly, especially inexperienced ones. But Gregory would not abide any perceived abuse of the judicial process — a trait which, in time, would bring the Jackson cause to grief.

On January 28, 1924, the parties converged on Milwaukee for the trial of the Jackson suit. Appearing on behalf of plaintiff Jackson was Cannon, assisted by associate counsel James D. Shaw. Hudnall, law firm partner Frank McNamara, and John C. Northrup of the Austrian firm represented the White Sox. During jury selection, Jackson and Happy Felsch, a local resident, took places in the rear of the courtroom while Comiskey sat at counsel's table, flanked by his team's attorneys. Unlike the criminal trial, jury selection proceeded expeditiously and a panel of ten men and two women was seated

Respected Wisconsin Circuit Court Judge John J. Gregory cited both Happy Felsch and Joe Jackson for perjury based on their testimony at the civil trial (courtesy Milwaukee Historical Society).

within hours.[17] None of the jurors professed great interest in baseball but most were at least casually acquainted with the Black Sox scandal. John E. Sanderson, an import company sales manager, was appointed jury foreman.[18]

In an opening address of one hour, Cannon harped on two themes: (1) the humble origins of his client, portrayed as one of 15 children[19] obliged to forego schooling to begin work in the mills at a tender age before ascending to baseball stardom, and (2) the power and duplicity of his employers, who took advantage of Jackson's illiteracy to do him injury. On the latter point, Cannon asserted that the White Sox had voided Jackson's contract on the basis of Clause 10, the contract provision that team secretary Henry Grabiner had duped Jackson into believing had been removed from the contract.[20] Turning next to the scandal, Cannon acknowledged that Jackson had been criminally charged in Chicago but declared that his client had been "acquitted after deliberations of five minutes" by the jury.[21] Cannon also conceded that certain members of the Sox team — namely, Eddie Cicotte, Chick Gandil, and Lefty Williams — had, in fact, colluded with gamblers to throw the 1919

World Series and that Jackson had received $5,000 from Williams. He maintained, however, that Jackson did not participate in the fix and indeed had no inkling that the Series had been rigged prior to receiving the $5,000. Cannon added that his client subsequently tried to inform Comiskey about his receipt of the money, only to be rebuffed by club officials, already wise to the fix.[22] Blameless, Jackson had been unjustly terminated and was, therefore, entitled to his unpaid salary for the 1921 and 1922 seasons.[23]

Speaking on behalf of the defendant White Sox, Hudnall was brief and blunt. Jackson had been discharged from team employ because he was a crook, the $5,000 payment admittedly accepted by Jackson being nothing less than "graft, pure and simple."[24] Hudnall further maintained that Comiskey, not Jackson, was the real victim in the case, the corruption of Jackson and the other Black Sox having necessitated the dismantling of a championship team, with a loss of $500,000 in anticipated revenue. Given this, Hudnall concluded, the Jackson suit had no merit.[25]

Cannon lost no time getting to the heart of his case, calling Jackson as the trial's first witness. After describing his background and career with the White Sox, Jackson denied involvement in the plot to throw the 1919 World Series, offering his statistics, a Series-best .375 batting average, a team-leading six RBIs, and error-free performance in the field, as proof of his clean play.[26] Jackson then reiterated the account of post–Series events recited in his April 1923 deposition — with minor deviations. This time, for example, Jackson placed the hotel room meeting with Williams on the evening that the Sox lost the final Series game, not several days afterward. He said that the $5,000 was both unexpected and unwelcome, as Jackson had not given fix leaders permission to use his name and had been unaware, until then, that they had done so.[27] "I don't want your money," Jackson told Williams. He also informed Williams that he would tell club owner Comiskey about their encounter in the morning.[28] But Jackson's efforts to speak to Comiskey were obstructed by Grabiner, who refused Jackson entry to the owner's office. "Go home," Grabiner told him. "We know what you want."[29]

The remainder of Jackson's direct examination focused on the circumstances surrounding the signing of his contract for the 1920-1921-1922 seasons. Shortly after this subject was introduced, Hudnall was on his feet with an anticipatory objection to any testimony that implicated the concept of condonation, a legal precept not pled in the Jackson complaint. Hudnall's concerns were well-founded, for condonation would add an entirely new dimension to the case, and one inimical to the White Sox interests. This is because condonation equates in law to forgiveness.[30] Applied to the Jackson case, condonation would permit recovery by plaintiff even if he had participated in the Series fix, provided it was shown that Sox management had been aware of Jackson's misconduct **before** the club tendered him a new contract. If that were the case but Chicago had chosen to re-sign him anyway, Jackson's Series misconduct would have been viewed as condoned or forgiven by the club—and thus, could not later be used as legitimate grounds for voiding the Jackson contract. At this juncture in the proceedings, however, Judge Gregory did not rule on the objection, apparently because he did not believe that a condonation claim was being asserted. But that situation would change as the case went on.

In the meantime, Jackson's testimony narrated the circumstances surrounding the signing of the contract. He related: (1) that he and Grabiner had discussed new contract terms in Joe's auto without his wife Katie being present; (2) that Jackson agreed to sign for less than the $10,000 per season that he and Katie had wanted; (3) that Grabiner filled in the terms on a contract form using a fountain pen; (4) that Grabiner assured him that the contract did not contain Clause 10, the standard termination on ten days' notice provision; (5) that Grabiner read the completed contract aloud to the illiterate Jackson to confirm the elimination of Clause 10; and (6) that so assured, Jackson signed the contract, balancing it against the steering wheel of his auto as he did so.[31] Jackson asked for but did not receive a copy of his new contract and did not learn of the retention of Clause 10 in the pact until he was suspended by the team late in the 1920 season.[32] Jackson added that he had not received the $8,000 salary stipulated in his contract for either the 1921 or the 1922 season and, once formally banished from organized baseball, had made only a few hundred dollars playing outlaw ball during those years.[33]

Many early press reviews judged Jackson an effective courtroom advocate in his own behalf. Trial coverage in the *Nebraska State Journal* was headlined "Find Shoeless Joe Excellent Witness,"[34] while the *Milwaukee Sentinel* informed readers that "Jackson made an excellent witness. He looked well on the witness stand. His answers came quickly and cleanly."[35] But such notices would undergo revision after Jackson was confronted with the central problem with his testimony—the almost complete irreconcilability of what Jackson had just told the jury under oath in this proceeding and what Jackson had told the Cook County grand jury while testifying under oath on September 28, 1920. Once a perfunctory objection to impeachment of Jackson by means of the grand jury record was denied by the court,[36] defense counsel Hudnall began the cross-examination that would ultimately dictate the outcome of the case.

Author Note: Perhaps the most enduring canard of the Black Sox case is the notion that the Cicotte, Jackson and Williams grand jury testimony vanished in late 1920. Almost as persistent is the claim that the players' statements remained lost until January 31, 1924, when the Jackson grand jury transcript mysteriously emerged from George Hudnall's briefcase.[37] As previously noted, it was only the original transcriptions of the Cicotte, Jackson, and Williams testimony that went missing, a problem that was easily solved by having the grand jury stenographers create new transcripts from their shorthand notes. At the 1921 Black Sox criminal trial, the Cicotte, Jackson, and Williams grand jury testimony was aired at tedious length during the suppression hearing and then was admitted in evidence in redacted form. As all this took place in open court and was the subject of extensive newspaper coverage — the *Chicago Tribune* reportage actually complained about the repetitious reading of grand jury transcripts — anyone following the case would have been conversant with what the players had said before the grand jury. In short, the Cicotte/Jackson/Williams grand jury testimony was virtually a matter of public record. Forty years later, however, Eliot Asinof's account of the Black Sox scandal put a creative spin on the situation, fashioning a melodramatic courtroom scene around the "surprise" production of the Jackson grand jury testimony in Milwaukee. See Asinof, *Eight Men Out,* 289–290. Whatever its literary merit, the scene as recounted by Asinof, and reiterated by later Black Sox writers, does not appear in the civil trial record and is, charitably speaking, most likely the product of artistic license.

The Jackson civil suit focused on the conduct of White Sox club secretary Harry Grabiner during 1920 contract negotiations with the illiterate Joe Jackson (courtesy National Baseball Hall of Fame Library, Cooperstown, NY).

Nor was there anything unfair or unethical about White Sox counsel confronting Jackson and others with statements that they had previously sworn were the truth. For the principle of grand jury secrecy does not empower witnesses to commit perjury with impunity at subsequent proceedings. Nor could surprise reasonably be claimed by the Jackson side. Defense possession of the grand jury record had been made obvious at the Cicotte and Williams deposition sessions. And while Sox lawyers were apparently less than forthright when inquiry about their possession of the Jackson grand jury transcript was made by plaintiff's counsel — the transcript was not utilized during the Jackson deposition for strategic reasons — this bit of sharp practice should not have lulled Jackson into a false sense of security about his risk of being confronted with his grand jury testimony. Finally, the citation of specific legal authority and precedent by Judge Gregory in his ruling on the Cannon objection belies the notion that defense use of the Jackson grand jury transcript caught anyone by surprise. Plainly, the judge knew in advance that use of the grand jury transcript during the defense cross of Jackson was a matter that would have to be ruled on and, hence, had the relevant legal authority at his fingertips.

Hudnall had prepared for cross-examination by parsing the Jackson grand jury testimony into select fragments. He would then confront Jackson with each self-incriminating detail of his previous account of fix-related events. When this strategy was deployed at trial, the Jackson reaction, whether preplanned or spontaneous, was surprising. And almost perverse. Jackson did not attempt to explain away the contradictions in his civil trial and grand jury testimony. Nor did he endeavor to harmonize the two. Instead, Jackson simply denied that he had spoken the words recorded in the grand jury record. According to Jackson, he never gave most of the testimony printed in black and white on the transcript pages.[38] When asked, for example, about his grand jury statement that Series fixers had "promised me $20,000 and paid me $5,000" (at JGJ4–9 to 10), Jackson did not assert that such testimony was untrue or try to rationalize it. Instead, he told Hudnall, "I didn't make that answer."[39] Or when asked about what Chick Gandil had told him about the fix payment shortchange (at JGJ6–10 to 13), Jackson's response was the same. He denied giving the testimony attributed to him in the grand jury transcript.[40] The following Hudnall-Jackson colloquy typifies the tenor of cross-examination:

HUDNALL: Were you asked and did you give this answer? Question: What did you say to Williams when he threw down the $5,000? Answer: I asked him what the hell had come off here (quoting JGJ6–25 to JGJ7–5).
JACKSON: No, sir. I don't know anything about that.
HUDNALL: And you did not so testify before the grand jury?
JACKSON: No, sir. I didn't.[41]

Similarly, when referred to his grand jury testimony about the "jazz" given the players by Abe Attell, Jackson denied the authenticity of the response reported at JGJ9–10 to 13:

HUDNALL: You didn't make any such answer before the grand jury?
JACKSON: No, sir.[42]

As Jackson's lawyers sat by helplessly, this dialogue went on at numbing length. Among other things, Jackson denied that he had given the answers contained in the transcript of his grand jury testimony about acceptance of the money delivered by Williams after Game Four. Insisted Jackson, "I didn't make any answer like you are reading from there. No, sir."[43] Regarding his grand jury testimony about the $10,000 bribe paid to Eddie Cicotte, Jackson replied, "I say that I did not make the answer that you read there."[44] Nor had Jackson testified about fix payments to Swede Risberg and Fred McMullin during his grand jury appearance. Hudnall: "Those questions were not asked and you did not make those answers?" Jackson: "No, sir."[45] Also repudiated by Jackson were transcript excerpts pertaining to pre–Series conversations with Gandil,[46] fix payment to Happy Felsch,[47] Katie Jackson's reaction to Joe's involvement in the fix,[48] and, by the author's count, 119 other particulars of Jackson's sworn grand jury testimony. No immediate consequences flowed from Jackson's performance on the stand. But before the proceedings closed, Judge Gregory would make his feelings known, emphatically.

At the conclusion of the Jackson testimony, Cannon sought to buttress his contention that Jackson had not been a participant in the throwing of the 1919 World Series. To that purpose, seasoned observers of the Series games were called to testify. Midwest Associated Press sports editor Charles W. Dunkley had covered the Series and informed the jury that "Jackson played good, I thought," citing plaintiff's .375 average at the plate. Dunkley conceded, however, his inability to determine if Jackson, or any other Series participant, had given "his best effort."[49] The testimony of AP sportswriter James C. Hamilton was much the same. On the one hand, Hamilton opined that Jackson had "played good ball" during the Series. On the other, the witness acknowledged that it is "impossible to tell if a player is doing his best."[50] That said, Hamilton had not suspected that Series games were being thrown while keeping score. Just one play struck Hamilton as dubious — Cicotte's attempt to cut off the Jackson throw to home plate in Game Four — and even that seemed shady only in retrospect.[51]

The plaintiff's case then proceeded into unfriendly territory, summoning White Sox officials to the witness stand. First up was Charles A. Comiskey, obliged to account for his conduct in the scandal.[52] Comiskey testified that his suspicions about the 1919 World Series were initially aroused by Mont Tennes, who had telephoned him at 5:00 A.M. on the morning of Game Two. After club employee Norris O'Neill, dispatched to confer with Tennes, had reported back, the Sox owner notified manager Kid Gleason that there were rumors of crooked play about, and directed him to bench any player whose performance was suspect.[53] Comiskey then conveyed his concerns to NL President John Heydler, who dismissed them, telling Comiskey that he had simply underestimated the strength of the Reds team.[54] Immediately after the Series was lost, Comiskey informed Chick Gandil and Happy Felsch that he intended to have fix rumors investigated and that if any Sox players were found to be corrupt, he was "going to put them out of business."[55] Comiskey reported that he then withheld the World Series checks due certain players and hired private detectives, but that no solid proof of a fix was uncovered.

Regarding Joe Jackson individually, the Comiskey testimony was largely beneficial to the plaintiff's cause. Whatever his assessment of the other Black Sox, Comiskey had observed nothing dishonest in Jackson's Series play. To the contrary, Jackson had "played good ball," Comiskey's only criticism being too shallow positioning on a Game One drive to left field that went over Jackson's head.[56] Nor did Comiskey suspect Jackson of crooked play at any other time during his six-season tenure with the club.[57] On random topics, Comiskey testified that he had not been involved in the procurement of Jackson's grand jury testimony by defense counsel. He imagined that the transcript had been obtained by the Austrian firm by means unknown to him.[58] Comiskey reported that he had spoken to sportswriter Hugh Fullerton about his suspicions shortly after the 1919 Series was over, but had been unaware of Bill Burns' involvement in the fix until the Cicotte admissions of late–September the following year.[59] As reflected in a November 1919 letter to Jackson, Comiskey had heard reports connecting Jackson's name to talk of corrupt Series play but had not been aware of Jackson's receipt of $5,000 from Lefty Williams during the games. If he had known of that matter, Comiskey would not have sent club secretary Grabiner to Georgia in February 1920 to sign Jackson to a new contract.[60]

After excerpts of the Comiskey deposition had been read into the record by Cannon, Harry Grabiner took the stand. He testified that the investigation of Series fix rumors was still in progress when he made the February 1920 trip south to see Jackson, but the play of the 1919 World Series was not discussed between them. Grabiner's sole purpose in going to Savannah was to sign Jackson for the upcoming season.[61] The rest of his testimony was devoted to contract-signing details. On that score, Grabiner maintained that Jackson never inquired about the presence of Clause 10 in his new contract; that negotiations focused entirely on salary and contract duration terms before a three-year, $8,000-per-season deal was reached; that Jackson signed the pact personally while seated inside the Jackson residence, and that Katie Jackson was present when he did so.[62] As for the terms inscribed on the contract, Grabiner added that he had inserted those into the pact using a steel pen. Grabiner had never used a fountain pen in his life.[63]

After Grabiner had been excused, Judge Gregory advised the jury that both sides stipulated the following: (1) that White Sox players Gandil, Cicotte, and Williams had entered a conspiracy to throw the 1919 World Series; (2) that plaintiff Jackson was "a good ballplayer"; and (3) that Jackson was "one of the best players in the league."[64] Cannon then closed plaintiff's case with expert testimony from Fred Luderus, a retired veteran of 12 NL seasons and a Milwaukee native.[65] Based on the statistical record — Luderus had not actually seen any of the 1919 World Series play — Luderus stated that Jackson had compiled "a wonderful batting average" in the Series, particularly as it had come against a Reds pitching staff that had been "the strongest in baseball" that season.[66] The Luderus opinion of Jackson's defensive play was equally glowing. Jackson's 18 putouts and one assist without an error constituted "a wonderful record for the World Series."[67] All in all, it was the witness' view that Jackson had posted the best record of any player in the Series.[68] Upon completion of the Luderus testimonial, Cannon rested the plaintiff's case.

Notes

1. The trial also encompassed the disputed 1917 World Series bonus but little attention was paid to that claim during trial.

2. The Jackson suit did not protest the one-sidedness of Clause 10 or otherwise challenge the legality of the standard 1920 MLB contract.

3. Defense counsel George B. Hudnall, quoted in the *Milwaukee Journal,* January 29, 1924.

4. Use of depositions in a criminal case is reserved for dire situations, such as to preserve the testimony of a terminally ill witness who may be deceased by time of trial. Otherwise, the Confrontation Clause of the Sixth Amendment mandates the courtroom appearance of witnesses giving evidence against the accused.

5. *Black's Law Dictionary,* 1301. This standard is called the preponderance of evidence.

6. As per a recently enacted Wisconsin statute.

7. Biographical sources for Cannon include the Menke profile in the *Atlanta Constitution,* July 17, 1921; another Cannon profile published in the *Boston Globe,* August 30, 1922; *The Biographical Dictionary of the United States Congress* (Cannon was a three-term Wisconsin congressman in the 1930s), and the Cannon obituary published in the *Chicago Tribune,* November 26, 1951.

8. As noted in Jim Nitz's comprehensive SABR BioProject profile of Happy Felsch, viewable at http://www.sabr.org/bioproj.cfm?a=v&v=1&bid=707&pid=438.

9. For the most part, Cannon's representation of Dempsey focused on fight film distribution rights. A lawsuit that Cannon later brought against Dempsey for unpaid services was eventually settled out of court, as reported in the *New York Times,* August 7, 1927.

10. See the *Washington Post,* August 18, 1922, *Boston Globe,* August 20, 1922, and *New York Times,* October 13, 1922. An agitator by nature, Cannon was later described as "the Leon Trotsky of the sporting business" by syndicated sports columnist turned political commentator Westbrook Pegler. See *Chicago Tribune,* March 30, 1927.

11. According to the *Boston Globe,* August 30, 1922.

12. The portrait of Hudnall is drawn from James Clark Fifield, *The American Bar, Vol. I* (New York: Fifield Company, 1918), 722, and reportage of the Jackson trial.

13. As reported in the *Chicago Tribune,* February 4, 1923.

14. See Gropman, 219–220. In addition, DA Zabel was indicted, and later cleared, on unrelated extortion charges. See *Chicago Tribune,* June 17, 1923.

15. As per Gropman, 220, placing the dismissal in December 1923, or about one month before trial proceedings commenced in the Jackson civil suit.

16. The sketch of Judge Gregory is drawn primarily from obituaries and testimonials published in Milwaukee newspapers following his death in late November 1939. Like the other Black Sox jurists, Gregory was an ardent baseball fan.

17. As per the *Milwaukee Journal/Milwaukee Sentinel,* January 29, 1924.

18. *Ibid.* Biographical information on jury foreman Sanderson was provided to the author by Black Sox expert Bob Hoie.

19. According to his biographers, Jackson was one of eight children. See David L. Fleitz, *Shoeless: The Life and Times of Joe Jackson* (Jefferson, NC: McFarland, 2001), 7; Frommer, 6.

20. As reported in the *Milwaukee Sentinel,* January 29, 1924. As is the norm, neither jury selection nor the opening statements of counsel appear in the Jackson trial transcripts.

21. As per the *Milwaukee Evening Sentinel,* January 29, 1924. Jury deliberations in the criminal trial actually consumed two hours, 47 minutes.

22. As reported in the *Milwaukee Journal* and *Milwaukee Sentinel,* January 29, 1924.

23. *Ibid.* The $18,000 damages sought by Cannon incorporated the 1917 bonus claim but no specific mention of that matter was noted in reportage of counsel's opening.

24. As per the *Milwaukee Sentinel,* January 29, 1924.

25. *Ibid.*

26. JTT, pp. 6–34.

27. JTT, pp. 69–71.

28. JTT, pp. 70–71.

29. JTT, pp. 71–72.

30. JTT, pp. 84–86. Condonation is the express or implied forgiveness of a wrongful act by its victim. See *Black's Law Dictionary,* 386.

31. JTT, pp. 89–92. Jackson had trusted Grabiner because the club secretary "had always been a fine man with me up to that deal, fair and square as he could possibly be."

32. JTT, pp. 92; 111–114.

33. JTT, pp. 118–123.

34. *Nebraska State Journal,* January 31, 1924.

35. *Milwaukee Sentinel,* January 30, 1924.

36. Specifically cited by the court in support of its ruling were *Murphy v. State,* 124 *Wisc.* 635, 102 *N.W.* 1087 (Sup. Ct. 1905), and the legal treatise *Jones on Evidence, Vol. 4,* Section 265.

37. Overlooked in this scenario is the fact that defense counsel Fallon had offered the transcript of the Jackson grand jury testimony in evidence during open court Attell extradition proceedings in June 1921.

38. Among the drawbacks of this strategy was that it required the work of the grand jury stenographer to be deemed incompetent or corrupt. Nor was Jackson's position helped by the fact that defense counsel at the Black Sox criminal trial had conceded the accuracy of the grand jury record. See again, *Chicago Daily Journal* and *Chicago Herald Examiner,* July 26, 1921. And tellingly, Jackson's civil counsel raised no claim that Hudnall's cross-examination was premised on an unreliable or inauthentic document.

39. JTT, p. 151.

40. JTT, p. 156.

41. JTT, pp. 159–160.
42. JTT, p. 162.
43. JTT, p. 220.
44. JTT, pp. 197–198.
45. JTT, p. 200.
46. JTT, p. 160.
47. JTT, p. 188.
48. JTT, pp. 154–155.
49. JTT, pp. 42–54. To accommodate the schedule of traveling witnesses, Dunkley and others testified as was convenient for them. The direct testimony of plaintiff Jackson, for example, was halted in order to put Dunkley on the stand. The narrative herein proceeds in chronological fashion but does not bifurcate the testimony of interrupted witnesses.
50. JTT, p. 59.
51. JTT, p. 62.
52. Unlike a criminal trial, defendants in civil litigation can be compelled to testify. Team owner Comiskey, moreover, was not technically a party to the suit. The lone defendant named in the Jackson complaint was the American League Baseball Club of Chicago, Comiskey's corporate alter ego.
53. JTT, pp. 344–345.
54. JTT, pp. 372–375.
55. JTT, pp. 375–378.
56. JTT, pp. 360–364. Comiskey was an expert on defensive positioning, having revolutionized play around first base during his playing days in the 1880s.
57. JTT, p. 412.
58. In Black Sox literature, it is sometimes insinuated that there was something sinister about defense procurement of the Jackson grand jury testimony. In this connection, it should be noted that prosecutors and counsel for crime victims routinely cooperate, as SAO attorneys and White Sox counsel Austrian had during the prosecution of the Black Sox case. Once the veil of grand jury secrecy was irrevocably lifted by admission of grand jury testimony in evidence during the ensuing criminal trial, there was no legal or ethical restraint on the dissemination of that testimony to civil litigants. Given that, provision of the Cicotte/Jackson/Williams grand jury testimony to the White Sox in defense of lawsuits initiated by the once accused was neither professionally nor morally inappropriate.
59. JTT, pp. 385–387.
60. JTT, pp. 341–342; 353–398.
61. JTT, p. 467; 483.
62. JTT, pp. 450–452; 473–475. Grabiner further related that an informal agreement was reached to have the club cover Katie Jackson's expenses for attending 1920 spring training.
63. JTT, p. 450; 475.
64. JTT, p. 490. A stipulation is an agreement between both sides in a lawsuit that a certain fact is true and uncontested.
65. Before the trial, Luderus and Jackson were not personally acquainted. Currently a minor league manager, Luderus had played his entire career in the National League and had only seen Jackson in action during a few spring training games.
66. JTT, p. 493.
67. JTT, p. 494.
68. JTT, p. 509.

21

The White Sox Defense and Late Trial Fireworks

Because of circumstances over which counsel had little control, the White Sox defense got off to a disjointed start, calling NL President John Heydler to the witness stand out of turn.[1] For the most part, Heydler's testimony corroborated the Comiskey account of how suspicions about 1919 Series play came to the attention of baseball executives. But defense efforts to elicit testimony about follow-up conversations between Heydler and Comiskey were excluded on hearsay grounds.[2] Former Judge Charles McDonald, now retired from the judiciary and a bank vice-president, proved a more substantial defense witness. At some length, McDonald repeated the testimony that he had provided at the criminal trial, an account plainly harmful to the Jackson side. In the process, McDonald added that Jackson had told him in chambers that "he had made no misplays that could be noticed by the ordinary person but that he did not play his best."[3] Jackson had also informed the witness that the Series fix payoff was supposed to be $100,000, with $20,000 to be distributed after each lost Series game[4]; that after Game Two, Gandil informed Jackson that the gamblers had double crossed the Sox players[5]; and that the Series fix participants were Gandil, Cicotte, Risberg, Williams, Felsch, Weaver, and himself.[6]

The defense then read excerpts of the Burns deposition to the jury.[7] This, however, was not particularly harmful to Jackson, as he had not been present at any of the fix meetings attended by Burns. Rather, Burns' inclusion of Jackson's name on his list of corrupt players was based entirely on what others had told Burns. But the next defense witness to take the stand would not be so benign, placing highly incriminating words directly into Jackson's mouth. He was Elbert M. Allen, the Cook County grand jury stenographer who had taken down Jackson's September 28, 1920, grand jury testimony. Allen had transcribed the Jackson testimony in shorthand and had then composed the typed transcript of that testimony for the State's Attorneys Office.[8] After certifying the accuracy of the transcript now in Hudnall's possession, Allen read the Jackson grand jury testimony aloud for the jury's benefit.[9] The art of overkill next was put on display by the defense, which summoned grand jury foreman Henry Brigham to the stand to corroborate Allen's uncontested testimony about the content of Jackson's grand jury testimony.[10] The Brigham appearance, however, afforded Jackson co-counsel Shaw the opportunity to remind the jury that Jackson had not actually admitted throwing Series games during his grand jury testimony. To the contrary, Jackson had told the grand jury that he had played to win.[11] Subsequently, trial time was consumed by the reading of more depositions, with that of Billy Maharg inflicting little injury on the Jackson cause. But the same could not be said of the second Lefty Williams deposition, replete with recitals of conversations, cash payments, and other fix-connected events implicating Jackson in the Series conspiracy.[12]

Testimony illuminating various Black Sox scandal details was supplied by White Sox corporation counsel Alfred Austrian. Austrian related that, shortly after the 1919 World Series was finished, Comiskey had confided to him his concern about the integrity of the Series. As a result, Comiskey retained John R. Hunter's Secret Service to probe fix rumors.[13] But no concrete proof of player corruption had been unearthed. That being the case, Austrian had advised Comiskey to retain the suspected players, as terminating their employment on unsubstantiated grounds might not be legally defensible.[14] After the Maharg exposé was published in late–September 1920, Eddie Cicotte, Joe Jackson, and later, Lefty Williams, were called to the Austrian office. Austrian, a non-baseball fan[15] who had never met any of the three previously, then recounted the particulars of the statements made in his presence by each ballplayer.[16] Austrian had then accompanied each player to the Cook County courthouse, but had not stayed around for their grand jury testimony. At a later point in the proceedings, the witness revealed that he had made the arrangements necessary for the grand jury appearance of Arnold Rothstein, who had been received beforehand in the Austrian office with personal counsel Hyman Turchin in tow.[17] Following completion of the Black Sox criminal trial in August 1921, Austrian had obtained transcripts of the Cicotte, Jackson, and Williams grand jury testimony from the State's Attorneys Office. Those transcripts were subsequently shipped to Milwaukee during preparation of the club's defense against the civil suits instituted by Jackson and the others.[18]

Next came syndicated sportswriter Hugh Fullerton, who testified about how he came to suspect a fix. Fullerton related that prior to Game One, he encountered old acquaintance Bill Burns, who advised the witness to "wise up" about betting on the Chisox to win the 1919 Series. Burns assured him, "The Reds are in."[19] But Fullerton had not taken Burns seriously and did not report any concern about Series integrity to Comiskey.[20] The timing and content of his post–Series columns notwithstanding, Fullerton testified that he had not been entirely satisfied that the 1919 World Series had been fixed until the confessions of the Sox players were published in late–September 1920.[21] Subsequent testimony by hotel bookkeeper Edward McNamara, the brief recall of Jackson to the witness box, and the reading of selected portions of the Jackson deposition supported the defense contention that Joe and Katie Jackson had stayed for several nights during the 1919 Series at the Lexington Hotel, the scene, according to Lefty Williams, of the $5,000 payoff to Jackson.[22] The defense then sought to further undermine Jackson's credibility by reading deposition excerpts wherein Katie Jackson contradicted her husband's account of events. This recital also permitted the defense to revisit once again the payoff to Jackson, this time from the perspective of his wife.[23] Following that, White Sox lawyers completed the payoff money trail via introduction of bank cashier Cornell's deposition.[24]

Although more harmful to Cannon's other clients, the statements made in the Cicotte deposition, again placing Jackson at the initial fix player meeting at the Ansonia Hotel, did further damage to the Jackson cause.[25] Next, the work of the Hunter detective agency was described to the jury by its namesake. In sum, the probe of Series fix rumors had been unproductive, John R. Hunter testifying that "there was nothing specific that [detectives] could connect up any of the players with" and that no verifiable "misconduct in the way of throwing the series" had been uncovered by his men.[26] Hunter was followed by grand jury stenographer Walter H. Smith, who attested to the accuracy of the grand jury testimony embedded in the depositions of Eddie Cicotte and Lefty Williams.[27] The defense then concluded with testimony from renowned handwriting expert John F. Tyrrell. Based upon comparison of the 1920 contract bearing Joe Jackson's signature to Jackson signature exemplars, Tyrrell concluded that Jackson had not signed the contract while balancing it upon the steering wheel of his automobile.[28]

The remaining testimony concerned Jackson's signature on his contract for the 1920-1921-1922 seasons. Called as a plaintiff's rebuttal witness, Happy Felsch testified that he, like Jackson, had signed his new 1920 season contract using a fountain pen supplied by Harry Grabiner.[29] But seemingly innocuous cross-examination by Hudnall seemed to unglue Felsch. Asked to identify his signature on several documents, including his 1920 contract, Felsch stunned all present by denying authorship, repeatedly. Even friendly cajoling by Cannon — "Just look at it, Happy, ... If that's your signature, say so" — failed to budge the panicked witness.[30] Felsch continued to deny that the signatures were his. Even when Judge Gregory took over the questioning, the answer was the same. The signatures had not been made by Felsch. Unhappily for Happy, signature exemplars that were then extracted from the witness quickly established the obvious: the repudiated signatures were plainly those of Felsch.[31] Now it was Judge Gregory who was unhappy, but the judge chose to bide his time, permitting counsel to conclude questioning of the witness. This afforded Felsch the chance to deny something else: participation in the conspiracy to throw the 1919 World Series. Nor, Felsch claimed, had he received "a penny" for corrupt Series play.[32]

Reckoning came the next morning when Judge Gregory preempted attorney plans and immediately directed Felsch back to the stand, outside the jury's presence. Present in the courtroom gallery for this event was Assistant Milwaukee County District Attorney Roland Steinle, attending the proceedings at Gregory's request.[33] Once everyone was in place, the judge announced that, in the court's view, Felsch had "defiantly" committed perjury. No expert was needed to authenticate the denied signatures, Gregory declared. Any lay person could tell that the signatures had been made by Felsch.[34] The court then beckoned the bailiffs and instructed them to take the witness into custody. The hapless Happy was removed from a somber and subdued courtroom.[35] His bail on a perjury citation was set at $2,000.

Once the jury was returned to its place,[36] Cannon resumed his rebuttal case by presenting handwriting expert W.W. Way. who testified that the same pen had been used to inscribe both the contract terms and the Jackson signature onto the player's 1920-1921-1922 contract. Way was also of the opinion that the pen in question was a fountain pen and that the Jackson signature had been written "awkwardly and clumsily."[37] The battle of experts then continued with Marquette University chemistry professor J. Vernon Steinle being summoned to the stand as a witness of the court. Steinle's testimony, however, did little to resolve the signature issues, being brief and inconclusive.[38] Lest plaintiff have the last word, the Sox defense subsequently called Harry Grabiner for surrebuttal testimony. First, Grabiner identified letters bearing signatures repudiated by Happy Felsch as club correspondence received from Felsch himself. Grabiner had also witnessed Felsch sign his 1920 contract, which did not involve use of a fountain pen. "I have never had a fountain pen," the witness reiterated.[39] The defense then returned handwriting expert Tyrrell to the stand to support the Grabiner testimony. In Tyrrell's opinion, the contract entries and signature on the 1920 Felsch pact displayed the fine line of a steel pen, not a fountain pen.[40] And on that tangential note, testimony in the Jackson civil case came to a close.

Notes

1. Heydler actually took the stand before the plaintiff rested, the testimony of plaintiff's expert Luderus being interrupted as a courtesy to the busy NL president.
2. JTT, pp. 502–505.
3. JTT, p. 552. McDonald had a "distinct recollection" of this particular admission.
4. JTT, p. 550.
5. JTT, p. 551.
6. JTT, p. 554. Jackson had omitted Fred McMullin from the fix roster.
7. See JTT, pp. 575–591; 686–708. Burns did not appear as a witness in the civil trial.
8. JTT, p. 599; 642.
9. JTT, pp. 603–640. In the process, Allen recited the 128 or so answers that Jackson had denied giving to the grand jury during his civil trial testimony two days earlier.
10. JTT, pp. 648–655.
11. JTT, p. 652.
12. JTT, pp. 710–740 (Maharg deposition); JTT, pp. 743–797 (first Williams deposition); JTT, pp. 802–870 (second Williams deposition). As with Bill Burns, neither Billy Maharg nor Lefty Williams was called to the witness stand during the civil trial.
13. JTT, pp. 889–891.
14. JTT, pp. 958–965. When recalled to the stand later in the trial, Comiskey testified that he had followed Austrian's advice about re-signing the fix suspects. See JTT, p. 1514.
15. JTT, pp. 910–912; 948–950. In the 17 years that he provided legal counsel to Comiskey and Cubs owner William Wrigley, Austrian reportedly attended only one ball game, as per the *Milwaukee Sentinel,* February 8, 1924. Apart from his family and the law, Austrian's interests were scholarly. According to his obituaries, Austrian was versed in the classics and collected original manuscripts and first editions. See *Chicago Tribune* and *New York Times,* January 27, 1932.
16. JTT, pp. 895–907: 1023–1027.
17. JTT, pp. 929–937.
18. JTT, pp. 910–912. Correspondence related to the transmittal of the transcripts to Hudnall is contained in CHM, Black Sox file, Box 1, Folder 7.
19. JTT, p. 1060.
20. JTT, pp. 1080–1081. Years later — after Comiskey's death and the expiration of the statute of limitations on a false testimony charge — Fullerton had an entirely different story, writing that he had informed Comiskey before Game One of talk that the Series was fixed. See *The Sporting News,* October 17, 1935.
21. JTT, pp. 1081–1084.
22. JTT, pp. 1105–1123. This phase of the case also included testimony by Red Faber (at JTT, pp. 1124–1143) on the mostly neglected 1917 World Series bonus claim. The Faber testimony supported the defense position that the bonus offer had not been made by Comiskey.
23. JTT, pp. 1130–1163.
24. JTT, pp. 1169–1179.
25. JTT, pp. 1213–1214.
26. JTT, pp. 1302–1320. For a fuller account of Hunter's work, see Gene Carney, "Comiskey's Detectives," *Baseball Research Journal,* Vol. 37, 2009, 108–116.
27. JTT, pp. 1352–1471.
28. JTT, pp. 1493–1504. Tyrrell's expertise would later be utilized in the Leopold & Loeb and Bruno Hauptmann (Lindbergh baby) murder trials. Handwriting expert John F. Tyrrell and like-named Black Sox prosecutor John F. Tyrrell were not related.
29. JTT, pp. 1566–1567.

30. Cannon's direction to Felsch is not contained in the trial record but was noted in contemporaneous civil trial reportage. See, e.g., *Chicago Tribune* and *Milwaukee Sentinel,* February 13, 1924.

31. JTT, pp. 1582–1587. Seizing the opportunity, Hudnall immediately moved to dismiss the pending Felsch suit, arguing, too cleverly, that Felsch could not base a claim on a contract that Felsch had just denied signing, as reported in the *Chicago Tribune,* February 13, 1924. The application was backhanded by Judge Gregory, who also denied a follow-up defense motion to strike the Felsch testimony from the trial record. See JTT, pp. 1592–1594.

32. JTT, pp. 1594–1597.

33. As reported in the *Chicago Tribune* and *Nebraska State Journal,* February 14, 1924.

34. JTT, pp. 1594–1595.

35. As reported in the *Chicago Tribune*, *Nebraska State Journal* and *Oakland Tribune,* February 14, 1924. Notwithstanding the hard stare that he had given Felsch earlier in the proceedings, Charles Comiskey appeared visibly distressed by the arrest of his former player, as reported in the *Milwaukee Sentinel,* February 14, 1924.

36. The court's citation of Felsch for perjury had taken place outside the jury's presence. Preventative action was taken by the court to shield the jury from learning of the event. In the meantime, bail was posted for Felsch and he was released from custody later in the day, as reported in the *Chicago Tribune* and *Oakland Tribune,* February 14, 1924.

37. JTT, pp. 1605–1623, implying without stating outright that the signer was balancing the contract on something like an automobile steering wheel while affixing his signature to the contract.

38. JTT, pp. 1624–1653.

39. JTT, pp. 1655–1659.

40. JTT, pp. 1660–1662.

22

Civil Case Endgame

With all of the evidence having been presented, Hudnall made several motions on behalf of the White Sox, including one for a directed verdict in favor of the ballclub. That was denied by the court without prejudice to its renewal after the jury had rendered its verdict. Hudnall also moved to strike any evidence of condonation that might have crept into the trial record, but that application was left unaddressed in the court's rulings.[1] The trial then proceeded to summations, with each side allotted three hours.[2] The order of address would be plaintiff, defense, then plaintiff again.

The closing remarks of plaintiff's counsel Shaw were designed more toward fostering juror empathy with Joe Jackson than to demonstrating the merits of his lawsuit. In this vein, Shaw "touched eloquently" on the ballplayer's blighted youth and the circumstances of his rise to baseball fame. But even an established star like Shoeless Joe Jackson was in an inequitable position when it came to bargaining his livelihood with wealthy and powerful team owners like Charles Comiskey. Still, Shaw argued, it "strained credulity" to accept Grabiner's claim that Jackson and the team secretary had not even discussed Jackson's desire to see Clause 10 deleted from his proposed new contract.[3]

When the defense turn came, "three distinguished lawyers ... pleaded fervently and eloquently" for a verdict in favor of the White Sox. Defense counsel summations commenced with an attack on the character of Jackson by Frank McNamara, affixing the time-tested Judas Iscariot label to the ballplayer. McNamara then ridiculed Jackson's account of his encounter with Grabiner, loudly telling the jury that "you can't believe one word that Jackson said, except his name and where he lives."[4] The personal attack on plaintiff was continued by John C. Northrup, who was "merciless in his denunciation of Jackson, calling his alleged perfidy to his employer one of the crimes that is beyond comprehension."[5] Matters of evidence, as opposed to character, were finally reached in the summation of lead defense counsel George Hudnall. Among other things, Hudnall observed that Jackson's account of his 1920 contract signing was uncorroborated by any other plaintiff's witness; that various aspects of Jackson's testimony regarding receipt of the $5,000 from Lefty Williams were contradicted by Katie Jackson in her deposition, and that Jackson's retention and personal use of that money substantiated his involvement in the plot to fix the 1919 World Series. Given Jackson's misconduct and the "best services" obligation in MLB player contracts, the White Sox termination of their pact with Jackson had been amply justified.[6]

Accorded the final say, plaintiff's lead counsel Cannon closed with a "powerful argument for a verdict that would restore to [Jackson] his honor and prestige among his fellow men."[7] Turning to the merits of the case, Cannon focused his rhetoric on the legal principle that the White Sox defense had long protested was not properly a part of plaintiff's case: condonation. The extant civil trial record is silent regarding when and on what basis the court sanctioned a condonation appeal to the jury. But clearly the court had done so and Cannon would now make the most of it.[8] In a nutshell, Cannon asserted that team officials had uncovered the World Series treachery of the Black Sox long before the time came to sign them to new contracts. But despite that knowledge, the team had chosen to sign Jackson and the others for the upcoming season anyway, effectively forgiving or condoning their Series misconduct in the process. Said Cannon, "White Sox management knew in 1919 about the crookedness of the World Series of that year, and yet next Spring was eager to sign Jackson to continue on their team for at least three years longer."[9] Having knowingly contracted with a scandal-tainted player in February 1920, the White Sox could not unilaterally terminate that pact six months later—when the public became cognizant of what club management had known all along.[10] Jackson was therefore entitled to his unpaid 1921 and 1922 salaries. Over repeated and oft-times sustained defense objection, a now weeping Cannon closed with an emotional flourish, ending

> his pleading for Jackson, whom he described as one of 15 children, obliged at twelve years of age to enter the unhealthy cotton mills of South Carolina to feed his brothers and sisters and begged the jury to restore his honor to him even if it didn't give him any money, so that he can go back home and again look his neighbor in the eye and tell the world that he has been falsely accused.[11]

At the conclusion of the Cannon address, the judge delivered his instructions to the jury. He noted that, as in most civil cases, Jackson, as the plaintiff, bore the burden of proof on disputed matters of fact. Turning next to the existence of Clause 10 in the 1920-1921-1922 Jackson contract, he made express reference to Jackson's illiteracy and his reliance on his wife during previous contract negotiations. Judge Gregory reminded the jury that, although both a conspiracy to throw the 1919 World Series and Jackson's acceptance of $5,000 from Lefty Williams were admitted by plaintiff, participation in the conspiracy was denied by Jackson. Thus, it was up to the jury to "determine whether Jackson was a party to it."[12] Regarding condonation, the legal principle that had taken center stage in the case, the court instructed the jury that the plaintiff again bore the burden of proving that "Comiskey had knowledge of the 1919 conspiracy to throw the World Series prior to signing Jackson for the 1920 season."[13]

To guide the jury's resolution of these issues, Judge Gregory gave them ten special interrogatories that were designed to guide the jurors through the various issues presented by the case and help them reach a just and rational verdict.[14] The first two dealt with the 1917 World Series bonus claim, a matter largely ignored during the proceedings.[15] Questions Three through Five asked the jury, in essence, to decide if club secretary Grabiner had misled Jackson about Clause 10 during 1920 contract negotiations. The next four were Black Sox scandal-related. Question Six asked if Jackson had conspired with Gandil, Williams, and the others to throw the 1919 Series. If he had, Question Seven probed whether Comiskey had been aware of Jackson's involvement in the fix when the White Sox signed Jackson for the 1920 season. Question Eight asked whether Jackson had received the $5,000 from Williams "before all the games of the 1919 World Series had been played." If Jackson was given the money after the Series was over, Question Nine asked whether the $5,000 was Jackson's prearranged share of conspiracy payoffs. The final question required assessment of specific monetary damages for breach of contract if the jury returned a verdict in plaintiff's favor.[16]

In evaluating the evidence, the jury was instructed to use its common sense and knowledge of human nature. It was to avoid passion and prejudice and to forget that a corporation was the party being sued. The jury was only to think of doing justice to both sides.[17] The agreement of ten jurors — favoring one side or the other — would be required for the twelve-member panel to reach a verdict. The jury was then excused to begin deliberations in private.

After the jury had filed from the courtroom, Judge Gregory remained seated on the bench. He then unexpectedly summoned Jackson to the well of the court, informing him that the court "now had a pained duty [to perform] with reference to you." With Jackson standing alone directly in front of the bench, the following exchange took place:

JUDGE GREGORY: You say you started working in a South Carolina cotton mill at age 13?

JACKSON: Yes, sir.

JUDGE GREGORY: Well, at that age I was a newsboy. But that does not give me the right to commit perjury now.[18]

Gregory then informed Jackson that "you stand here self-convicted of the crime of perjury. You came to the wrong state, to the wrong city, to the wrong court." The judge directed bailiffs to take Jackson into custody.[19] To observers, Jackson appeared stunned by the court's pronouncement, his mouth agape. He quickly recovered his composure, however, and assumed a stoic demeanor while being escorted from the courtroom.[20] The judge then set Jackson's bail at $5,000, more than twice the bail placed on Happy Felsch a day earlier.[21]

Sometime after Jackson had been removed, Judge Gregory recalled the jury to the courtroom. Seeking to avoid jury discovery of the situation and, hence, a likely mistrial, he informed the jurors that unspecified courtroom action had been taken in their absence but that they were not to speculate on the nature of that action. Nor were the jurors to read newspaper accounts of the trial until after they had rendered a verdict and been discharged from service. And to further safeguard the jury from contamination via news of Jackson's arrest, the panel was advised that, for those same unspecified reasons, it was being placed under sheriffs' guard and would be sequestered until a judgment was rendered. With that, the jury was excused to resume its deliberations. But before he left the bench, Judge Gregory told the lawyers that "when the jury has returned its verdict, I shall have something more to say on this case."[22]

The following morning, the normally genial judge was still in high dudgeon. Citing the irreconcilability of the testimony that Jackson had given at trial and his testimony before the Cook County grand jury, the judge repeated his view that Jackson "stands self-convicted and self-accused of perjury.[23] Either his testimony here or his testimony before the Chicago grand jury was false. I think the false testimony was given here."[24] In any event, the court was making this statement now "before receiving the verdict of the jury because I will not be influenced or guided by the action of the jury."[25] The judge then turned his wrath on Cannon, criticizing his summation as "not pleading for justice but pleading for mercy. Asking for damages of $5 when suing for $18,000. If plaintiff Jackson requires mercy, he must ask the court for it," not the jury.[26] Judge Gregory then left the bench. But before the day was out, the jury would return a verdict that would do little to improve his mood.

Notes

1. JTT, pp. 1667–1668.
2. As per the *Chicago Tribune* and *Oakland Tribune,* February 14, 1924.
3. As reported in the *Milwaukee Evening Sentinel,* February 13, 1924. In civil matters, the omission of summations from the trial transcript is not unusual and the CBM transcript of the Jackson case does not contain the closing remarks of counsel.
4. As summarized and quoted in the *Milwaukee Evening Sentinel,* February 14, 1924.
5. *Ibid.*
6. As per the *Milwaukee Evening Sentinel,* February 15, 1924.
7. As per the *Milwaukee Sentinel,* February 15, 1924.
8. Although no trace of a plaintiff-favorable ruling on condonation resides in the CBM trial transcript or trial reportage, manifestly somewhere along the line Judge Gregory sanctioned a condonation appeal to the jury.
9. As quoted in the *Milwaukee Sentinel,* February 15, 1924.
10. *Ibid.*
11. *Ibid.*
12. The court's final instructions to the jury are not contained in the CBM trial transcript. The exposition herein is derived from the reportage of the *Milwaukee Journal, Milwaukee Sentinel* and *Milwaukee Evening Sentinel,* February 14 and 15, 1924.
13. *Ibid.*
14. The use of jury questions — known as interrogatories — is a common feature in the trial of civil cases, particularly complex ones.
15. The ten special interrogatories were published verbatim in the *Milwaukee Journal,* February 14, 1924, *Milwaukee Sentinel,* February 15, 1924, and elsewhere.
16. As per the *Milwaukee Journal,* February 14, 1924, and *Milwaukee Sentinel,* February 15, 1924.
17. As per the *Milwaukee Sentinel,* February 15, 1924.
18. As reported in the *Milwaukee Journal,* February 15, 1924.
19. *Ibid.*
20. As per the *Milwaukee Sentinel,* February 15, 1924.
21. JTT, p. 1686.
22. As per the *Milwaukee Sentinel,* February 15, 1924. See, also, *Milwaukee Journal,* February 15, 1924.
23. JTT, pp. 1686–1687. See, also, *Milwaukee Evening Sentinel,* February 15, 1924. The perjury-related crime of false swearing can be deemed a sort of self-accusing, self-convicting offense. In one of its forms, false swearing does not require demonstration that a particular statement given under oath was false. Conviction can rest upon proof that the accused uttered inconsistent statements on the same subject matter while under oath at different judicial proceedings. It does not matter which of the two inconsistent statements is false, just that one of them has to be (e.g., giving two different birth dates).
24. As per the *Milwaukee Evening Sentinel,* February 15, 1924.
25. JTT, pp. 1687–1688.
26. JTT, pp. 1689–1690.

23

The Jury's Judgment and Its Aftermath

After several hours in custody, Joe Jackson was released on bond, his freedom secured by Joseph A. Padway and George Damman, two Milwaukee attorneys who had earlier posted bond for Happy Felsch.[1] The next morning, Jackson was back in the courtroom regaling local reporters with stories while the jury was out.[2] He also denied that he had committed perjury. "I told the truth, as far as I remembered it," maintained Jackson. "Those lawyers, they had everything before them in writing. I had to depend on my memory and what happened was a long time ago. Maybe in some things I was mistaken, but I didn't do no lying — not that I know of."[3]

The Jackson discourse came to an abrupt halt when word was received that the jury had reached a verdict. Without waiting for the trial's principals to reassemble — of the attorneys, only defense counsel Northrup was in or near the courtroom — Judge Gregory had the jury brought in. The verdict was promptly received and it was a triumph for Jackson. Via a special verdict form signed by jury foreman Sanderson, the panel answered every interrogatory in Jackson's favor.[4] More particularly, the jury had determined that Comiskey had, in fact, offered the 1917 White Sox players the disputed World Series bonus; that Harry Grabiner had misled Jackson about the retention of Clause 10 in his 1920-1921-1922 contract; that Jackson had not conspired to throw the 1919 World Series; that Jackson had not received the $5,000 from Lefty Williams while the Series was in progress, and that Jackson had not accepted the money in connection with participation in the Series fix.[5] Breach of contract damages were set at $16,711.04. But no additional sum was awarded plaintiff on the 1917 Series bonus claim.[6]

Judge Gregory greeted the verdict with astonishment and indignation. As jurors sat frozen in their seats, the judge lit into them. "You have failed to discharge your duty," Gregory chided. "How you could answer some of those questions in the manner you have, the court cannot understand. Jackson stands before this court a convicted perjurer and has been committed to jail. It did not need a court or a jury to determine that. Jackson determined that for himself."[7] With that, Gregory dismissed the panel from the courtroom. Not waiting for the arrival of plaintiff's counsel, the court then solicited applications from the defense. A hastily collected Hudnall obliged. "I move that the verdict be set aside on the ground that it is based on a conspiracy to defeat justice and founded on perjury," he said. "You can file a written motion to that effect," snapped Gregory in reply. The court, on its own motion, was setting aside the jury's verdict, specifying fraud and perjured testimony as its grounds.[8]

As they left the courtroom, smiling White Sox lawyers declined comment on this startling turn of events[9] but plaintiff's counsel Cannon was not so bashful. Reached by telephone at his office, Cannon complained that "Judge Gregory may be perfectly right in this matter. But I don't see how the verdict can be set aside without hearing argument from counsel on both sides. We haven't had a chance to be heard yet."[10] Vowing to persevere on his client's behalf, Cannon took solace in the jury's judgment. "We view the victory obtained by Jackson in this case from a jury of twelve men and women to be so far reaching as to bring about Jackson's ultimate return to organized baseball," he said optimistically.[11]

Insight into the jury's thinking was provided in post-trial interviews granted by panel foreman John E. Sanderson. In the process, Sanderson took considerable luster off the Jackson triumph.[12] Sanderson revealed that the jury had not believed Jackson's testimony and had disregarded it entirely while deciding the facts.[13] Regarding the disputed circumstances of the 1920 contract signing, the jury specifically rejected Jackson's claim that he had signed his new contract while balancing it against his auto's steering wheel. Rather, the jury concluded that the contract had been signed inside the Jackson residence as Harry Grabiner testified, but that, critically, Katie Jackson had not been present.[14] Nor did the jury's verdict represent much vindication of Jackson's World Series conduct. As far as Sanderson himself was concerned, Jackson knew that the $5,000 received from Williams had come from gamblers trying to rig the Series. At least to that extent, Jackson was therefore involved in the fix conspiracy.[15] Despite that, the jury had decided the case in Jackson's favor. Its judgment was founded on the principle of condonation, the theory that had been so feared by White Sox attorneys.

Sanderson explained that the jury was convinced that Comiskey and other club officials had become aware of Jackson's involvement in the fix soon after the 1919 Series was over. Yet club management had chosen to offer Jackson a new contract anyway and had therefore condoned Jackson's Series misconduct.[16] Given that, subsequent public exposure of Jackson's betrayal of the team did not afford the White Sox a legitimate basis for terminating his contract.[17] Jackson was therefore entitled to his withheld salary. Calculating the White Sox to have been in breach of its contractual obligations to Jackson for two years (the 1921 and 1922 seasons) and two weeks (a paycheck owed Jackson for the end of the 1920 season), the jury awarded him back pay at his contract salary rates.[18] Having resolved the case thusly, no apologies on behalf of the jury were offered by Sanderson, the scolding of Judge Gregory notwithstanding. He maintained that the jurors had done their "full duty, based on the testimony and our common sense."[19]

The stunning developments that brought the trial to a close prompted reaction from many quarters. Back in Chicago, Charles Comiskey informed the press that "he would continue to fight crookedness in baseball and if the sport could not be kept clean, he would get out."[20] Meanwhile in Milwaukee, Katie Jackson stood by her husband whom, Katie believed, would never tell a lie in court.[21] Katie's sentiments were overshadowed by those of Milwaukee County District Attorney George A. Shaughnessy, who announced his intention to secure a transcript of Jackson's trial testimony. "We will go over it carefully to see if there is anything that seems to warrant prosecution for perjury," the DA stated. "If we find anything, we will make complaint, a warrant will be issued and Jackson re-arrested."[22] The proceedings before Judge Gregory, however, were not yet over. To formalize the court's ruling from the bench, Sox defense counsel Hudnall submitted an order for Judge Gregory to sign. Plaintiff's counsel Cannon countered by filling a motion for entry of the judgment and award returned by the jury. Both applications would be entertained by the court at a later date.[23] In the meantime, Jackson retained former Milwaukee County DA Wilfred C. Zabel to defend him on any forthcoming perjury charge.[24] Jackson then went home to Savannah.

On May 27, 1924, a formal order nullifying the jury verdict was signed by Judge Gregory. The order specified that there was no credible evidence to support the jury's answers to the special interrogatories and that the verdict was based wholly on perjured testimony. On that basis, the jury's award was vacated and the Jackson complaint dismissed with prejudice.[25] In due course, Jackson appealed to the Wisconsin Supreme Court, asserting that the trial court had no authority to overturn a jury's verdict on the grounds cited in its order.[26] Thereafter, the matter proceeded at the leisurely pace congenial to appellate courts.

On October 20, 1925, the Wisconsin Supreme Court dismissed the Jackson appeal, apparently on the basis of procedural deficiencies.[27] Or perhaps the appeal was abandoned by the Jackson side in contemplation of an out-of-court resolution of the case, as several Black Sox authors relate that the case eventually ended in settlement.[28] At this late date, the ultimate disposition of the matter cannot be stated with certainty. But whatever the final outcome, it went unnoted in the press, for the Jackson civil suit was no longer a matter of much public interest.

Notes

1. Jackson was released at 10:00 P.M.

2. At least one newsman was impressed, reporting that Jackson's "years of experience in the big leagues and his travels throughout the country, together with his natural disposition have given him an address that no one would associate with illiteracy," as per the *Milwaukee Journal,* February 15, 1924.

3. *Ibid.*

4. As reported in the *Milwaukee Evening Sentinel,* February 15, 1924.

5. As particularized in the *Milwaukee Journal,* February 15, 1924.

6. JTT, p. 1694. The trial transcript does not indicate the jury vote but most published accounts placed it at 11–1 in Jackson's favor. See, e.g., *Milwaukee Journal,* February 15, 1924, and *Atlanta Constitution,* February 16, 1924. In one post-verdict interview, however, jury foreman Sanderson stated that the original vote was 10–2 but turned unanimous in favor of the plaintiff by the time that a fifth ballot was taken. See *Milwaukee Evening Sentinel,* February 15, 1924. Given that the assent of only ten jurors was required to return a verdict, the taking of additional ballots is curious.

7. JTT, pp. 1694–1695. See, also, *Milwaukee Evening Sentinel,* February 15, 1924.

8. JTT, p. 1696. See, also, *Milwaukee Journal* and *Milwaukee Evening Sentinel,* February 15, 1924.

9. As per the *Milwaukee Evening Sentinel,* February 15, 1924.

10. As quoted in the *Milwaukee Journal,* February 15, 1924.

11. As quoted in the *Chicago Tribune,* February 15, 1924, and *Atlanta Constitution* and *Nebraska State Journal,* February 16, 1924.

12. Although Sanderson claimed only to speak for himself, it is the author's experience that post-verdict remarks by the jury foreman, particularly one as obviously intelligent as Sanderson, usually reflect the sentiments of the panel as a whole.

13. As reported in the *Milwaukee Journal* and *Milwaukee Evening Sentinel,* February 15, 1924.

14. *Ibid.*

15. As reported in the *Milwaukee Journal,* February 15, 1924. This particular assertion is at odds with the jury response to the sixth question: *Did plaintiff Jackson unlawfully conspire with Gandil, ... to lose or throw any of the baseball games of the 1919 World Series?* Answer: *No.*

16. The issue of condonation was expressly addressed in the seventh question, but the jury's response to the preceding query made that question superfluous. The seventh question was, therefore, left unanswered by the jury.

17. As per the *Milwaukee Journal,* February 15, 1924. Specifically, club awareness of Jackson's involvement in the fix was inferred from Comiskey's failure to confront Jackson about Series rumors and from the character of the Hunter investigation, which the jury viewed as being designed more to cover up player wrongdoing than expose it.

18. *Ibid.*

19. As reported in the *Milwaukee Evening Sentinel,* February 15, 1924.

20. As quoted in the *Milwaukee Journal,* February 15, 1924. Similar Comiskey comments appeared in the *Chicago Tribune,* February 15, 1924.

21. As reported in the *Milwaukee Journal,* February 17, 1924.

22. As per the *Milwaukee Journal,* February 16, 1924, and *Chicago Tribune,* February 17, 1924. The perjury arrest of Jackson ordered by Judge Gregory was a contempt of court-type sanction. Criminal proceedings against Jackson could only be instituted by a law enforcement agency, like the District Attorney's Office.

23. As per the *Milwaukee Evening Sentinel* and *Milwaukee Journal,* February 16, 1924. Judge Gregory's ruling was not final, and hence subject to appeal, until it was embodied in a formal order signed by the court.

24. As reported in the *Chicago Tribune,* February 20, 1924. Zabel, Jackson's new lawyer, was the former Milwaukee District Attorney named as recipient of the bootleg champagne in the Cannon bribery indictment of February 1923.

25. As briefly noted in the *New York Times,* May 28, 1924. A copy of the court's order is contained in CHM, Black Sox file, Box 1, Folder 8.

26. As had been previewed for the press by Cannon associate A.W. Richter. See *Chicago Tribune* and *Los Angeles Times,* April 25, 1924.

27. As reported in the *Chicago Tribune,* October 21, 1925.

28. See, e.g., Ginsburg, 155; Carney, "Notes from the Shadows of Cooperstown," No. 298, June 30, 2003, and *Burying the Black Sox,* 7. Jackson biographer Gropman equivocates, writing that it "appears" that the case was settled to "forestall an appeal," in *Say It Ain't So, Joe!,* 227. Mike Nola, official historian of the Shoeless Joe Jackson Virtual Hall of Fame and perhaps the foremost authority on Joe Jackson, could not verify the out-of-court settlement assertion. Nor could the author document it. But late settlement of litigation, even by the prevailing party at trial, is hardly an unheard of legal phenomenon.

24

Resolution of the Remaining Lawsuits

The trial of the Jackson civil case was the last legal proceeding that shed any light on the Black Sox scandal. The remaining lawsuits — the still-pending civil actions of Happy Felsch, Swede Risberg, and Buck Weaver — limped to inconclusive and little noticed conclusions. To some extent, pursuit of the Felsch and Risberg suits may have been chilled by the prospect of criminal prosecution of the plaintiffs. In early April 1924, Milwaukee DA Shaughnessy, now satisfied that false testimony had, in fact, been uttered at the recent Jackson civil trial, directed that warrants be obtained for the arrest of Felsch and Jackson.[1] On May 19, 1924, a not guilty plea to a perjury criminal complaint was entered by Felsch.[2] In due course, the matter would be scheduled for a preliminary hearing and then trial.[3] Given the peril of this now pending criminal prosecution, testimony at another civil trial would obviously place Felsch, and perhaps Risberg, as well, in further jeopardy. But an even larger impediment to forward movement of the Felsch and Risberg lawsuits was the attitude of Judge Gregory, thoroughly disaffected by both the testimony of Jackson and Felsch and the conduct of plaintiff's attorney Raymond Cannon during the trial of Jackson's suit. Gregory had little appetite for a rerun of that case in his courtroom anytime soon.

Judge Gregory's disinclination to afford the Black Sox litigation more time on his calendar was driven home to Cannon on May 23, 1924, shortly before the formal order vacating the jury judgment and dismissing the Jackson suit was entered by the court. On the docket that date was a Cannon motion to set an immediate trial date for the Felsch and/or Risberg action. The application, however, was opposed by counsel for the White Sox, citing the ill health of Comiskey. The team owner had recently undergone surgery and would require considerable time to recuperate. That was all Gregory needed to hear: further proceedings in the Felsch/Risberg were postponed indefinitely.[4] From there, the litigation turned ugly and personal. On August 24, 1924, Cannon obtained a show cause order that sought to have Comiskey held in contempt for exaggerating his illness.[5] This precipitated an acrimonious hearing before Judge Gregory in which antagonisms on all sides were placed on display. At the end of the proceedings, the court determined that grounds for sanctions against Comiskey had not been shown and discharged the order. As previously, the Felsch and Risberg lawsuits would remain adjourned without date.[6]

With his pending actions becalmed, Cannon cast his eyes on a new litigation target: Commissioner Landis. A new grievance would center on shares of second-place finish money for the 1920 season withheld from Jackson, Felsch, and Risberg. On October 28, 1924, a declaration of intent to initiate suit was filed by Cannon.[7] Concerned about the debilitating effect that representing Black Sox was having on his firm's practice,[8] Cannon tried to distance this latest suit from the scandal. "The money claimed has absolutely nothing to do with the 1919 World Series," he proclaimed, "but that which was lawfully earned and to which the players are rightfully entitled."[9]

Filed in Milwaukee, the suit notice was accompanied by requirement that Landis submit to immediate deposition. On November 3, 1924, the Commissioner and his local attorney, Cannon nemesis George B. Hudnall, appeared before court commissioner Max W. Nohl to face the Cannon inquisition. But to the disappointment of gathered reporters, the proceedings were tame, completely "devoid of fireworks."[10] During two and one-half hours of questioning, Landis remained unruffled, informing Cannon that the decision to withhold second-place money from Black Sox players had been proposed by team owners, not him.[11] The sanction had also been endorsed by league presidents Heydler and Johnson.[12] Landis was unsure about what would eventually become of the confiscated shares "but his guess was that it would go to the 16 clubs in the major leagues."[13] In any event, it would not be Landis' call.

At session's end, Hudnall opined that if Cannon wanted to sue, his actions should be commenced against the team owners, not Commissioner Landis.[14] Cannon viewed the situation differently, as all executive power in major league baseball now was vested in the Commissioner. The team owners would do as Landis bade them.[15] Even so, litigation over such relatively small sums seemed unproductive. No record was found by the author showing that litigation was ever initiated. Little more was heard of the controversy for the next year. Then, at a December 10, 1925, meeting of team owners, disposition of the 1920 second-place shares withheld from the Black Sox was announced. The money would be distributed to their teammates, "those players who proved that they had no connection to the plot to throw the series to Cincinnati."[16]

In the end, the White Sox outlasted Raymond J. Cannon. In February 1925, the Felsch and Risberg suits were settled, with each plaintiff accepting a small fraction of the damages originally sought. Felsch received his final two salary paychecks for the 1920 season ($583.33 each), with interest and incurred costs — a recovery of $1,575.35 total.[17] Risberg got less, a nuisance-value award of $401.31.[18] With that, the Black Sox lawsuits were reduced to one: the Weaver suit still pending in federal district court in Chicago. But before the scene shifted to Chicago, there were still a few matters to be resolved locally.

Settlement of the Felsch and Risberg suits did not bring scandal-related proceedings in Milwaukee entirely to a close. There were still the looming perjury charges against Happy Felsch and Joe Jackson. DA Shaughnessy's elevation to a judgeship in July 1924 effected a change of administration at the district attorney's office but not a perceptible difference in attitude regarding the charges. On December 19, 1924, new Milwaukee DA Eugene Wengert announced that a new complaint had been drafted against Jackson. This process would replace the prior charge, as that "had not been filed through proper chanels,"[19] and would promptly be served on Jackson in Georgia in order to "obtain proper jurisdiction" over the accused.[20]

On May 18, 1925, Felsch appeared before Judge Gregory to enter a negotiated plea of guilty to the offense of false swearing, a lesser included offense of the original perjury charge. Upon accepting the plea, the court sentenced Felsch to a one-year term of probation and dismissed the underlying perjury complaint.[21] That same date, Jackson failed to appear for pretrial proceedings before Judge George F. Page. Attorney Cannon attempted to excuse his client's absence, explaining that Jackson was then on a barnstorming trip with a team from Waycross, Georgia. The court was unmoved. Jackson's $1,000 bond was declared forfeited and a bench warrant was issued for his arrest.[22] When news of the situation reached Jackson, he expressed surprise. Jackson was not aware that court proceedings had been scheduled and intended "to get in touch directly" with Cannon.[23] After that, no judicial proceedings on the Jackson perjury charge are known to have been conducted. The matter apparently languished, with no resolution publicly announced. Decades later, however, a Milwaukee newspaper would report that the Jackson perjury charge was ultimately dismissed.[24]

While matters in the Felsch, Risberg and Jackson cases were winding down, the Weaver suit plodded to disposition. Unlike the situation in Milwaukee, the Weaver litigation was conducted in a low-key and professionally cordial manner. The principal attorneys, Charles A. Williams for plaintiff Weaver and Alfred S. Austrian for the defendant White Sox, were both eminent members of the Chicago bar and active in Republican Party politics.[25]

The lawyers, however, were unable to reach agreement on a settlement, the White Sox rejecting the $5,000 figure proposed by Williams at a December 1923 pretrial hearing. From February 1924 on, the Weaver suit appears to have been carried on the district court trial list. But nothing more was printed about the case until a brief item appeared in the *Chicago Tribune* of November 20, 1925. It stated that the Weaver suit had been dismissed by Chief Judge George A. Carpenter after plaintiff's counsel Williams failed to appear in court, presumably for another trial call. In addition to dismissal, Judge Carpenter also imposed court costs on the plaintiff.[26] A formal order terminating the Weaver lawsuit was subsequently entered on December 31, 1925.[27]

As in the case of Joe Jackson, Black Sox authors have reported that Weaver and the White Sox later reached an out-of-court settlement.[28] In one of his final internet postings, the late Gene Carney related that the settlement was reached in 1930, with Weaver getting $3,500, or approximately half his unpaid 1921 salary.[29] According to scandal chronicler Dan Ginsburg, "Weaver always viewed this [settlement] as exoneration and additional proof of his innocence."[30] If so, it would be about the only satisfaction that Weaver would ever derive from the Black Sox scandal.

Notes

1. As reported in the *Chicago Tribune*, April 10, 1924.
2. As reported in the *Los Angeles Times*, May 20, 1924. Presumably, a personal appearance by Jackson, now back in Georgia, was waived for arraignment on the complaint.
3. Except in extraordinary situations, grand juries were not empanelled in Milwaukee. On most charges, a preliminary hearing was conducted instead. The differences between how a criminal case was prosecuted in Milwaukee, as opposed to Chicago, were explained by Shaughnessy (by then a judge) in the *Chicago Tribune*, January 12, 1925.
4. As reported in the *Chicago Tribune*, May 25, 1924, and documented in CHM, Black Sox file, Box 1, Folder 8. The proceedings were adjourned notwithstanding the fact that Comiskey was only a witness, not a party to the Felsch/Risberg suits. As with the Jackson action, only the White Sox corporation was named as a defendant by the plaintiffs.
5. As per documents in CHM, Black Sox file, Box 1, Folder 8. In support of their adjournment arguments, Sox lawyers presented a certification about Comiskey's medical condition signed by his physician, Dr. Philip H. Kreuscher.
6. Judge Gregory's ruling on the order to show cause was rendered on September 19, 1924.
7. As reported in the *Atlanta Constitution*, *Hartford Courant* and *Los Angeles Times*, October 29, 1924.
8. Major league ballplayers, in particular, were put off by Cannon's continued representation of the Black Sox and, by the end of 1924, Cannon's attempt to form a new players' union had collapsed, according to Fleitz, 255.
9. As quoted in the *Chicago Tribune*, November 3, 1924.
10. *Ibid.*
11. As per the *Chicago Tribune*, November 4, 1924, which reported that Landis pro-

duced the minutes of the owners meeting to corroborate his testimony. See, also, *Decatur* (Ill.) *Review,* November 4, 1924. The move to exclude the Black Sox from a share of 1920 second place money was actually initiated by "the honorable Sox," as reported in the *Lousville Courier-Journal,* November 20, 1920.

12. As per the *Chicago Tribune* and *Washington Post,* November 4, 1924.

13. As per the *New York Times,* November 4, 1924.

14. As reported in the *Chicago Tribune,* November 4, 1924.

15. *Ibid.*

16. As per the *Atlanta Constitution,* December 11, 1925.

17. As per Carney, "New Light on an Old Scandal," 75.

18. *Ibid.* More particularly, Risberg was granted a $288.88 settlement award, plus $75.23 in accrued interest, and reimbursed court costs of $37.20.

19. As reported in the *Chicago Tribune,* December 20, 1924. Complainant on the new process was ADA George Skogmo, as per the *Dunkirk* (NY) *Evening Observer,* December 29, 1924.

20. As per the *Atlanta Constitution, Boston Globe* and *Hartford Courant,* December 30, 1924.

21. As reported in the *Milwaukee Sentinel,* May 20, 1925. See, also, the SABR BioProject profile of Felsch.

22. As reported in the *Milwaukee Sentinal/Sheboygan Press,* May 18, 1925.

23. As per the *Atlanta Constitution,* May 20, 1925.

24. According to the *Milwaukee Journal,* March 13, 1986. February and April 2010 letters to the Milwaukee County District Attorneys Office from the author regarding the disposition of the Jackson perjury complaint were unanswered.

25. A youthful former judge, the Charles A. Williams who represented Weaver is not to be confused with another Charles A. Williams, an older Democrat elected to the bench in the early 1920s and the presiding judge in a number of high-profile Chicago murder trials.

26. As per the *Chicago Tribune,* November 20, 1925.

27. As per a docket entry in the Weaver case preserved at the National Archives in Chicago.

28. See, e.g., Ginsburg, 148; Stein, 177 (but erroneously placing the settlement in 1924).

29. See Carney, "Notes from the Shadows of Cooperstown," No. 487, May 17, 2009.

30. Ginsburg, 148.

25

Treatment of Judicial Proceedings in the Black Sox Canon

Public interest in the Black Sox scandal crested with the criminal trial conducted in Chicago during the summer of 1921. Following the post-acquittal banishment of the accused players by Commissioner Landis, the attention of baseball fans reverted to the diamond, where an exciting 1921 season culminated in an historic intra–New York City World Series between the Giants and the Yankees.[1] From there, both fandom and the media moved on. Apart from the Milwaukee papers, only passing press notice was accorded the trial of the Jackson civil suit in early 1924, while virtually no attention was paid to the later resolution of the Felsch, Risberg, and Weaver litigation. As years passed, the Black Sox scandal receded into memory, with interest only revived from time to time by the random sports column,[2] anecdotal recollection,[3] or, beginning with the death of Joe Jackson in December 1951, the obituary of a Black Sox player.[4]

Although not a book about the Black Sox scandal, Leo Katcher's 1958 biography of Arnold Rothstein provided a brief account of the 1919 World Series fix. In same, Rothstein was portrayed not so much as the fix financier, but as a knowing but passive presence whose name, reputation, and vaunted wealth allowed the fix to be perpetrated by underlings, with Rothstein himself then cashing in handsomely on advance knowledge that the Series outcome was rigged.[5] Katcher also identified the shadowy fix operative *Brown* as Nat Evans, a capable Rothstein lieutenant and Rothstein's junior partner in casino ventures in Saratoga and Long Island. According to Katcher, Rachael Brown was yet another Rothstein operative, Rothstein's female bookkeeper who was supposedly in attendance in Cincinnati and Chicago to assist Evans in fix negotiations. This latter claim, however, seems far-fetched, as Rothstein's real-life bookkeeper was a man named Samuel Brown and no one has ever connected Samuel Brown to the 1919 World Series fix.[6] Nor did anyone conversant with fix details — Black Sox player, fix participant, prosecution or defense witness — ever place a female anywhere near the scandal action. In sum, the female Rachael Brown described by Katcher (who was only a youth during Rothstein's heyday and had no first-hand knowledge of Rothstein) is likely apocryphal.[7]

In 1960, the Black Sox scandal was revisited at some length when the first volume of Harold and Dorothy Seymour's esteemed trilogy on baseball history was published.[8] But by the time that the Seymours were doing their Black Sox research in the late 1950s, the transcript of the criminal trial had disappeared from court archives in Chicago. This necessitated reliance on secondary sources and resulted in error creeping into their account of the Black Sox saga.[9] Among other things, *Baseball: The Golden Age* states that Buck Herzog appeared before the grand jury;[10] that Joe Jackson testified about "moving slowly to balls hit to him, making throws that fell short, and deliberately striking out with runners in scoring position";[11] that two Clean Sox (inferentially, Byrd Lynn and Harvey McClellan) testified that some of the suspected players had purposely dumped games during the 1920 season;[12] and that Eddie Cicotte's landlady (Henrietta Kelley) "came to [Comiskey] after the Series end and told of overhearing Cicotte's suspicious remark."[13] None of these things happened.

Three years later, this regrettable situation recurred when *Eight Men Out* by Eliot Asinof was published. Asinof presented a spell-binding account of the Black Sox scandal, but one that was marred by many dubious details, many of which appear to have been supplied to the author by Abe Attell.[14] An engrossing storyteller not overly fussy about historical accuracy, the Little Champ himself is presumably the source for the fiction that he was "raised in San Francisco with the name Albert Knoehr."[15] In fact, Abraham Washington Attell was the second of three prominent boxers born to Jonas Attell and his wife, the former Sarah Semel.[16] Attell also duped Asinof regarding his motives, prompting the author to write uncritically that "Rothstein's partner, Nat Evans, dies in 1959, permitting Abe Attell, another ex-Rothstein associate, to reveal his participation in the fix."[17] In fact, Evans, highly regarded as a sportsman by the New York boxing and turf press, was long dead by then, having died on February 6, 1935.[18] But Abe Attell is not to be blamed for Asinof misstatements such as "George M. Cohan testified" before the grand jury[19]; that Eddie Cicotte admitted making deliberate misplays in Game One and Game Four[20]; that George Gorman, a middle-aged former congressman admitted to the bar in 1895 was "a worried young man" when assigned to handle the Black Sox prosecution;[21] that Carl Zork and Ben Franklin were part of the Attell contingent at the Sinton Hotel;[22] and that prosecution witness Billy Maharg took the stand after defendant David Zelcer had testified.[23] Asinof got those matters wrong on his own.[24] No useful purpose is served by chronicling how such factual errors, and those of Victor Luhrs,[25] David Quentin Voigt,[26] and other Black Sox commentators, were recycled in the scandal literature that followed. Suffice it to say that longstanding errata are now encrusted in the Black Sox canon.

Specific examination of the judicial proceedings generated by the Black Sox scandal has been sparse, and confined almost entirely to the criminal trial.[27] Little need be said about the insipid re-imagining of the trial presented in a January 1961 episode of the television docudrama series *Witness.*[28] As history, the production did not rise to the level of travesty. A far more estimable treatment of the criminal proceedings was offered in a 1988 article by University of Tennessee law professor James Kirby.[29] In Kirby's view, the accused were guilty as charged but were the beneficiaries of hyper-technical judicial rulings and the vagaries of conspiracy law.[30] A decade later, a diametrically different position — at least as it pertained to Joe Jackson — was espoused in faux legal pleadings submitted to present MLB Commissioner Bud Selig by Chicago lawyer Louis R. Hegeman.[31] Based upon a selective exposition of the judicial record, Hegeman proclaimed the innocence of Jackson (and Buck Weaver, as well), while advocating his petition's stated objective: removal of Joe Jackson from baseball's ineligible list.

A few years later, a revival of interest in the Black Sox scandal became the mission of one man: Gene Carney. An avid baseball fan and longtime researcher, Carney had developed a following in the 1990s via his blog *Notes from the Shadows of Cooperstown,* an eclectic mélange of history, commentary, poetry, and whimsy related to the game. But in September 2002, he abandoned this format to focus the blog exclusively on the subject that had become a near obsession for him — the Black Sox affair. For the next seven years, Carney filed near-weekly dispatches chock-full of Black Sox-related miscellany: character sketches on scandal actors, large and small; insightful speculation on the motivation of fix participants; new information on 1919 Sox player salaries; details of the civil litigation related to the scandal; surveys of contemporaneous scandal reportage, including the by-then long forgotten exposés of *Collyer's Eye,* and more.

In 2006, Carney realized an ambition to reach a broader audience via publication of his book, *Burying the Black Sox.* For Black Sox aficionados, the book became a research touchstone and it was a deserving winner of the 2007 Larry Ritter Award for Deadball Era baseball research. But *Burying the Black*

Sox is not an easy read, eccentrically organized — Carney begins his account of the Black Sox saga with commentary on the January 1924 trial of Joe Jackson's civil suit — and handicapped by the absence of a firm editorial hand.[32] That said, the book, like the Carney blog, is a cornucopia of Black Sox information and insight, much of it related to the litigation spawned by the scandal. Nor did Carney rest upon publication of his book. He was among the first researchers to plumb the long-lost Black Sox documents acquired by the Chicago History Museum in December 2007. As was his wont, Carney then shared his discoveries with Black Sox aficionados via a series of informative articles and internet posts.[33] Carney was also the driving force behind the establishment of the Society for American Baseball Research's Black Sox Scandal Research committee. Tragically, Gene Carney did not get to enjoy the fruits of this particular labor. He died unexpectedly while on vacation in Alaska, only weeks before the Black Sox committee had its inaugural meeting at the 2009 SABR convention in Washington, D.C.

This work is a direct product of that first committee meeting, having begun as a report to the committee membership on the "crime and punishment" aspect of the Black Sox scandal. As stated in the preface, this work does not aspire to be the definitive treatment of the Black Sox affair. Instead, its objective has been to provide a thorough, informative, and reliable account of the judicial proceedings precipitated by the outcome of the 1919 World Series, matters not always accurately portrayed or well understood in Black Sox literature. To achieve this purpose, the narrative has striven to be comprehensive, not polemical. For this, essentially, is a reference work, not a polemic or an opinion piece. In the end, it is for the reader to determine whether justice was done in the judicial proceedings spawned by the Black Sox scandal. If such judgments are better informed for having read this text, the book has accomplished its objective.

Notes

1. For a splendid account of the season, see Lyle Spatz and Steve Steinberg, *1921: The Yankees, the Giants and the Battle for Baseball Supremacy in New York* (Lincoln: University of Nebraska Press, 2010).

2. See, e.g., John E. Wray and J. Roy Stockton, "Ban Johnson's Own Story," *St. Louis Post-Dispatch,* March 3, 1929; Damon Runyon, "Attell Keeps Secret of Big Sports Scandal," *Washington Post,* October 4, 1939; Shirley Povich, "Say It Ain't So, Joe," *Washington Post,* April 11, 1941. See, also, Shoeless Joe Jackson, as told to Furman Bisher, "This Is the Truth," *Sport,* October 1949.

3. See, e.g., the Fowler biography of William J. Fallon (1931); Caroline Rothstein's memoir (1934); James T. Farrell, *My Baseball Diary* (New York: A.S. Barnes, 1957).

4. Jackson died on December 5, 1951, followed by Fred McMullin in November 1952 and Buck Weaver in January 1956.

5. Leo Katcher, *The Big Bankroll: The Life and Times of Arnold Rothstein* (New York: DaCapo Press, 1958).

6. Samuel Brown's role as Rothstein confidant and bookkeeper was amply noted in press coverage of the probate battle over Rothstein's deathbed will. See, e.g., *New York Times,* November 17 and 18, and December 24, 1928.

7. For more on the Rachael Brown controversy, see Lamb, "A Black Sox Mystery," 5–11.

8. Harold Seymour and Dorothy Seymour Mills, *Baseball: The Golden Age* (New York: Oxford University Press, 1960).

9. These observations are in no way intended as disparagement of the Seymours, whose work, even fifty years after publication, remains magisterial.

10. Seymour and Mills, *Baseball: The Golden Age,* 290.

11. *Ibid.,* 303.

12. *Ibid.,* 305.

13. *Ibid.,* 335.

14. Asinof's reliance on Attell for inside fix details is reflected in the Asinof papers at the Chicago History Museum and acknowledged by Asinof in *Bleeding Between the Lines,* 103–109. Before *Eight Men Out* was published, Asinof had served as ghostwriter for a Black Sox-related magazine article with an Abe Attell byline that appeared in *Cavalier,* October 1961.

15. Asinof, *Eight Men Out,* 26.

16. Older brother Caesar Attell was a respectable West Coast lightweight, while younger brother Monte Attell captured the world bantamweight championship in 1909, making Monte and Abe Attell the first brothers ever to hold world boxing titles simultaneously. The complete Attell family tree from 1878 to present has been posted on-line by Abe Attell's great, great grandnephew.

17. Asinof, *Eight Men Out,* xii.

18. As per Pietrusza, *Rothstein,* 362.

19. Asinof, *Eight Men Out,* 158.

20. *Ibid.,* 172–173.

21. *Ibid.,* 227.

22. *Ibid.,* 231.

23. *Ibid.,* 255. Apparently for copyright protection purposes, Asinof created *Harry F.*, an entirely fictional goon cast as the cause of Lefty Williams' dreaful Game Eight performance. See *Eight Men Out,* 113–114.

24. For more pointed criticism of Asinof, see Daniel Voelker and Paul Duffy, "It Ain't So, Kid. It Just Ain't So: History's Apology to Shoeless Joe Jackson, Charles Comiskey and Chicago's Black Sox," *Chicago Lawyer,* September 2009.

25. In *The Great Baseball Mystery: The 1919 World Series* (South Brunswick, NJ: A.S. Barnes, 1966), Luhrs erroneously portrays Mont Tennes as a grand jury witness (pp. 121–122); has Eddie Cicotte and Joe Jackson admitting deliberate misplays during their grand jury appearances (pp. 127–128); depicts Rachael Brown as a Boston gambler and a fix operative distinct from the *Brown* who parlayed with the Black Sox at the Warner Hotel (p. 142), and maintains that Fred McMullin was not charged in the criminal case (p. 186).

26. The brief scandal account of Voigt, a distinguished baseball historian, in *American Baseball, Vol. II: From Commissioners to Continental Expansion* (Norman: University of Oklahoma Press, 1970), is surprisingly inept. Among other things, Voigt has Buck Weaver admitting fix complicity to Comiskey (p. 127); has Lefty Williams telling the grand jury that Series fixers had threatened his wife (p. 129); asserts that Eddie Cicotte made "extra money betting on the Reds to win fixed games" (p. 129), and states that the purported disappearance of the Cicotte, Jackson, and Williams grand jury testimony made it possible

for those players "to repudiate their confessions" (p. 129). None of these contentions has even an arguable basis in the record.

27. Gene Carney's *Burying the Black Sox,* which begins with an extended consideration of the Jackson civil trial, is a notable exception.

28. For a synopsis of this moronic dramatization, see Carney, *Burying the Black Sox,* 266–269.

29. See again, James Kirby, "The Year They Fixed the World Series," *American Bar Association Journal,* February 1, 1988.

30. *Ibid.,* 69.

31. Bearing the title *In the Matter of Joseph Jefferson "Shoeless Joe" Jackson, a deceased ballplayer,* the Hegeman petition is reproduced in Gropman, Appendix L, 315–354.

32. For a mixed review of *Burying the Black Sox,* see Irv Goldfarb, "Tugging on Superman's Cape: A Critique of Carney," Black Sox Scandal Research Committee newsletter, Vol. 3, No. 2, December 2011, 4–5.

33. Informative Carney articles appeared in the *Baseball Research Journal,* while discoveries from his research visit to the Chicago History Museum were revealed in *Notes from the Shadows of Cooperstown,* Nos. 489–493, May 31 to June 15, 2009. Gene Carney's final contribution to Black Sox scholarship ("Eddie Cicotte on the Day That Shook Baseball") was published posthumously in *Base Ball: A Journal of the Early Game,* Vol. 3, No. 2, Fall 2009.

Glossary of Black Sox Persons and Places

Michael Ahern: Accomplished Chicago attorney. Co-counsel with law firm partner Thomas D. Nash for defendants Weaver, Felsch, and Risberg at Black Sox criminal trial. The two lawyers also represented absent defendant McMullin. Ahern later served as attorney for Al Capone. Suffered fatal heart attack at age 56 in September 1943.

Elbert M. Allen: Cook County grand jury stenographer. Took down grand jury testimony of Joe Jackson. Authenticated transcript of Jackson testimony as witness for White Sox defense at Milwaukee trial of Jackson civil suit.

Ansonia Hotel/New York: Luxurious Beaux-Arts residential hotel located on Manhattan's west side. Scene of initial meetings regarding fix of 1919 World Series. Erected in 1904 and currently a condominium apartment building. On National Register of Historic Places.

Astor Hotel/New York: Hotel grill room was scene of Arnold Rothstein's rebuff of fix overtures of Bill Burns and Billy Maharg.

Abe Attell: Former world featherweight boxing champion and sometime bodyguard of Arnold Rothstein. Inveterate hustler, hooked up with David Zelcer/Bennett to back fix proposal of Bill Burns. Indicted by Cook County grand jury for his role in Series fix but successfully resisted extradition to Chicago. Principal informant of fix details for Eliot Asinof in early 1960s. A member of various boxing halls of fame. The Little Champ died in 1970, age 86.

Alfred S. Austrian: Longtime counsel for the White Sox corporation. Interviewed Eddie Cicotte, Joe Jackson, and Lefty Williams in his law office prior to their grand jury appearances. Witness at both the criminal and civil trials. Scholarly man without interest in baseball. Died in January 1932 after extended period of failing health, age 61.

Charles V. Barrett: Chicago attorney and Republican Party powerbroker. Lawyer for American League President Ban Johnson during the scandal period and younger brother of AL special counsel George F. Barrett. Died of a heart attack following an appendectomy on New Year's Eve 1931, age 49.

George F. Barrett: Recently retired Chicago circuit court judge retained to represent interests of the American League during Black Sox criminal proceedings. Like brother Charles, a close political ally of Cook County State's Attorney Crowe at time of Black Sox scandal. Suffered fatal cerebral hemorrhage in March 1937, age 57.

William Barry: Foreman of the criminal trial jury that acquitted Black Sox defendants.

Kid (Henry) Becker: Notorious St. Louis gambler and reputed mastermind of stillborn plan to fix 1918 World Series. Shot to death in April 1919, age 36.

Curley (Joseph) Bennett: Tammany Hall foot soldier and sometime steerer/bodyguard for Arnold Rothstein. Not involved in 1919 World Series fix but occasionally confused with David Zelcer, the fixer who adopted the alias "Bennett" when dealing with corrupted Sox players.

Rube (John) Benton: Southpaw NY Giants pitcher. Testified before grand jury about knowledge of World Series fix and accused Hal Chase, Buck Herzog, and Heinie Zimmerman of unrelated bribe attempts. Not called as a witness in Black Sox criminal trial. 150–144 record in 15 major league seasons. Died in a 1937 auto crash, age 50.

Henry Berger: Combative co-counsel for defendant Carl Zork at Black Sox criminal trial. Former Cook County prosecutor and active in local Democratic Party politics. Killed by falling building construction material while walking a Chicago street in November 1929, age 43.

Babe (William) Borton: Captain/first baseman of the 1919 PCL champion Vernon Tigers. Suspended for suspected bribery of opposition players in August 1920. Later indicted by a Los Angeles grand jury but charges dismissed by court on technical grounds. Banished from organized baseball in January 1921. Batted .270 in parts of four major league seasons. Died in July 1954, age 65.

Abraham Braunstein: Small-time gambler known in NYC gaming circles as *Rachel Brown*. Presumed by East Coast newspapers to be the fixer indicted by the Cook County grand jury as Rachael Brown but involvement in 1919 World Series plot improbable. In and out of a Saratoga (NY) County courtroom on local charges in early 1921 but no effort made to extradite Braunstein/Brown to Chicago. Relocated to Los Angeles and running a storefront bookmaking operation at time of death in September 1936.

Henry Brigham: Automobile company president appointed foreman of Cook County grand jury that conducted original Black Sox probe. Later testified on behalf of White Sox defense at trial of Jackson civil suit.

Rachael Brown: Name assigned by grand jury to fix front man from New York working with Sport Sullivan. Parleyed with Sox players at Warner Hotel about throwing the Series. Indicted but never made an appearance in Chicago court. True identity never conclusively established but various Black Sox authors assert that this Brown was actually NYC gambler and Rothstein lieutenant Nat Evans.

John E. Bruce: Secretary of defunct National Commission and minor prosecution witness at Black Sox criminal trial.

Frederick Burnham: An attorney at the Austrian law firm and the pretrial handler of the Weaver suit for the White Sox corporation.

Bill Burns: Texas gambler and World Series fix middleman. Indicted by Cook County grand jury but turned State's evidence. Chief prosecution witness at Black Sox trial. Provided deposition for White Sox defense in Jackson civil case. Journeyman left-handed pitcher known as "Sleepy Bill" during his playing days. Died in 1953, age 73.

Raymond J. Cannon: Aggressive Milwaukee attorney and counsel for Happy Felsch, Swede Risberg, and Joe Jackson in post-banishment civil litigation. Attempt to organize a new MLB players union failed. Disbarred for ambulance chasing and other untoward professional conduct in July 1929. Reinstated to law practice in 1932. Three-term Democratic congressman in 1930s. Subsequent bids for elective office failed. The "stormy petrel of Wisconsin politics" died at home in his sleep in November 1951. He was 60.

Daniel P. Cassidy: Detroit civil attorney and longtime friend of Eddie Cicotte. Served as nominal defense counsel for Cicotte during Black Sox criminal trial. Advised Cicotte during ensuing civil litigation.

Hal Chase: Gifted first baseman and widely suspected game-fixer. On margins of plot to fix 1919 World Series but exact fix role indistinct. Indicted by Cook County grand jury but successfully fought effort to extradite him from California. Persona non grata in organized baseball following release by Giants in February 1920. Spent years playing outlaw ball in the West. Died in 1947 from effects of various ailments aggravated by chronic alcoholism. He was 64.

Eddie Cicotte: Ace of the 1919 White Sox pitching staff and a reputed fix leader among the players. Confessed fix involvement inside Austrian office and before grand jury. Indicted. Testified at mid-trial suppression hearing during Black Sox criminal trial. Acquitted of charges but promptly banned from organized baseball by Commissioner Landis. Reluctant deposition witness during ensuing civil litigation. Silent about scandal thereafter. Lifetime record 209–148. Died in 1969, age 84.

Eddie Collins: Second baseman and captain of the 1919 White Sox. Alibi witness for Black Sox players at criminal trial. Gave deposition for White Sox during civil litigation refuting 1917 World Series bonus claim asserted by Felsch, Risberg, and Jackson. Exceptional player: 3,315 hits/lifetime .333 BA. Retired after 1930 season. Inducted into Hall of Fame in 1939. Executive for Boston Red Sox at death following a stroke in March 1951, age 63.

Shano (John) Collins: Dependable White Sox outfielder/first baseman. Named as representative player-victim in indictments returned in March 1921 by second grand jury panel. Brief defense witness for Black Sox players at criminal trial. Batted .264 over 16 MLB seasons. Died in native Massachusetts in 1955, age 69.

Bert Collyer: Canadian-born publisher of *Collyer's Eye,* the horse racing trade sheet that broke early scandal stories. Scheduled grand jury witness but never called to testify. Died in Chicago, July 1938, age 61.

Charles A. Comiskey: Renowned player, manager, and team owner. Head of Chicago White Sox from founding in 1900. Testified about club inquiries into rumors about fix of 1919 Series before grand jury and at criminal trial of indicted players. Gave deposition and testified at trial of Jackson civil suit in Milwaukee. Died of heart disease in 1931, age 72. Inducted into Hall of Fame in 1939.

Comiskey Park/Chicago: Southside home stadium of the White Sox. Scene of Games Three, Four, Five and Eight of the 1919 World Series. Cornerstone laid in 1910. Razed in 1991.

Congress Hotel/Chicago: Located near Grant Park and originally called the Auditorium Annex. Managed by Paul Gores, agent for transmission of 1919 World Series bet winnings to Abe Attell. Later, site of Lee Magee admission of 1918 game fix plot to NL President Heydler and Cubs boss Veeck. Opened for Columbian Exhibition in 1893. Still in operation today as the Congress Plaza.

Cook County Courthouse/Chicago: Site of Black Sox grand jury probes and criminal trial. Erected in 1893. Use as courthouse discontinued in 1929. Now houses law firms and business offices. Placed on National Register of Historic Places in 1984.

J.J. Cooke: Former Chicago jurist retained as additional criminal trial counsel by Midwestern gambler defendants Zelcer and Levi.

John J. Cornell: Savannah bank cashier who provided deposition for White Sox defense in Jackson civil suit.

Robert E. Crowe: Circuit Court judge who won the Cook County State's Attorney election in midst of Black Sox grand jury probe. Unilaterally dismissed initial indictments in March 1921, then superintended re-indictment of Black Sox a week later. Did not appear for prosecution during criminal trial but dismissed charges against remaining defendants following acquittal of main Black Sox defendants in August 1921. Later chief prosecutor in the infamous Leopold & Loeb murder trial. A major force in Chicago Republican Party circles. Died in 1958, age 79.

James Crusinberry: *Chicago Tribune* sportswriter and important early grand jury witness. Revealed authorship of influential Loomis letter in late life 1956 magazine article.

Jack Davis: Des Moines gambler and companion of defendant David Zelcer during 1919 World Series. Unclear if Davis testified for Zelcer defense during criminal trial.

William E. Dever: Respected circuit court judge whose denial of prosecution adjournment request and assignment of a peremptory trial date precipitated SAO dismissal of the original Black Sox indictments. Did not participate in later scandal-related proceedings. Elected mayor of Chicago as reform Democrat candidate in 1923. Served one term. Died in September 1929, age 67.

Gregory T. Dillon: *Chicago Daily News* reporter and Zork defense witness at Black Sox criminal trial.

Thomas F. Donnelly: New York State Supreme Court justice who assumed Attell extradition proceedings at mid-hearing. Denied extradition and granted Attell release on habeas corpus.

Larry Doyle: NY Giants infielder and minor grand jury witness.

Jean Dubuc: Former NY Giants pitcher. Provided corroboration to grand jury of Benton testimony about Hal Chase/Bill Burns contact just prior to start of 1919 World Series.

Charles W. Dunkley: Midwest Associated Press sports editor and plaintiff's witness at trial of Jackson civil suit.

Charles Ebbets: Owner of the Brooklyn Dodgers. Appeared briefly before the Cook County grand jury to respond to fix rumors about the 1920 Cleveland/Brooklyn World Series.

Clyde Elliott: Motion picture production company president and avid White Sox fan. Accompanied club officials to St. Louis during post–Series inquiry into fix rumors. Grand jury witness and publicly critical of fix inaction by White Sox brass.

Nat Evans: Polished NYC gambler and junior partner in Rothstein casino ventures. Name briefly mentioned in grand jury testimony of Charles Weeghman but otherwise unconnected to scandal during his lifetime. Respected as sportsman by boxing and turf press. Died in 1935. Fix involvement first alleged in Leo Katcher's 1958 biography of Arnold Rothstein. Five years later, Evans identified as fix operative "Brown" by Asinof in *Eight Men Out.* Surname may actually have been *Evens.*

Red (Urban) Faber: Standout White Sox hurler sidelined by ailments/injury for the 1919 World Series. Suspected teammates of crooked play during 1920 season. Gave deposition and testified on White Sox behalf regarding 1917 Series bonus claim during Jackson civil suit. Record 254–213 over twenty MLB seasons, all with Chicago. Veterans Committee Hall of Fame inductee in 1964. Died September 1976, age 88.

William J. Fallon: Gifted and unscrupulous, "The Great Mouthpiece" had a meteoric career as NYC criminal defense lawyer. Reputed architect of Rothstein grand jury strategy and attorney for Abe Attell at NY extradition hearing. Notoriety and profligate living brought about collapse of law practice in mid–1920s. Dodged conviction on a jury tampering charge and later avoided disbarment, but law practice never revived. Near bankrupt when died of a heart attack in 1927, age 41. Friend and periodic client John McGraw footed the bill for Fallon's casket.

Happy (Oscar) Felsch: Amiable White Sox center fielder on brink of stardom when scandal erupted. Confessed scandal involvement to a Chicago reporter and indicted by

Cook County grand jury. Acquitted at trial but banished from organized baseball by Commissioner Landis. Disastrous appearance as rebuttal witness for plaintiff Jackson at trial of civil suit in Milwaukee. Arrested for perjury. Later pled guilty to reduced charge of false swearing. Played outlaw ball into middle age. Old and ailing, Felsch admitted Series fix participation, and throwing games during the 1920 season as well, to Asinof in early 1960s. Died in Milwaukee in 1964, age 72.

Art Fletcher: Former NY Giants player and coach. Minor grand jury witness.

Otto Floto: *Kansas City Post* sports editor. Supplied AL President Johnson with info about Kansas City connection to suspect August 1920 Cubs-Phillies game. Grand jury probe of that game morphed into Black Sox inquiry.

Ben Franklin: St. Louis gambler. Confederate of Carl Zork in post–Game 3 fix revival effort. Charged in superseding Black Sox indictments returned in March 1921. Prosecution of Franklin severed from other defendants on eve of trial on grounds of illness. Charges dismissed following acquittal of Black Sox in August 1921. Sometimes referred to as *Frankel* (original family surname still being used by relatives in Des Moines) in Black Sox literature.

Hugo M. Friend: Trial judge in Black Sox criminal case. College track star and Olympic Games medalist in his youth. Appointed to bench in September 1920 and judicially inexperienced at time of Black Sox trial. Served on Illinois trial and appellate courts for another 45 years. Avid baseball fan died of a heart attack in May 1966, reportedly while listening to a White Sox game on radio. Age 83.

A. Morgan Frumberg: Prominent St. Louis attorney. Lead counsel for Black Sox defendants Carl Zork and Ben Franklin.

Hugh Fullerton: Syndicated sports columnist. Penned first notable articles questioning integrity of 1919 World Series. Longtime friend of team owner Comiskey and White Sox defense witness at Jackson civil trial. Revised account of scandal-related events in 1935 column. Died in Florida in December 1945, age 72.

Chick (Arnold) Gandil: White Sox first baseman and alleged fix ringleader among players. Did not return to Chisox for 1920 season following salary dispute. Indicted but acquitted at Black Sox criminal trial in August 1921. Immediately banished from baseball by Commissioner Landis. Admitted Series plot but maintained that players did not go through with fix in 1956 *Sports Illustrated* article. Died in California in 1970, age 83.

Joe Gedeon: St. Louis Browns infielder. Friend of fellow Californians Swede Risberg and Fred McMullin. Won fix-informed bets on 1919 World Series. Grand jury witness in October 1920 and March 1921. Testified about attending mid–Series fix revival meetings held by gamblers at Chicago hotel. Listed as State's witness for Black Sox criminal trial but not called to testify during prosecution's direct case. Application to use as prosecution rebuttal witness denied by Judge Friend. Banished from organized baseball by Commissioner Landis in November 1921. First scandal-connected player to die, succumbing to cirrhosis of liver/bronchial pneumonia in May 1941, age 47.

Kid (William) Gleason: White Sox manager in 1919. Testified about post–Series investigative trip to St. Louis during grand jury appearance. Minor prosecution witness as well as defense alibi witness at Black Sox criminal trial. Pitcher, then infielder during 22-year MLB playing career. Piloted Sox through 1923 season. Died ten years later, age 66.

George E. Goreman: Represented the Black Sox case to the grand jury March 1921 and thereafter served as lead trial prosecutor. One-term U.S. Congressman (1913–1915). In private law practice with former SA Crowe when he suffered a fatal heart attack in January 1935, age 61.

Harry Grabiner: White Sox club secretary. Prosecution and defense witness at Black Sox criminal trial. Testimony about 1920 surge in franchise revenue deemed most important testimony in entire case by jury foreman Barry. Deposition and trial witness in Jackson civil suit. Circumstances of his signing of Jackson to 1920 contract were central issue in Jackson litigation. Grabiner was a Cleveland Indians executive at time of death in 1948. Grabiner diary, now lost, was main source of Black Sox revelations in Bill Veeck, Jr., 1965 book *The Hustler's Handbook.*

John J. Gregory: Presiding judge in Jackson, Felsch, and Risberg lawsuits. Cited both Jackson and Felsch for perjury during 1924 trial of Jackson suit. Died of complications from a fall at age 67 in November 1939, shortly after reelection to the Wisconsin bench for a seventh time. Highly esteemed in Milwaukee legal community.

George Guenther: Able Chicago criminal defense attorney and longtime law partner of Benedict J. Short, with whom he often appeared in court. Low profile co-counsel with Short for Joe Jackson and Lefty Williams at Black Sox criminal trial.

Philip Hahn: Cincinnati betting commissioner. Vigorously disputed leaked Benton grand jury testimony about having inside fix knowledge.

Sam Hall: *Chicago Herald Examiner* sports editor and chairman of the aborted sportswriter inquiry into suspect Cubs-Phillies game. Gave early grand jury opinion testimony of little consequence.

James C. Hamilton: Associated Press sportswriter and plaintiff's witness at trial of Jackson civil suit.

Claude Hendrix: Scheduled Cubs starting pitcher for August 31, 1920 game against Phillies. Replaced by manager Mitchell following receipt of fix reports. Did not accompany team on late 1920 season road trip and released by Chicago in February 1921. Never pitched in major leagues thereafter. Accused of planning to dump Phillies game by Kansas City sports editor Otto Floto.

Al Herr: Circulation manager for *The Sporting News* and minor grand jury witness.

Garry (August) Herrmann: National Commission chairman and Cincinnati Reds president. Testified about NL scandal investigations during grand jury appearance. Testified for prosecution about technical World Series matters during Black Sox criminal trial. Resigned after 25 years as Reds boss after 1927 season. Died of diabetes/arteriosclerosis complications in April 1931, age 71.

Buck (Charles) Herzog: Scrappy Chicago Cubs infielder accused by Rube Benton of game-fixing attempt. Strong Herzog denials backed up by NL President Heydler, who publicly exonerated Herzog. Slashed after late–September 1920 exhibition game in Joliet by scandal-incensed fan who may have mistaken Buck Herzog for the just indicted Buck Weaver. Herzog later served as baseball coach at US Naval Academy. Near destitute when died of tuberculosis in September 1953, age 67.

John Heydler: National League president. Minor witness at grand jury and Jackson civil trial.

Maclay Hoyne: Controversial two-term Cook County State's Attorney. Lost Democratic Party primary in re-nomination bid at outset of Black Sox grand jury proceedings and then left town on vacation. Bumptiously reinserted himself into probe after publicly questioning its legitimacy from NYC. Censured for lax oversight of Chicago District Sanitary Board but escaped disbarment in 1932. Died after long illness in 1939, age 66.

George B. Hudnall: Prominent Wisconsin political figure and corporate attorney. Retained as local Milwaukee counsel for White Sox in lawsuits instituted by Felsch, Risberg, and Jackson. Lead defense counsel at trial of Jackson civil suit. Later represented Commissioner Landis at pre-suit deposition about 1920 second-place money withheld from Black Sox.

John R. Hunter: Head of eponymous private detective agency retained by White Sox owner Comiskey to investigate 1919 World Series fix rumors. Reports of his agency later described by Comiskey as insufficient basis for taking action against suspected players. Testified for White Sox defense during trial of Jackson civil suit.

James Isaminger: *Philadelphia North American* sportswriter who broke Maharg expose of Series fix in late September 1920. Behind-the-scenes ally of AL President Johnson in getting Black Sox case ready for criminal trial.

Katie Jackson: Maiden name: Wynn. Married neighbor Joe Jackson at age 15 in 1908. Had vaudeville-touring husband served with divorce papers and arrested in March 1915, but quickly reconciled with him. Katie's deposition used by White Sox defense in trial of Jackson civil suit. Vocal in support of husband's honesty after perjury citation during civil trial. Married for over forty years at time of Joe's death in 1951. Katie died in April 1959, age 66.

Joe Jackson: The legendary "Shoeless Joe" rose from impoverished childhood to baseball stardom. Made admissions about fix of 1919 World Series in Judge McDonald's chambers and before grand jury in late September 1920. Indicted on fix-related charges. Testified at mid-trial suppression hearing. Acquitted of criminal charges in August 1921 but promptly banned from organized baseball by Commissioner Landis. Jury award in 1924 breach-of-contract suit against White Sox overturned by trial judge who had Jackson arrested for giving perjured testimony as trial witness. Played outlaw ball into middle age and maintained non-involvement in Series fix for remainder of his life. Successful small businessman despite lifelong illiteracy. Lifetime .356 BA is third highest in MLB history. Died of heart attack in December 1951, age 63.

Hugh Jennings: Tigers manager summoned to enlighten the grand jury regarding the gambling climate in Detroit but proved of little use on the subject.

Ban Johnson: Founder and president of the American League. Major force behind the grand jury probe of 1919 World Series fix allegations and appeared three times as a grand jury witness. Also testified during March 1921 grand jury re-presentment of matter. Behind-the-scene promoter/financier of SAO prosecution of Black Sox case. Listed as prosecution witness but not called to testify at trial. Accused by Black Sox defense lawyers of instigating prosecution to injure Chisox owner Comiskey, a former friend now in a bitter public feud with Johnson. Declined via counsel to appear on behalf of White Sox defense at trial of Jackson civil suit. Gradually lost executive power to Commissioner Landis in 1920s. Retired in 1927. Died in 1931 of diabetes complications, age 67. Charter member of Hall of Fame.

Albert Kafka: Gandil landlord and defense witness at Black Sox criminal trial.

Benny Kauff: Federal League star and NY Giants outfielder. Grand jury witness regarding NL matters. Acquitted of auto theft ring-related charges in New York but banned from organized baseball by Commissioner Landis. Worked as clothing salesman in later life. Died of a cerebral hemorrhage in November 1961, age 71.

Thomas Kearney: St. Louis bookmaker and associate of Harry Redmon and Joe Pesch. Fix informant for Ban Johnson but failed to appear for scheduled grand jury testimony.

Sid Keener: Young sports editor for *St. Louis Times* at time of scandal. Conducted own private investigation of Series fix rumors in St. Louis. Results conveyed to SAO and counsel for defendant Carl Zork. Testified as fact witness for Zork defense at Black Sox criminal trial. Hall of Fame director from 1952 to 1963. Died in Florida in 1981, age 92.

Henrietta Kelley: In-season landlady for various White Sox players. May have been sister of Eddie Cicotte. Reportedly overheard Cicotte make incriminating comment at boarding house. Reluctant grand jury witness who publicly disclaimed having any info pertinent to Black Sox probe.

William J. Kelly: Boston attorney and counsel for defendant Sport Sullivan. Supposedly blackmailed Arnold Rothstein via possession of scandal-related affidavits. Subsequently disbarred on blackmail grounds in unrelated matter.

George Kenney: Secretary to Cook County State's Attorney Maclay Hoyne. Mistrusted by Black Sox grand jury prosecutors. Reputed thief of grand jury material from SAO offices.

Dickie Kerr: Diminutive lefty won two 1919 Series games for Sox. 21-game winner in 1920. Hostile defense alibi witness at Black Sox criminal trial. Long suspected Eddie Cicotte, Buck Weaver, and other Sox teammates of throwing games during 1920 season and unforgiving. Placed on ineligible list by Commissioner Landis following 1922 contract impasse with White Sox. Subsequently reinstated but arm gone. Longtime minor league manager. Converted pitcher Stan Musial to outfield after shoulder injury. Died in 1963, age 69.

Kenesaw Mountain Landis: Tempestuous Chicago federal judge appointed commissioner of baseball in November 1920. Banished Black Sox players the day after their acquittal in court. Continued to sit on federal bench while Commissioner until he resigned under congressional pressure in February 1922. Autocratic administrator of game for 24 years. Still serving as Commissioner at time of death in 1944, age 78. Inducted into Hall of Fame the same year.

Nemo (Harry) Leibold: Smallish White Sox outfielder named for comic strip character "Little Nemo." Had miserable 1919 Series, batting .056. Brief defense witness at Black Sox criminal trial. Longtime minor league manager after 13-year MLB career was over. Died in 1977, age 84.

Ben Levi: Des Moines gambler and brother-in-law of David Zelcer. Originally from Kokomo, Indiana. He and brother Lou Levi originally considered attempt to corrupt 1919 Cincinnati Reds. Later suspected of joining with others in effort to fix Series through White Sox players. A particular prosecution target of AL President Ban Johnson and charged in superseding indictments returned by Cook County grand jury in March 1921. Charges dismissed at mid-trial on lack of evidence grounds by Judge Friend.

Lou Levi: Brother of Ben. Observed in company of Abe Attell in Cincinnati during 1919 World Series and reportedly won big betting on Reds. Named as defendant in superseding Black Sox indictments. Charges dismissed mid-trial due to evidential insufficiency.

H.C. Lewinson: St. Louis attorney and low-visibility member of Zork/Franklin legal defense team.

Lexington Hotel/Chicago: Southside luxury hotel with dubious reputation. Scene of Lefty Williams transfer of $5,000 to Joe Jackson after Game Four. Erected 1892. Served as headquarters for Al Capone in late 1920s. Demolished in 1995.

Ota P. Lightfoot: Black Sox case grand jury prosecutor.

Harry Long: Chicago Board of Trade clerk. Testified before grand jury regarding bets placed on 1919 World Series as agent of Sport Sullivan.

J.H. Lowenblatt: St. Louis jeweler and character witness for Zork defense at Black Sox criminal trial.

Fred Luderus: Retired National League first baseman and expert witness for plaintiff Jackson at trial of civil suit.

Max Luster: Lead counsel for defendants Zelcer and Levi at Black Sox criminal trial.

J.L. Mackall: NY Giants team trainer and minor grand jury witness.

Lee Magee: Born Leopold Christopher Hoernschemeyer. Itinerant NL infielder and Hal Chase accomplice banned from baseball in early 1920 following admission of game-fixing. Lost civil suit for damages instituted against Chicago Cubs following release. Drifted into obscurity. Died in 1966, age 76.

Harl Maggert: Veteran Salt Lake City Bees outfielder indicted for accepting bribe from Vernon captain Babe Borton. Charges dismissed on legal technicality. Worked in family coal business after banishment from baseball. Batted .250 in two brief major league stints. His son, also named Harl, played outfield for the Boston Bees in 1938. Died in California in January 1963, age 79.

Billy Maharg: Journeyman Philadelphia pugilist and Phillies go-fer. Working at local Ford auto plant when enlisted into plot to fix 1919 World Series by his friend Bill Burns. Published newspaper interview in late September 1920 broke scandal open. Testified as prosecution witness at Black Sox criminal trial and provided deposition for White Sox defense in Jackson civil suit. Died in hometown of Philadelphia in 1953, age 72.

Christy Mathewson: All-time NY Giants pitching great. Managed Reds from 1916 until late in 1918 season when accepted commission as US Army officer. Gassed in training accident and never fully recovered. Covered 1919 World Series as special correspondent for *New York Times* and authored post–Series column dismissing fix rumors. Died of tuberculosis in Saranac Lake, NY, in 1925, age 45. One of initial five players elected to Hall of Fame.

William P. McCarthy: Pacific Coast League president when scandal erupted in August 1920. Swift banishment of suspect players following December 1920 dismissal of criminal charges by court provided Black Sox scandal instruction and precedent for Commissioner Landis.

Charles A. McDonald: Presiding judge of Chicago criminal courts in Fall 1920. Instructed grand jury to investigate Cubs-Phillies game fix rumors. Converted grand jury into special investigative panel after Black Sox revelations emerged. Witness for prosecution at Black Sox criminal trial and for White Sox defense at trial of Jackson civil suit. Resigned from bench in 1922. High profile Illinois special prosecutor in late 1920s. Appointed by federal courts as master in chancery in 1934 and still serving at time of death in March 1951, age 86.

John McGraw: Authoritarian manager of NY Giants. Testified about NL-related matters during Cook County grand jury probe. Indicted in New York for violation of Volstead Act following an October 1920 Lambs Club incident that left actor John Slavin with a fractured skull. At trial, defended by William J. Fallon, who obtained a swift acquittal from jury. Resigned as Giants manager in 1930 due to illness. Died of cancer two years later, age 60. Inducted into Hall of Fame in 1937.

Fred McMullin: White Sox utility man from Los Angeles. Accounts of how McMullin gained entry into 1919 Series fix differ. Allegedly assumed role of player-gambler conduit when Gandil did not return to White Sox for 1920 season. Indicted by both original Black Sox grand jury and March 1921 panel but did not arrive in Chicago in time to stand trial with other accused. Charges against McMullin dismissed by SAO following verdict. Lived quietly thereafter, working on motion picture sets and for LA marshal's service. Suffering from heart disease when felled by stroke in November 1952, age 61.

Edward McNamara: Desk clerk at Lexington Hotel in Chicago and witness for White Sox defense at trial of Jackson civil suit.

Frank McNamara: Name partner in Milwaukee law firm that represented White Sox in civil litigation and co-counsel for Sox defense in trial of Jackson case.

E.P. Melrose: Indiana newspaper executive and fact/character witness for Zork defense at Black Sox criminal trial.

Milwaukee County Courthouse/Milwaukee: Site of trial of Jackson civil suit in January–February 1924. Erected in 1873, the second county courthouse built on the location. Decommissioned in 1931 and razed in 1937. Now site of a Milwaukee park.

Fred Mitchell: Chicago Cubs manager who pulled Claude Hendrix from starting assignment in favor of staff ace Grover Alexander after August 31, 1920, game fix rumors relayed to him by club president Veeck. Testified about matter before Cook County grand jury.

Morrison Hotel/Chicago: Scene of boasts about Series fix allegedly made by gambler defendant Carl Zork. Billed as tallest hotel in America after building addition completed in 1927. Razed in 1965.

John Caldwell Myers: Assistant New York County District Attorney and lead prosecutor at Attell extradition hearing.

Thomas D. Nash: Noted Chicago attorney and influential Democratic Party politico. Lead defense counsel for Buck Weaver, Swede Risberg, and Happy Felsch at criminal trial. Longtime partner of Black Sox defense co-counsel Michael Ahern. Died following a lengthy illness in 1955, age 69.

Charles K. Nims: Lost World Series bet to Abe Attell. Named as representative bettor-victim in superseding Black Sox case indictment. Charge dismissed following revelation of extortion attempt by Nims at office of defense counsel Berger.

John C. Northrup: Senior attorney at Austrian firm and co-counsel for White Sox defense at trial of Jackson civil suit.

James C. O'Brien: Former Cook County Assistant State's Attorney retained by AL President Johnson to represent league interests in Black Sox proceedings. Thereafter, switched sides to defend Chick Gandil. Called "Ropes" in press because of number of murderers who he obtained hanging verdicts for as prosecutor. Often prosecuted high-profile cases in tandem with ASA John Prystalski, later his partner in private practice. In late 1920s, O'Brien served as assistant to Illinois Special Prosecutor Charles A. McDonald. Facing disbarment for padding bills as attorney for Chicago Sanitary District Board when he died suddenly of a stroke in November 1931. O'Brien was 56.

Norris O'Neill: White Sox front office employee who accompanied manager Gleason on post–Series investigative trip to St. Louis. Testified about trip before grand jury.

John Owen: Former Cook County ASA and law firm partner of Gandil defense attorneys James O'Brien and John Prystalski. A *Chicago Daily News* photo depicts Owen in consultation with Gandil and O'Brien in courthouse corridor but extent of Owen's participation in Black Sox trial, if any, is unknown.

Sam Pass: Best man at Ray Schalk's wedding and sidekick of Chisox players. Lost heavily betting on Sox in 1919 Series, including wagers made with Abe Attell. Witness at grand jury proceedings in September 1920 and March 1921. Refused to identify Attell in court at June 1921 extradition hearing held in New York (after secretly accepting betting losses reimbursement from Attell lawyer Fallon).

Joe Pesch: St. Louis pool hall operator and gambler. Passed along word of 1919 Series fix to traveling companion Harry Redmon. Refused to contribute to fix revival fund being collected by Midwest gamblers after Sox won Game 3. Testified before Cook County grand jury that returned superseding Black Sox indictments in March 1921, but not called to witness stand at criminal trial. Committed suicide in 1923.

Raymond Prettyman: Chicago dentist and Weaver family friend. Testified before grand jury in October 1920 but published accounts of testimony in conflict. Posted bond for Buck Weaver following return of original Black Sox indictments.

Edward A. Prindiville: Former First Assistant Cook County State's Attorney retained as special prosecutor for Black Sox criminal trial. Delivered State's summation to jury.

John Prystalski: Low-key co-counsel for Chick Gandil at Black Sox criminal trial. Former Cook County Assistant State's Attorney oft-times teamed with ASA James O'Brien in high profile prosecutions. Prystalski was the duo's cross-examiner. Left SAO in December 1920 to enter private practice with O'Brien and former ASA John Owen. Had been sitting as a Circuit Court judge in Chicago for 17 years when he died of pneumonia in November 1950. He was 69.

J.C. Punch: St. Louis insurance broker and Zork defense character witness.

Nate Raymond: Swarthy West Coast gambler indicted by Los Angeles grand jury as mastermind of corruption of 1919 PCL pennant race. Charges later dismissed on technical grounds. A participant in November 1928 Manhattan card game that ended with fatal shooting of Arnold Rothstein. Later imprisoned on forgery conviction. Invariably referred to as "Nigger Nate" in the press.

Redland Field/Cincinnati: Home grounds of the Cincinnati Reds. Site of Games One, Two, Five, and Six of 1919 World Series. Name changed to Crosley Field in 1934. Demolished in 1972.

Harry Redmon: Owner of Majestic Theater in East St. Louis and heavy 1919 World Series betting loser. Informed White Sox officials of fix during private post–Series meetings in St. Louis and Chicago. Later informed AL President Johnson. Testified before Cook County grand juries in October 1920 and March 1921. Combustible prosecution witness during the Black Sox trial, daring defense counsel Berger to repeat cross-examination insinuations to Redmon's face outside the courthouse.

Hartley Replogle: Lead grand jury prosecutor in initial Black Sox probe. Testified as prosecution witness at mid-trial suppression hearing.

Swede (Charles) Risberg: Tough-guy shortstop on 1919 White Sox and reputed Series fix enforcer. Acquitted of criminal charges at Black Sox trial but immediately banned from organized baseball by Commissioner Landis. Initiated big-dollar civil lawsuit against White Sox in Milwaukee but settled for a pittance. Later testified before Commissioner Landis at public hearing into allegations that 1917 Sox had bribed Tigers. Played outlaw ball in West with Hal Chase and other banned Sox. Later earned living as dairy farmer and bar owner. Died in California nursing home on 81st birthday in 1975. Risberg was the last surviving Black Sox.

Fred Roosenfeld: St. Louis furniture dealer and Zork defense character witness.

Arnold Rothstein: NYC underworld banker and reputed financier of 1919 Series fix. Indignantly denied fix involvement to Cook County grand jury and publicly exonerated by SAO and Sox attorney Austrian. Later accused of arranging theft of grand jury transcripts by AL President Johnson, whom Rothstein threatened to sue (but did not). At trial of Fuller & McGee bucket shop operators in 1923, Rothstein barraged by questions about connection to fix but responded with insulting non-answers. Shot during Manhattan card game on November 5, 1928. Lingered for about 12 hours before dying, refusing to name his assailant while conscious.

Dutch (Walter) Ruether: Pitching and batting star for Reds during 1919 World Series. Made brief appearance as defense witness at Black Sox criminal trial. Ended career with 1927 NY Yankees. Overall 137–95 in 11 seasons. Filed $2 million defamation suit against Eliot Asinof and publishers after *Eight Men Out* was released in 1963. Settled out of court. Died in 1970, age 76.

Bill Rumler: PCL batting champ in 1919 for Salt Lake City but indicted for accepting bribe from Vernon captain Babe Borton. Steadfastly maintained innocence. Charges dismissed on legal technicality but banned from organized baseball. Reinstated in December 1928 and hit .386 for Hollywood Stars in 1929 at age 38. Later held various government posts in hometown of Milford, Nebraska, until death in May 1966, age 75.

Julian C. Ryer: Chicago attorney and plaintiff co-counsel in the Weaver civil suit instituted against the White Sox.

John E. Sanderson: Foreman of the jury at the trial of the Jackson civil suit in Milwaukee. Post-trial interviews provided rationale for jury's verdict. Son-in-law of former Missouri Attorney General and Governor Elliott Woolfolk Major.

Ray Schalk: Feisty White Sox catcher who reportedly raged at Eddie Cicotte during Game One and attacked Lefty Williams after Game Two, but turned mum thereafter. Proved of little use to those investigating fix of 1919 World Series. Brief appearance on witness stand as both a prosecution and defense witness during Black Sox criminal trial. Later gave deposition for White Sox regarding disputed 1917 World Series bonus claim during civil litigation. Refused to speak about scandal for the remainder of his life. Veterans Committee Hall of Fame selection in 1955. Died in 1970, age 77.

Harold Schwind: Clerk at Sherman Hotel in Chicago during 1919 World Series. Appeared as alibi witness for Zelcer defense, later as prosecution rebuttal witness during Black Sox criminal trial.

James P. Sex: San Francisco attorney who represented Hal Chase at late 1920 season expulsion hearings conducted by Mission League officials. Successfully resisted extradition to Chicago on Chase's behalf in April 1921.

James O. Seys: Chicago Cubs team secretary and stakeholder for 1919 World Series bets placed by Abe Attell and Lou Levi. Testified at initial Cook County grand jury proceedings and was prosecution witness at Attell extradition proceedings in New York. Also appeared as prosecution witness at Black Sox criminal trial.

James D. Shaw: Co-counsel for plaintiff Jackson at 1924 trial of civil suit in Milwaukee.

Sherman Hotel/Chicago: Chicago headquarters for gambler defendants Abe Attell and David Zelcer during 1919 World Series and scene of mid–Series fix revival meeting of Midwest gamblers. Erected in 1911 and premier Chicago night spot and jazz venue during the 1920s. Torn down in 1980.

Benedict J. Short: Prominent Chicago criminal defense attorney and lead counsel for Joe Jackson and Lefty Williams at Black Sox trial. Gave final defense summation at close of case. First Assistant Cook County State's Attorney from 1909 to 1912. Practiced law for more than 50 years. Died in March 1947, age 77.

Sinton Hotel/Cincinnati: Away-game living quarters for White Sox during the 1919 Series and Cincinnati base of operations for gamblers. Site of fix meeting between corrupted Sox players and Bill Burns, Abe Attell, and "Bennett" prior to Series start. Room 708 site of player payoff after Sox loss in Game Two. Erected in 1909 and named for wealthy 19th century Ohio industrialist. Razed in 1964.

Walter J. Smith: Cook County grand jury stenographer. Took down grand jury testimony of Eddie Cicotte and Lefty Williams. Prosecution witness at criminal trial and appeared on behalf of White Sox defense at trial of Jackson civil suit.

J.G. Taylor Spink: Publisher of *The Sporting News* and official scorer of the 1919 World Series. Minor grand jury and Black Sox criminal trial witness.

J. Vernon Steinle: Assistant professor of chemistry at Marquette University and neutral expert witness summoned by court at trial of Jackson civil suit. No known relation to Milwaukee ADA Roland Steinle.

Harry Stephenson: White Sox trainer and defense witness at Black Sox criminal trial. Testified that Swede Risberg complained of a cold and was using medication during the 1919 Series.

Charles Stoneham: NY Giants team owner and brief grand jury witness.

Sport (Joseph) Sullivan: Boston bookmaker and fix front man at meeting with corrupted Sox players at Warner Hotel in Chicago. Loudly protested indictment by Cook County grand jury in October 1920 and threatened to reveal fix knowledge to Chicago prosecutors. Then dropped from view. Widespread report that Sullivan had fled to Canada or Mexico contradicted by Boston police, who reported seeing Sullivan in city on near daily basis during winter of 1920–1921. Named as defendant in superseding indictment returned in March 1921 but did not appear in court for trial. Last publicly reported sighting involved ejection from Yankee Stadium during Game Seven of 1926 World Series. Fictionalized Sport Sullivan served as protagonist in Brendan Boyd's Black Sox novel *Blue Ruin* but little is actually known about Sullivan's post-scandal life.

John J. Talty: Former judge and St. Louis mayoral candidate. Testified as character witness for Zork defense at Black Sox criminal trial.

Mont (Jacob) Tennes: Kingpin Chicago gambler and horse racing odds maker. Publicly denied leaked Weeghman grand jury testimony about imparting advance knowledge of World Series fix to Weeghman. Offered to repeat denial to grand jury but not called to testify. Sox owner Comiskey testified at criminal and civil trials that he was first alerted to Series fix by a Tennes telephone call on morning of Game Two. Tennes reportedly lost $80,000 betting on hometown White Sox in Series. Noted philanthropist in later years. Died in 1941, age 68.

John M. Tierney: New York State Supreme Court Justice sitting in the Bronx. Presided over Attell extradition hearing before relinquishing proceedings to Justice Thomas F. Donnelly.

Fred Toney: NY Giants pitcher and minor grand jury witness.

John F. Tyrrell: Black Sox trial prosecutor, formerly of Barrett law firm. Handled technical and procedural issues during Black Sox proceedings. Expert on election law violations. Active in Chicago Republican Party politics and Illinois State Republican Party chairman in 1937.

John F. Tyrrell: Renowned handwriting expert and document examiner from Milwaukee. Testified for White Sox defense during trial of Jackson civil suit. No relation to Black Sox prosecutor of the same name.

William L. Veeck, Sr.: Chicago Cubs president. Publicized rumors of attempt to fix Cubs-Phillies game of August 31, 1920, and hired Burns Detective Agency to investigate. Also invited inquiry into matter by NL officials and Chicago sportswriters. Later testified before grand jury that fix report was most likely a ruse of gamblers seeking to influence game betting odds. Father of Bill Veeck, Jr., flamboyant part-owner of Cleveland Indians, St. Louis Browns, and Chicago White Sox.

Warner Hotel/Chicago: Southside Chicago residential hotel. Long used as in-season residence by White Sox players. Site of pre–Series meeting between Black Sox and fix front men Sullivan and Brown. Also reported scene of Gandil rejection of new fix proposal made by Bill Burns after Game Three. Named for owner Charles M. Warner and torn down as part of early 1950s urban renewal project.

W.W. Way: Handwriting expert and rebuttal expert witness for plaintiff Jackson at trial of civil suit.

Buck (George) Weaver: Popular White Sox third baseman. Protested innocence from the moment his name was connected to 1919 World Series fix. Acquitted at criminal trial in August 1921 but immediately banished from game by Commissioner Landis. Instituted breach-of-contract suit against White Sox in October 1921 but suit dragged on until being dismissed by federal court in late 1925. Out-of-court settlement reportedly reached thereafter. Petitions for reinstatement denied by Commissioners Landis and Chandler. Working as racetrack pari-mutuel clerk when stricken by fatal heart attack on a Chicago street in January 1956. Weaver was 66.

Charles Weeghman: Former owner of Chicago Cubs and racetrack regular. Testified before Cook County grand jury about advance World Series info allegedly given to him in Saratoga by Mont Tennes. Leaked Weeghman testimony publicly contradicted by Tennes. Died of a stroke in 1938, age 64.

Roy Wilkinson: Second-line White Sox pitcher and defense alibi witness at Black Sox trial.

Charles A. Williams: Chicago attorney and primary counsel for plaintiff Weaver in civil breach-of-contract action initiated against White Sox.

Lefty (Claude) Williams: Regular-season 23-game winner for 1919 White Sox but 0–3 in World Series. Admitted fix involvement in Austrian office and then before grand jury in late September 1920. Mid-trial suppression hearing witness at Black Sox criminal trial. Acquitted of charges but immediately banned from organized ball by Commissioner Landis. Reluctant deposition witness in subsequent civil litigation instituted by former Sox teammates. Played outlaw ball in west with Hal Chase. Moved to California and worked in landscape and plant nursery business. Remained silent about scandal for rest of life. Died in November 1959, age 66.

Frank R. Willis: Los Angeles County Superior Court judge. Dismissed indictments returned in PCL scandal on ground that game-fixing was not proscribed by California criminal law: such conduct only constituted a breach of contract, a civil matter. Rationale rejected by Judge Friend in pretrial rulings in Black Sox case.

David Zelcer: Oldest of four gamblers from Des Moines. Accused of teaming up with Abe Attell in fix dealings in and about the Sinton Hotel in Cincinnati. Identified as fix operative named "Bennett" at Black Sox trial by prosecution witnesses Bill Burns and Billy Maharg. Testified in own defense at trial and acquitted with other defendants. Continued gambling activities until death in 1945, age 68. Surname misspelled as *Zelser* in superseding indictments and Black Sox trial reportage.

Carl Zork: Owner of Supreme Shirtwaist Company, manufacturer of ladies apparel in St. Louis, and a serious gambler. Longstanding acquaintance of Abe Attell. Associate of Kid Becker and other Midwestern gamblers. Charged in superseding indictments returned by Cook County grand jury in March 1921 but acquitted at Black Sox trial. Died of heart attack in St. Louis in January 1947, age about 68.

Bibliography

Books

Alexander, Charles C. *John McGraw*. New York: Penguin, 1988.

Anderson, David W. *More Than Merkle: A History of the Best and Most Exciting Baseball Season in Human History*. Lincoln: University of Nebraska Press, 2000.

Asinof, Eliot. *Bleeding Between the Lines*. New York: Holt, Rinehart and Winston, 1979.

_____. *Eight Men Out*. New York: Henry Holt, 1963.

Axelson, Gustaf W. *Commy: The Life Story of Charles A. Comiskey*. Chicago: Reilly & Lee, 1919.

Boyd, Brendan. *Blue Ruin: A Novel of the 1919 World Series*. New York: HarperCollins, 1991, not used as a factual source.

Carney, Gene. *Burying the Black Sox: How Baseball's Cover-Up of the 1919 World Series Fix Almost Succeeded*. Washington, DC: Potomac Books, 2006.

Cook, William A. *August "Garry" Herrmann: A Baseball Biography*. Jefferson, NC: McFarland, 2008.

_____. *The Louisville Grays Scandal of 1877: The Taint of Gambling at the Dawn of the National League*. Jefferson, NC: McFarland, 2005.

_____. *The 1919 World Series: What Really Happened*. Jefferson, NC: McFarland, 2001.

Dellinger, Susan. *Red Legs and Black Sox: Edd Roush and the Untold Story of the 1919 World Series*. Cincinnati: Emmis Books, 2006.

Deveney, Sean. *The Original Curse: Did the Cubs Throw the 1918 World Series to Babe Ruth's Red Sox and Incite the Black Sox Scandal?* New York: McGraw-Hill, 2010.

Dewey, Donald, and Nicholas Acocella. *The Black Prince of Baseball: Hal Chase and the Mythology of the Game*. Toronto: Sport Classic Books, 2004.

Dinger, Ed. *A Prince at First: The Fictional Autobiography of Hal Chase*. Jefferson, NC: McFarland, 2002, not used as a factual source.

Farrell, James T. *My Baseball Diary*. New York: A.S. Barnes, 1957.

Fifield, James Clark. *The American Bar, Vol. I*. New York: Fifield, 1918.

Fleitz, David L. *Shoeless: The Life and Times of Joe Jackson*. Jefferson, NC: McFarland, 2001.

Fowler, Gene. *The Great Mouthpiece: A Life Story of William J. Fallon*. New York: Covici, Friede, 1931.

Frommer, Harvey *Shoeless Joe and Ragtime Baseball*. Dallas: Taylor, 1992.

Garner, Bryan A., ed. *Black's Law Dictionary*, 9th ed. St. Paul: West, 2009.

Ginsburg, Daniel E. *The Fix Is In: A History of Baseball Gambling and Game Fixing Scandals*. Jefferson, NC: McFarland, 1995.

Greenberg, Eric Rolfe. *The Celebrant.* Lincoln: University of Nebraska Press, 1983, not used as a factual source.

Gropman, Donald. *Say It Ain't So, Joe! The True Story of Shoeless Joe Jackson*, rev. 2nd ed. New York: Citadel Press, 1992.

Huhn, Rick. *Eddie Collins: A Baseball Biography*. Jefferson, NC: McFarland, 2008.

Katcher, Leo. *The Big Bankroll: The Life and Times of Arnold Rothstein*. New York: DaCapo Press, 1958.

Kohout, Martin Donell. *Hal Chase: The Defiant Life and Turbulent Times of Baseball's Biggest Crook*. Jefferson, NC: McFarland, 2001.

Lowry, Philip J. *Green Cathedrals: The Ultimate Celebration of Major League and Negro League Ballparks*, rev. 3rd ed. New York: Walker, 2006.

Luhrs, Victor. *The Great Baseball Mystery: The 1919 World Series*. South Brunswick, NJ: A.S. Barnes, 1966.

Mansch, Larry D. *Rube Marquard: The Life and Times of a Baseball Hall of Famer*. Jefferson, NC: McFarland, 1998.

Murdock, Eugene C. *Ban Johnson: Czar of Baseball*. Westport, CT: Greenwood Publishing, 1982.

Pietrusza, David. *Judge and Jury: The Life and Times of Judge Kenesaw Mountain Landis*. South Bend, IN: Diamond Communications, 1998.

_____. *Rothstein: The Life, Times, and Murder of the Criminal Genius Who Fixed the 1919 World Series*. New York: Carroll & Graf, 2003.

Reichler, Joseph L., ed. *The Baseball Encyclopedia*, 4th ed. New York: Macmillan, 1979.

Rothstein, Caroline. *Now I'll Tell*. New York: Vanguard Press, 1934.

Ryczek, William J. *Baseball's First Inning: A History of the National Pastime through the Civil War*. Jefferson, NC: McFarland, 2009.

_______. *Blackguards and Red Stockings: A History of the National Association, 1871 to 1875*. Wallingford, CT: Colebrook Press, 1992.

Seymour, Harold, and Dorothy Mills Seymour. *Baseball: The Golden Age*. New York: Oxford University Press, 1960.

Shatzkin, Mike, ed. *The Ballplayers: Baseball's Ultimate Biographical Reference*. New York: Arbor House, 1990.

Spatz, Lyle, and Steve Steinberg. *1921: The Yankees, the Giants, and the Battle for Baseball Supremacy in New York*. Lincoln: University of Nebraska Press, 2010.

Stein, Irving M. *The Ginger Kid: The Buck Weaver Story*. Dubuque: Brown & Benchmark, 1992.

Stinson, Mitchell Conrad. *Edd Roush: A Biography of the Cincinnati Reds Star*. Jefferson, NC: McFarland, 2010.

Thorn, John. *Baseball in the Garden of Eden: The Secret History of the Early Game*. New York: Simon & Schuster, 2011.

Thorn, John, Pete Palmer, and Michael Gershman, eds. *Total Baseball*. Kingston, NY: Total Sports, 7th ed. 2001.

Veeck, Jr., Bill, with Ed Linn. *The Hustler's Handbook*. New York: Fireside Books, 1965.

Voigt, David Quentin. *American Baseball, Vol. II: From Commissioners to Continental Expansion*. Norman: University of Oklahoma Press, 1970.

Wilbert, Warren N., and William C. Hageman. *The 1917 White Sox: Their World Championship Season*. Jefferson, NC: McFarland, 2004.

Articles

Attell, Abe. "The World Series Fix." *Cavalier,* October 1961.

Carney, Gene. "Comiskey's Detectives." *Baseball Research Journal,* Vol. 37, 2009.

_____. "Eddie Cicotte on the Day that Shook Baseball." *Base Ball: A Journal of the Early Game,* Vol. 3, No. 2, Fall 2009.

_____. "New Light on an Old Scandal." *Baseball Research Journal,* Vol. 35, 2007.

Christian, Ralph. "Beyond Eight Men Out: The Des Moines Connection to the Black Sox Scandal." SABR Conference presentation, 2003.

Crusinberry, James. "A Newsman's Biggest Story." *Sports Illustrated,* September 17, 1956.

Gandil, Chick, as told to Mel Durslag. "This Is My Story of the Black Sox Series." *Sports Illustrated,* September 17, 1956.

Gerlach, Larry R. "The Bad News Bees: Salt Lake City and the 1919 Pacific Coast League Scandal." *Base Ball: A Journal of the Early Game,* Vol. 6, No. 1, Spring 2012.

Goldfarb, Irv. "Tugging on Superman's Cape: A Critique of Carney." Black Sox Scandal Research Committee newsletter, December 2011.

Hoie, Bob. "1919 Baseball Salaries and the Mythically Underpaid Chicago White Sox." *Base Ball: A Journal of the Early Game,* Vol. 6, No. 1, Spring 2012.

Hynd, Alan. "The Great World Series Baseball Mystery." *True Detective,* November 1938.

Jackson, Joe, as told to Furman Bisher. "This Is the Truth." *Sport,* October 1949.

Kirby, James. "The Year They Fixed the World Series." *American Bar Association Journal,* February 1, 1988.

Lamb, William F. "A Black Sox Mystery: The Identity of Defendant Rachael Brown." *Base Ball, A Journal of the Early Game,* Vol. 4, No. 2, Fall 2010.

_____. The People of Illinois v. Edward V. Cicotte, et al.: The Initial Grand Jury Proceedings in the Black Sox Case." *Base Ball: A Journal of the Early Game,* Vol. 6, No. 1, Spring 2012.

Lardner, John R., Jr. "Remember the Black Sox?" *Saturday Evening Post,* April 30, 1938.

Voelker, Daniel, and Paul Duffy. "It Ain't So, Kid. It Just Ain't So: History's Apology to Shoeless Joe Jackson, Charles Comiskey, and Chicago's Black Sox." *Chicago Lawyer,* September 2009.

Internet

Abe Attell family history at *http://www.familytreemaker.geneology.com/users/t/h/o/Eric-Thomsen/index.htm.*

Billy Maharg boxing record at *http://boxrec.com.*

Black Sox criminal court records at *http://www.cookcountyclerkofcourt.org.*

The Black Sox Trial: An Account, by Douglas Linder at *http://www.law.umkc.edu/faculty/projects/ ftrials/blacksoxaccount.html.*

Black Sox Scandal transcripts at *http://www.1919blacksox.com/transcripts.html.*

Mont Tennes, King of Gamblers at *chicagocrimescenes.blogspot.com/2009/04/mont-tennes-king-of-gamblers.html.*

1919 Black Sox Group at *http://groups.yahoo.com/group.1919BlackSox.*

SABR Bioproject profiles of Eddie Cicotte, Eddie Collins, Charles Comiskey, Red Faber, Happy Felsch, Chick Gandil, Joe Gedeon, Kid Gleason, Buck Herzog, Shoeless Joe Jackson, Billy Maharg, Fred McMullin, Swede Risberg, Ray Schalk, Buck Weaver, and Lefty Williams at *http://www.sabr.org.bioproj.*

U.S. Census records via *http://www.ancestry.com.*

Other Sources

Black Sox file, Chicago History Museum, Chicago, Illinois.

Black Sox file, Giamatti Research Center, National Baseball Hall of Fame and Museum, Cooperstown, New York.

Chicago newspaper archives at the Chicago Public Library/Harold Washington Branch.
Eliot Asinof papers, Chicago History Museum, Chicago, Illinois.
Gene Carney, "Notes from the Shadows of Cooperstown," No. 268 (September 24, 2002) to No. 493 (June 15, 2009), inclusive, and selected excerpts from the Gene Carney papers, archived at the Shoeless Joe Jackson Museum and Library, Greenville, South Carolina.
Transcript of Jackson v. American League Club Baseball Club of Chicago, January-February 1924 civil trial, Chicago Baseball Museum, Chicago, Illinois.
Docket entries and other documents re George Weaver v. American League Baseball Club of Chicago, National Archives and Administration building, Chicago, Illinois.

INDEX

Numbers in ***bold italics*** indicate pages with photographs.